YOUR A-Z GUIDE FOR BUILDING AGILE AND
TASK-BASED SCHEDULES

MICROSOFT PROJECT 2019

B.A.S.I.C.S.

JERRY REED, PMP, MCP
AND YOLANDA REED

Available in Video!
https://msproject.vhs.tv

Over 200 COLOR Images!

Microsoft
CERTIFIED
Professional

JERRY REED, PMP
Microsoft-Certified Professional

Yolanda Reed
Co-Author, Editor

Credits

All non-software images used in this book are licensed from **Adobe® Stock**.

The cover image was designed by **Yolanda Reed**.

All image modifications were designed by **Yolanda Reed and Jerry Reed**.

Simplified Project Management Training
www.pmplicity.com

Published by: PMplicity®

ISBN: 978-0997-9775-23

Print Run Number: 1

Author Reviews

Excellent course. Well-organized. Instructor Reed took a very difficult software program and broke it down into digestible bites, explaining the "why" behind each feature. I especially appreciate the practical approach, helping us understand when and why to use each feature and that the way we use MS Project will vary for each project environment. I came into this class with zero experience with MS Project. I feel I now have all the basic tools needed to successfully run projects using MS Project. Thank you, Instructor Reed! *– Student Feedback*

Excellent knowledge of course topic; valuable real world experience; well organized; clear communicator – Student Feedback

… it was nice to have someone who was working and applying what he knew in a real environment. Jerry had very good lessons leaned from past experience that I will use with my teams – Student Feedback

He is very qualified. He is interesting and energetic. – Student Feedback

Excellent instructor. Really brings the information down-to-earth but is clearly incredibly knowledgeable of the software program and project management in general. **– Student Feedback**

Clearly you have provided your students with an outstanding learning experience and you have provided UCLA Extension with the quality of instruction that we seek in all our programs.

–UCLA Distinguished Instructor Award Committee

Foreword

sim·plic·i·ty

the condition of being easy to understand or do

Thank you for learning with PMplicity®! Our goal is to teach Project Management concepts with simplicity.

Each chapter in this book is also available as a streaming video! The series includes a 30-day free trial, software demonstrations and bonus material.

Watch the free trailer at https://msproject.vhx.tv.

Practice Exercises

If you knew that someone learned to drive by reading a manual, you'd probably hesitate to share the road with them. Some training requires hands-on experience. Learning Microsoft Project falls into this category.

Beginning with Chapter 3 and ending with Chapter 17, you'll find a "Challenge" practice exercise covering the lessons and software features reviewed in the chapter. The exercises include simple steps to reinforce learning and help you progress toward proficiency.

Website

Solutions to the "Challenge" practice exercises can be found on the companion website:

www.mspbasics.com

Videos!

When you see the symbol below at the end of a chapter, you'll find videos from the Microsoft Project B.A.S.I.C.S. video series! You can watch them for free on the companion website above. If you like them, sign up for a 30-day trial and stream the entire series at https://msproject.vhx.tv.

VIDEO

Brief Contents

Introduction xii

PART ONE: Laying the Foundation 1

    Chapter 1 Why Not use Excel for Scheduling? 2

    Chapter 2 Navigating the Project 2019 Interface 10

    Chapter 3 Understanding the Work Breakdown Structure 33

    Chapter 4 Understanding Tasks 42

    Chapter 5 Understanding Settings 60

    Chapter 6 Selecting the Right Scheduling Method 82

PART TWO: Building Your Schedule 96

    Chapter 7 Building Your Schedule 97

    Chapter 8 Adding Resources to Your Schedule 113

    Chapter 9 Adding Calendars to Your Schedule 130

    Chapter 10 Documenting Your Schedule 144

    Chapter 11 Compressing Your Schedule 157

    Chapter 12 Constraining Your Schedule 174

    Chapter 13 Leveling Your Resources 183

    Chapter 14 Inspecting Your Schedule 205

PART THREE: Executing Your Schedule 223

    Chapter 15 Executing Your Schedule 224

    Chapter 16 Tracking Project Costs 247

    Chapter 17 Creating Project Status Reports 265

    Chapter 18 Consolidating and Linking Schedules 280

    Chapter 19 Closing Your Project 291

    Chapter 20 Customizing Microsoft Project 2019 299

    Chapter 21 Twenty FAQs 320

PART FOUR: Executing Agile Projects 336

    Chapter 22 Understanding Agile Projects 337

    Chapter 23 Using the Kanban Features 344

    Chapter 24 Using the Scrum Features 358

    Chapter 25 An Agile Use Case – Putting it All Together 370

Contents

Introduction xii

How this Book is Organized xiii

PART ONE: Laying the Foundation 1

  Chapter 1 Why Not use Excel for Scheduling? 2

    Why Not Use Excel? 3

    Microsoft Project in Project Management Practice 6

    Bonus Video 8

    Now You Can 9

  Chapter 2 Navigating the Project 2019 Interface 10

    The Project 2019 Interface 11

    Views: Working with Your Project Data 20

    Now You Can 32

  Chapter 3 Understanding the Work Breakdown Structure 33

    Defining the WBS 34

    Building the WBS 34

    Top-down and Bottom-up Planning 36

    Important Points about the WBS 36

    CHALLENGE – Practice Exercise 40

    Now You Can 41

  Chapter 4 Understanding Tasks 42

    What is a Task? 43

    Creating Tasks 43

    Naming Tasks 44

    Task Duration 44

    Scheduling Mode 44

    Understanding Summary Tasks 44

    Creating Summary Tasks 45

    Using Milestones 46

    Creating Milestones 47

    Displaying the Project Summary Task 47

    Mastering Task Relationships: Using the Predecessors Field 48

    CHALLENGE – Practice Exercise 54

Now You Can 59

Chapter 5 Understanding Settings 60

Scheduling Modes 61

Understanding the Duration Equation.. 70

Understanding Effort-Driven Scheduling 71

Understanding Task Type 73

CHALLENGE – Practice Exercise 75

Now You Can 81

Chapter 6 Selecting the Right Scheduling Method 82

Understanding the Two Scheduling Methods... 83

Comparing the Two Scheduling Methods 87

Selecting the Right Scheduling Method 88

Adjusting the Settings... 89

CHALLENGE – Practice Exercise 92

Now You Can 94

Part One Summary 95

PART TWO: Building Your Schedule.. 96

Chapter 7 Building Your Schedule 97

Using the B.A.S.I.C.S Acronym 98

CHALLENGE – Practice Exercise 107

Now You Can 112

Chapter 8 Adding Resources to Your Schedule 113

Understanding Resource Types 114

Creating Resources and Adding Resource Information 114

Fields in the Resource Sheet... 115

Important Information about Max Units 117

Adding Additional Resource Information 118

Assigning Resources 119

CHALLENGE – Practice Exercise 122

Now You Can 129

Chapter 9 Adding Calendars to Your Schedule 130

Understanding the Microsoft Project Work Week 131

Base Calendars 131

The Project Calendar 131

Resource Calendars 133

Task Calendars 134

Create a Custom Base Calendar for the Project Calendar 136

Calendar Precedence 136

Elapsed Duration 137

CHALLENGE – Practice Exercise 138

Now You Can 143

Chapter 10 Documenting Your Schedule 144

Why Document Your Schedule? 145

Entering Document Properties 145

Adding Task Notes 146

Adding Hyperlinks to Tasks 147

Adding Resource Notes 149

Adding Hyperlinks to Resources 150

Adding Files to Task and Resources 151

CHALLENGE – Practice Exercise 154

Now You Can 156

Chapter 11 Compressing Your Schedule 157

Why Compress Your Schedule? 158

KEY TERMS – Learning to Talk the Talk 158

Understanding the Critical Path 159

Highlighting the Critical Path 159

How to Compress a Schedule 161

Using the Task Path Feature 164

Adding Deadlines to Tasks 164

CHALLENGE – Practice Exercise 167

Now You Can 173

Chapter 12 Constraining Your Schedule 174

Constraint Types 175

Scheduling from the Start or Finish Date 176

Applying Constraints to Tasks 177

When to Use and Not Use Constraints 178

Scheduling Conflicts and the Planning Wizard 178

CHALLENGE – Practice Exercise 179

Now You Can 182

Chapter 13 Leveling Your Resources 183

Resource Leveling 184

Max. Units 184

Analyzing Over-Allocations – Using the Resource Usage View 185

Resource Leveling Methods 186

Automatic Resource Leveling 187

Leveling Resources Manually 190

CHALLENGE – Practice Exercise 197

Now You Can 204

Chapter 14 Inspecting Your Schedule 205

Why Inspect Your Schedule? 206

Things to Inspect 206

KEY TERMS – Learning to Talk the Talk 207

Sorting Project Data 207

Note: 208

Grouping Project Data 210

Filtering Project Data 214

Using the Task Inspector 218

Bonus Video 220

Now You Can 221

Part Two Summary 222

PART THREE: Executing Your Schedule 223

Chapter 15 Executing Your Schedule 224

The Execution Phase – Starting the Project! 225

Baselines 226

Interim Plans 227

Using the Interim Plan to Copy Baselines 228

Clearing Baselines and Interim Plans 228

Viewing Baseline Information 229

Moving the Project 229

Collecting Progress Data (Actuals) 230

Tracking Fields 231

Viewing Expected Outcomes 231

Entering Progress Data (Actuals) 232

Updating the Schedule 237

Using the Tracking Gantt 237

Inactivating Tasks.. 238

Challenge – Practice Exercise... 239

Now You Can 246

Chapter 16 Tracking Project Costs... 247

Variance.. 248

Earned Value Metrics... 248

Assigning a Project Budget 249

Comparing Budget to Cost and Viewing Cost Variance... 252

Viewing Earned Value Metrics... 253

Using Reports to View Cost and Earned Value Metrics... 254

Challenge – Practice Exercise... 256

Now You Can 264

Chapter 17 Creating Project Status Reports 265

Sharing Gantt Chart Reports.. 266

Using the Copy Picture Feature... 266

Using the Timeline View 267

Using Built-in Reports to Share Project Status.. 270

Using the Copy Report Feature.. 272

Challenge – Practice Exercise... 274

Now You Can 279

Chapter 18 Consolidating and Linking Schedules 280

Consolidating Project Plans 281

Why Consolidate Project Plans?.. 281

Creating a Consolidated Project Plan... 282

Managing Resources in a Master Project – Creating Resource Pools 283

Linking Schedules – Creating Inter-Project Dependencies....................................... 286

Bonus Video.. 289

Now You Can 290

Chapter 19 Closing Your Project.. 291

Why Close Your Project?... 292

How to Close Your Project 292

Compare Final Results to Planned Estimates – Using the Compare Projects Feature.............. 293

Creating a Project Template 296

Now You Can 298

Chapter 20 Customizing Microsoft Project 2019 299

Ten Useful Project 2019 Customizations 300

Now You Can 319

Chapter 21 Twenty FAQs 320

1 - What Does Microsoft Project Do? 321

2 - What Can Project Do That Excel Can't? 321

3 - How Do You Read a Microsoft Project Timeline? 321

4 - Can I use Microsoft Project 2019 like I Used the Prior Versions? 322

5 - What is a Milestone? 323

6 - What are Those Red Men? 323

7 - How Do I Get Rid of Those Question Marks? 324

8 - Should I Enter Start and Finish Dates? 325

9 - How Do I Set the Project Start Date? 325

10 - Why Do I Get a Constraint Indicator When I Enter a Date? 326

11 - How Do I Get Rid of a Constraint? 326

12 - How Can I Fix My Project Outline? 327

13 - What is a Baseline and Do I Need One? 328

14 - How Can I Use the Templates to Get Started Quickly? 329

15 - What is the First Thing I Should Do to Build a Schedule? 329

16 - What is Task Mode 330

17 - What Does "New Tasks: Manually Scheduled" Mean? 330

18 - Where Do I Enter Resource Names? 330

19 - What Goes in the Predecessors Field? 331

20 - What are the steps for Building a Schedule in Microsoft Project 2019? 332

PART FOUR: Executing Agile Projects 333

Chapter 22 Understanding Agile Projects 334

Agile Business Drivers 335

Agile Basics 336

Kanban and Scrum Basics 336

Using Kanban 337

Using Scrum 338

Selecting the Right Approach 339

Now You Can 340

Chapter 23 Using the Kanban Features 341

Starting a Kanban Project 342

Understanding the Kanban Board 343

Using the Kanban Ribbon..344

Using the Waterfall Project Command 350

Kanban Use Cases..351

Conclusion 353

Now You Can 354

Chapter 24 Using the Scrum Features 355

Starting a Scum Project...356

Understanding the Sprint Planning Board 356

Using the Scrum Ribbon 358

Conclusion 365

Now You Can 366

Chapter 25 An Agile Use Case - Putting it All Together...367

Project Description 368

Step 1 – Select a Scheduling Methodology 368

Step 2 – Start the Scrum Project 369

Step 3 – Enter Tasks...370

Step 4 – Set the Project Start Date 370

Step 5 – Generate a New Sprint...371

Step 6 – Add Resource Names and Work Estimates 373

Step 7 – Organize Task by Sprints 373

Step 8 – Update Board Status for the Current Sprint...374

Step 9 – Enter Progress data and pull Agile Reports..376

Step 10 –Pull the Agile Report: "Boards – Task Status" 377

Step 11 – Pull the Agile Report: "Boards – Work Status"..378

Step 12 – Pull the Agile Report: "Current Sprint – Task Status"...379

Step 13 – Pull the Agile Report: "Current Sprint – Work Status" 380

Step 14 – Pull the Agile Report: "Sprint Status"...381

Conclusion 382

Now You Can 383

Video Series...384

More Resources..385

Glossary..386

Index...395

Introduction

"When will you finish the project?" This question stumps many working professionals. We make calls, trade favors and pressure resources, when what we really need is a schedule. Whether you're managing an Agile or a traditional project, you can use Microsoft Project to build a schedule in a few basic steps. It's time to rethink the notion that Project is difficult to learn or that you must be a software genius to use it. This book was created for everyday professionals who want to build reliable schedules and communicate clear updates through project completion. It challenges the notion that Project is difficult to learn by organizing lessons around a simple acronym. B.A.S.I.C.S. reflects the natural progression of a project and provides a context for learning new software features. Learning through practical application leads to better retention and has proven to be effective in classroom and online settings.

I'm Jerry Reed. I've managed projects for over 20 years at AT&T. I developed the B.A.S.I.C.S. acronym and scheduling approach while teaching Project Management courses at UCLA Extension. I've taught Microsoft Project courses through five software updates and have observed that scheduling fundamentals don't change with new software releases.

To build a schedule in *any* version of Project, you must:

1. **B**reak Down the Project
2. **A**djust the Settings
3. **S**tructure the Tasks
4. **I**nitialize the Durations
5. **C**onnect the Tasks and
6. **S**tart the Project

This practical approach will guide you in building your project schedule. Keeping the focus on practical use will make Microsoft Project easier to learn. This book is also available as a streaming video series at https://msproject.vhx.tv.

How this Book is Organized

This book is organized into four parts:

Part One, "Laying the Foundation", introduces you to Microsoft Project, helps you understand what it does and explains important scheduling fundamentals, like developing a Work Breakdown Structure, task relationships and the two ways to build a schedule. You'll also get an overview of the software and discover how it can simplify your project management efforts. This section is essential if you're new to Microsoft Project. Experienced users will also find this section helpful, as it fills a knowledge gap that addresses common scheduling challenges, such as selecting the wrong scheduling method.

Part Two, "Building Your Schedule", explores the Microsoft Project features that are most essential for building a schedule. In this section, you'll learn to build your schedule, using the 6 steps in the **B.A.S.I.C.S.** scheduling approach, and the key fundamentals supporting each step. You'll also learn how to create, level and manage resources, and how to compress your schedule to meet critical deadlines.

Part Three, "Executing Your Schedule", focusses on executing your project and tracking it to completion. You'll learn key execution practices such as setting a baseline, entering progress data and tracking costs. You'll also learn to create dynamic status reports and how Project interfaces with other Microsoft applications. Finally, you'll learn advanced features, such as how to create a Master schedule and establish dependencies between projects. This section concludes with guidelines for closing your project and customizing Project to fit your scheduling needs.

Part Four, "Executing Agile Projects", covers the most significant update to Project 2019 – Agile scheduling features. If you're fuzzy about Agile concepts, this section will sharpen the picture for you. We'll review the business drivers behind the Agile movement, key Agile concepts and use cases for the new Scrum and Kanban features. We'll close this section by putting those features to use with a full-fledged Agile software development project.

PART ONE: Laying the Foundation

IN PART ONE, you'll learn fundamental concepts for building a schedule with Microsoft Project, including a comparison of Excel to Project as a scheduling solution, an overview of the software, instructions for preparing a Work Breakdown Structure, an overview of tasks, milestones and task relationships, an overview of Project 2019 settings, an overview of the two scheduling approaches and guidance on selecting the right approach for your project. You'll also learn key skills measured by Microsoft Project Exam 74-343.

Chapter 1 Why Not use Excel for Scheduling?

IN THIS CHAPTER:

- Excel or Project?

- Microsoft Project in Project Management Practice

- Competitive Advantages of using Microsoft Project

- Microsoft Project and the Triple Constraints

In this chapter, we'll address the question, "Why not use Excel for Scheduling?" When you're done, you'll be able to explain the benefits of scheduling with Microsoft Project over Excel, how Microsoft Project is used in today's Project Management environment, the Competitive Advantages of using Microsoft Project and how it relates to the Triple Constraints.

Why Not Use Excel?

Microsoft Project is the premier scheduling solution across many industries, yet more professionals (including Project Managers) develop schedules using Excel than Project. Why is this? Perhaps because Excel is familiar, intuitive and everyone has it. Developing a schedule is as simple as listing task names, dates, and a predecessor for each task.

Figure 1 below shows a House Painting schedule using Excel. The schedule shows that if you started painting a house on 6/1/20, you'd finish in 20 days (not counting weekends) on 6/26/20. Easy enough. So... why not use Excel for scheduling?

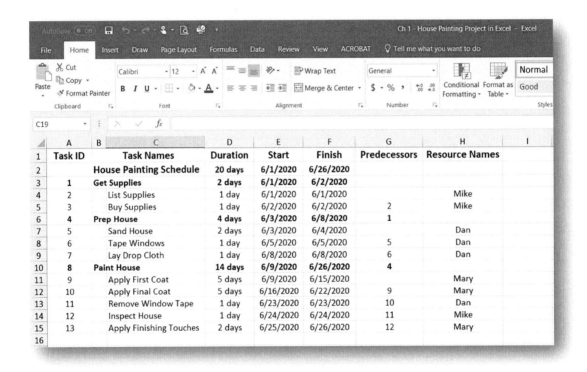

Figure 1 – *House Painting* Schedule in Excel

If no changes are needed and the schedule is executed according to plan, the Excel schedule may work fine. But let's assume you underestimated the duration of one of the tasks. For example, Task 5 (Sand House), will take 3 days instead of 2 days. How would you make this adjustment in Excel?

To begin, the duration of Task 5 must be changed to 3 days and the finish date must be changed to 6/5/20. Then, you'll need to manually adjust the start and finish dates of every other task impacted by this change. *Figure 2* below shows the updated House Painting schedule. Each highlighted cell was impacted by the change.

	A	B	C	D	E	F	G	H	I
1	Task ID		Task Names	Duration	Start	Finish	Predecessors	Resource Names	
2			House Painting Schedule	21 days	6/1/2020	6/29/2020			
3	1		Get Supplies	2 days	6/1/2020	6/2/2020			
4	2		List Supplies	1 day	6/1/2020	6/1/2020		Mike	
5	3		Buy Supplies	1 day	6/2/2020	6/2/2020	2	Mike	
6	4		Prep House	5 days	6/3/2020	6/9/2020	1		
7	5		Sand House	3 days	6/3/2020	6/5/2020		Dan	
8	6		Tape Windows	1 day	6/8/2020	6/8/2020	5	Dan	
9	7		Lay Drop Cloth	1 day	6/9/2020	6/9/2020	6	Dan	
10	8		Paint House	14 days	6/10/2020	6/29/2020	4		
11	9		Apply First Coat	5 days	6/10/2020	6/16/2020		Mary	
12	10		Apply Final Coat	5 days	6/17/2020	6/23/2020	9	Mary	
13	11		Remove Window Tape	1 day	6/24/2020	6/24/2020	10	Dan	
14	12		Inspect House	1 day	6/25/2020	6/25/2020	11	Mike	
15	13		Apply Finishing Touches	2 days	6/26/2020	6/29/2020	12	Mary	
16									

Figure 2 – Updated *House Painting* Schedule in Excel

As you can see, quite a few tasks were impacted. Imagine the number of manual changes you'd have to make if the schedule were more complex. Moreover, what are the chances of missing one of the impacted cells? Certainly, higher than if these adjustments were automated. Excel enthusiasts might suggest creating formulas to automate the changes throughout the schedule. But note that the tasks in this schedule occur one after the other, which is not always the case. Creating formulas to account for each task dependency would be inefficient.

Not only is it time consuming, but it becomes less efficient and more prone to error as the number of tasks increases. Also, formulas won't allow you to see key scheduling information such as the **Critical Path**. The Critical Path is the series of tasks that must occur on time for the overall project to meet its deadline. As I often tell students, if you're programming Excel to calculate the Critical Path, your talents are being misappropriated!

Now, we'll look at scheduling in Microsoft Project. *Figure 3* below shows the same House Painting schedule in Microsoft Project. The House Painting schedule is shown in the pane on the left. The pane on the right shows a graphical representation of the timeline. This is called a **Gantt Chart**. Project automatically generates this chart from the scheduling information on the left. We'll discuss the Gantt chart in more detail in Chapter 2.

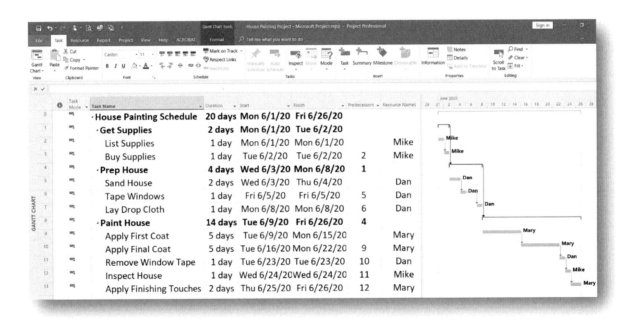

Figure 3 - *House Painting* Schedule in Microsoft Project

Updating the schedule in Project is as easy as changing the duration of the "Sand House" task from 2 days to 3 days. *Figure 4* below shows the result of this update in Project.

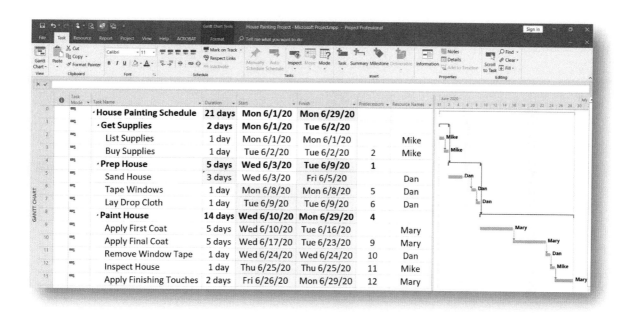

Figure 4 – Updated *House Painting* Schedule in Microsoft Project

After the duration for the "Sand House" task was updated, Project automatically updated each impacted task, using the task dependencies. Non-working times, like weekends and vacation days were also factored into the update. Project also automatically highlighted all updated fields in blue, so you'll know what changes were made. This feature is called **Change Highlighting**. Because the scheduling updates are automated in Project, users can be confident that all impacted values are adjusted.

Project can also tell you the cost impact of scheduling updates. For example, the Sand House task was delayed 1 day. If you've added cost information, like resource pay rates to your schedule, Project will automatically update the cost of the task. With its powerful scheduling engine, Project is designed to help develop and manage schedules, resources and costs.

Microsoft Project in Project Management Practice

PMs who Don't

Surprisingly, scheduling software such as Microsoft Project is optional in many project management environments. The general view is that Project Managers should have the freedom to choose how to build their schedules. I've observed this in my own industry, with clients, and with students who work in fields such as oil, entertainment, medical, event planning, and software development. Exceptions include the construction, defense and aerospace industries. Students who are new to project management are generally shocked that Microsoft Project is optional. They ask, *"How can PMs keep projects on track without a true scheduling solution?"* The answer is – we make calls, trade favors and pressure resources.

The view that scheduling software is optional, limits, rather than liberates project managers. It allows schedules to be determined by business pressures rather than by task dependencies. It also undermines key aspects of the project manager's role, such as advising stakeholders on project dependencies, developing realistic options for compressing schedules and conveying the cost impact of doing so. This practice often results in unrealistic schedules and project delays.

Competitive Advantages

Mastering a tool like Microsoft Project can distinguish you in the field. Project Managers who use Microsoft Project enjoy competitive advantages over their peers. Their project updates are more clear, reliable, and useful to decision makers. They appear well-informed about their projects and gain the confidence of project sponsors. They provide better status updates, better risk assessments, better budget assessments and they build credibility faster with project teams and senior leadership.

Microsoft Project and the Triple Constraints

Perhaps the best business case for using Microsoft Project in project management practice is its utility in balancing the **Triple Constraints** (project management jargon for the trade-off between scope, schedule and cost when managing a project). For example, if a project has a complex scope and must be delivered quickly, then the cost will be high. If the cost is *too* high, it can be reduced by changing the scope of the project or relaxing the timeline.

Here's an example of the Triple Constraints in practice and how Project can help you manage the tradeoffs. Your project is to build 10,000 widgets. Your client has $10,000 and needs the widgets in 10 weeks. You tell your client that $10,000 can't pay for sufficient labor to build 10,000 widgets in 10 weeks. You'll need 20 weeks. Your client insists on 10 weeks. You then suggest he reduce the number of widgets from 10,000 to 5,000 to meet the 10-week deadline. But, your client insists on 10,000 widgets. You then educate your client on the trade-offs of the Triple Constraints. You explain, that to produce 10,000 widgets in 10 weeks, you will need to hire more resources, which will increase the cost to $20,000. You and your client on your way to an agreement. But how did you gather the project intelligence to advise your client on the precise cost increase? Or the exact number of weeks you would need based on the budget? Or precisely how many widgets you could build, if the duration and budget were frozen? You guessed it – Microsoft Project! Microsoft Project allows you to quickly assess the effects of scope, time, and cost restrictions. It's designed to measure these tradeoffs using the three parameters in its scheduling formula – Duration, Work, and Units. With Microsoft Project, you can negotiate better timelines and deliver projects faster than colleagues who use Excel for scheduling.

We've now reviewed the benefits of scheduling with Microsoft Project over Excel, how Microsoft Projects is used in today's project management environment, the competitive advantages of using Microsoft Project and how it relates to the Triple Constraints.

Bonus Video

VIDEO

To watch this chapter as a video, click the link above. Or, visit www.mspbasics.com. Select Practice Exercise Solutions" from the menu and select "Chapter 1".

Now You Can

- Explain the benefits of scheduling with Microsoft Project over Excel

- Explain how Microsoft Project is used in today's Project Management

  Environment

- Explain the Competitive Advantages of using Microsoft Project

- Explain how Microsoft Project relates to the Triple Constraints

Chapter 2 Navigating the Project 2019 Interface

IN THIS CHAPTER:

- The Project 2019 Interface

- The Ribbon

- Changing Views

- Choosing the Right View

- The Backstage View

In the last chapter, we reviewed the benefits of scheduling with Microsoft Project over Excel. In this chapter, you'll learn to navigate the Project 2019 interface. You'll learn to use the ribbon to perform commands, change views to see project information in various ways and access the backstage view to manage files and adjust project settings. When you're done, you'll be able to find the features and commands you'll need to build your schedule.

The Project 2019 Interface

Figure 5 below shows the opening view in Microsoft Project 2019.

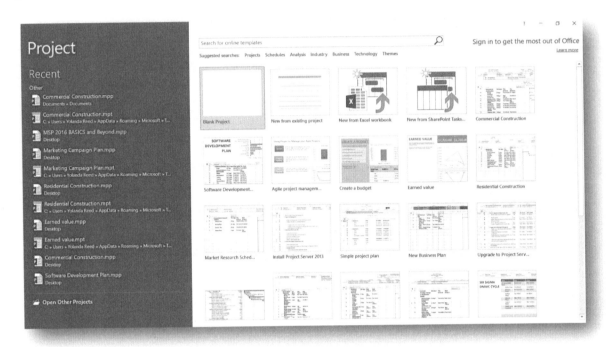

Figure 5 – The Opening View

In the green area on the left, you'll find links to recently saved project files. Click any file name to quickly open the file. Select "Open Other Projects" to search for other files. On the right, you'll find starter templates for typical business and personal projects. The templates are hosted on a companion website, so you must be connected to the internet to use them. If you don't find a template that fits your project, you'll need to build a schedule from scratch. You'll be able to do that when you complete this book.

Note: Throughout this book, the terms Schedule, Plan and Project Plan will be used interchangeably to reference a Microsoft Project file.

We'll start our tour of the interface by opening a Blank Project. In the opening view, select "Blank Project" to create a new project plan. Your screen should look like *Figure 6* below. This view is called the **Gantt Chart View**. It's the most commonly used view in Project and it's where you'll build your schedule. When your schedule is built, it shows the tasks in your schedule, and depicts their relationship with one another.

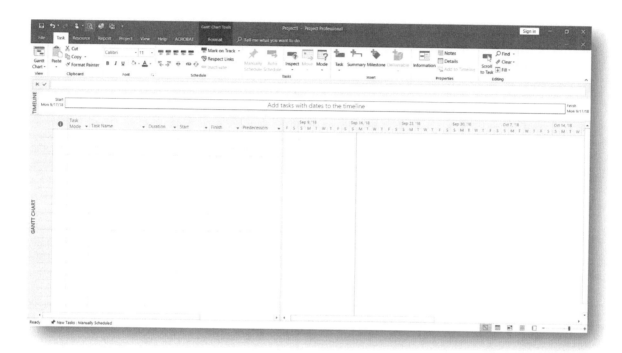

Figure 6 – The Gantt Chart View

Using *Figure 7* below, let's review the Gantt Chart view, one section at a time.

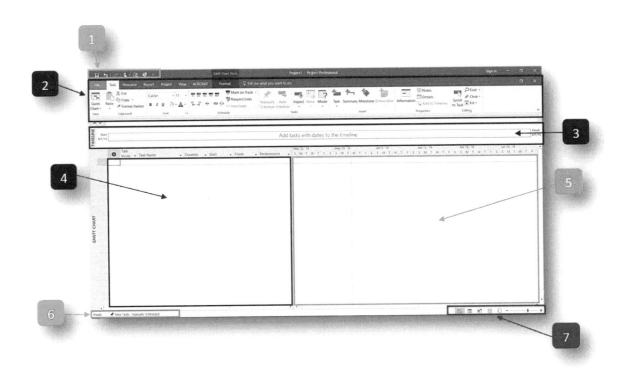

Figure 7 – The Gantt Chart View Section-by-Section

Section 1

Section 1 is called the **Quick Access Toolbar**. It contains icons for frequently used commands, so you can quickly navigate the Project interface. By default, some commonly used commands are already included on the toolbar, like *Save* and *Print*. However, Project allows you to customize the toolbar to add the quick access commands *you* use most. We'll demonstrate how to customize the Quick Access Toolbar in Chapter 20, "Customizing Microsoft Project 2019".

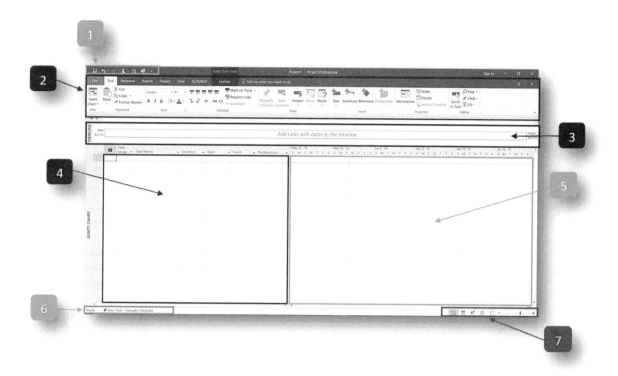

Figure 7 – The Gantt Chart View Section-by-Section

Section 2

Section 2 is called the **Ribbon**. Think of the ribbon as your toolbox. It contains all the tools you'll need to build and manage your schedule. The ribbon is organized by tabs, which makes it easy to find the functions you need. Each tab contains icons for actions you can perform. The icons vary from tab to tab and are organized into groups of related commands, separated by gray lines. You can hover over most of the icons to get a description of their function.

There are seven tabs on the ribbon – **File**, **Task**, **Resource**, **Report**, **Project**, **View**, and **Format**. The Task tab is selected by default. The options on this tab are task-related. The options on the Resource tab are resource-related, and so forth. The Format tab is also a contextual tab, meaning, the actions you can perform will vary depending on the view you're in and the item selected. A contextual label for the view will appear above the Format tab. For example, in the Gantt Chart View, the "Gantt Chart Tools" label appears, and the commands pertain to the Gantt chart.

Note: If you have Office 2019, and a compatible version of Adobe Acrobat, you can also enable the **Acrobat** tab, where you can create and share Project files in the Adobe PDF format.

Next to the File tab, you'll find a handy feature added to Project 2019 – the "**Tell me what you want to do**" search box. If you've used earlier versions of Project, you'll appreciate this upgrade. It's not just a search box, it's a function finder. For example, if you can't remember how to set the project start date, type in "start" and the relevant icons appear. Need to set a baseline? Type in "baseline" and the relevant icons appear. You no longer have to recall which tab the function lives on.

If you're new to Project, the variety of tools on each tab can be daunting. But consider the ribbon, like your toolbox at home. While there are many tools to choose from, generally, you'll only use a select few. The hammer and screwdriver will suffice for most jobs – whereas the saw is only used occasionally. The same is true for the tools on the Project ribbon. You'll only use a few commands on each tab to build and manage your schedule. Here's an overview of the most commonly used commands on each tab.

The File tab is used to access the *Backstage* view, which we'll discuss later in the chapter. The most commonly used commands on the Task tab are the **Gantt Chart** icon pick list (to change the view), the **Indent Task** and **Outdent Task** commands (to create your outline), and the **Information** command (to change task details).

On the Resource tab, the most commonly used commands are the **Assign Resources** command (to assign resources to tasks) and the **Level Resources** command (to level overallocated resources).

On the Report tab, you'll find eye-catching reports to communicate project status. Project automatically generates these reports as you develop your schedule. Once your plan is fully developed, just select the report you want.

The Project tab is used to make changes that impact the entire project. The most commonly used commands on this tab are the **Project Information** command (to set the project start date) and the **Change Working Time** command (to specify non-working days, like vacation days and special work schedules.).

Use the View tab to display your project data in various views. This tab contains several features you can use to sort, filter and group project data in various tables, diagrams and charts. The most commonly used commands on this tab are the **Entire Project** command (to zoom out to show the entire Gantt Chart), the **Timeline** checkbox (to toggle the Timeline view on or off) and the **Details** checkbox (to split the view).

The last tab is the Format tab. The most commonly used commands on this tab are the **Critical Path** checkbox (to display the critical path in the Gantt Chart), and the **Project Summary Task** checkbox (to display the Project Summary Task, which is the task that summarizes your entire project).

Section 3

Section 3 is called the **Timeline View**. Depending on how your version of Project is configured, the Timeline will be displayed when you open a new project. As mentioned earlier, you can toggle the Timeline on or off with the Timeline checkbox, located on the View tab, in the Split View group. The Timeline is a customizable summary of the project schedule. The timeline will be empty until project data is entered. Once you enter project data, you can customize the Timeline to show key milestones in your project. When you're communicating project status, this feature will come in handy. You'll learn how to customize the Timeline view in Chapter 17, "Creating Project Status Reports".

PROJECT 2016 UPDATE – Multiple Timelines

Project 2016 now allows you to create multiple timelines. This can be useful if you want to group similar tasks together and show them on different timelines.

Section 4

Section 4 is called the **Entry Table.** This is where you'll build your schedule. You'll enter task names, structure your outline, and add scheduling details, like Durations and Predecessors into this table. The Entry table is the default table in the Gantt chart view. Project includes several other tables, which display different project information.

When you're building your schedule, you'll want to use the default Entry table. When you begin executing your schedule, you'll find useful fields in the "Cost" and "Variance" tables. We'll review how to change tables later in the chapter.

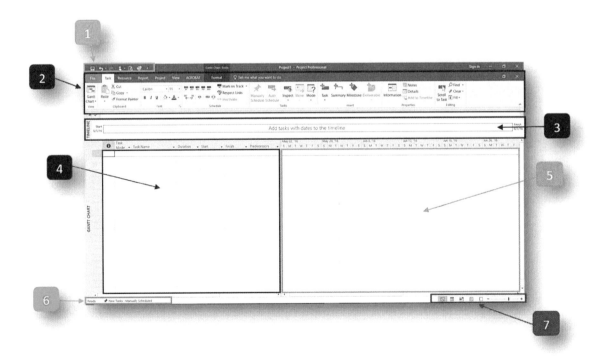

Section 5

Section 5 is called the **Gantt Chart**. As you enter scheduling data into the Entry table, Project will create a Gantt Chart that graphically depicts the task durations, start and finish dates and dependencies. The vertical green gridline indicates the current date. The thick, vertical gray lines indicate non-working days. By default, weekends and non-working days.

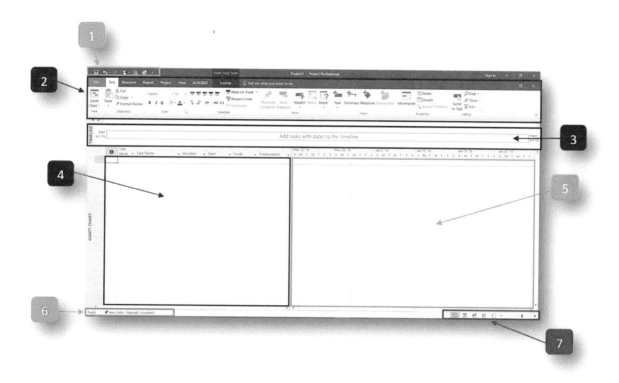

Above the Gantt chart is the **Timescale**, which depicts units of time. You can adjust the timescale to show increments ranging from minutes to years. On the **View** tab, in the **Zoom** group, use the "Timescale" pick-list to adjust the units. Each row of the Timescale is called a tier. There are three tiers – Top, Middle and Bottom. By default, only the middle and bottom tiers are displayed, with the middle tier is set to "weeks" and the bottom tier set to "days". You can customize the timescale by double-clicking it.

Section 6

Section 6 is called the **Status Bar**. This area shows the scheduling mode for new tasks. It will also show any filter applied to the current view. The "New Tasks: Manually Scheduled" notification means that all new tasks will be scheduled in the *Manual* scheduling mode. In Project 2019, users can create a schedule in the **Automatic** or **Manual** scheduling mode. Microsoft refers to this as "user-controlled scheduling". We'll review the two scheduling modes in more detail in Chapter 5, "Understanding Scheduling Settings".

Section 7

Section 7 contains **Quick Access** shortcuts to commonly used Views. Using these icons, you can quickly access the Gantt Chart, Task Usage, Team Planner and Resource Sheet views. The Report icon, allows you to quickly view reports. Use the zoom slider to zoom in and out of the current view. This is also a quick way to adjust the Timescale.

We've now reviewed the components of the Gantt chart view, the area where you'll build your schedule!

Views: Working with Your Project Data

A **View** is the active screen you're working in that displays a subset of your project data. There are three types of views in Project: task views, resource views, and assignment views. For example, the Gantt Chart view is a *task* view because it primarily displays task information such as task names, task durations and task relationships. In each data is displayed in different formats, including tables, charts and diagrams.

Changing Views

There are several ways to change the view. A quick way is to use the **Gantt Chart** command on the **Task** tab. In the bottom-left corner of the ribbon, select the pick-list from the **Gantt Chart** command to find a list of commonly used views (*Figure 8 below*).

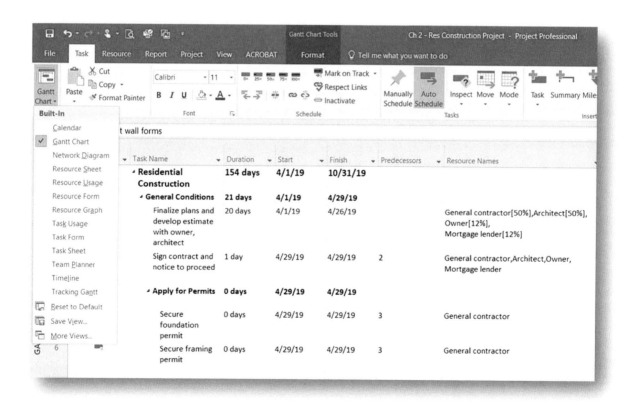

Figure 8 – Gantt Chart Command - View Pick-List

Here's a brief description and snapshot of each view:

- **Calendar View** – This view displays tasks and task durations in a calendar format. (*Figure 9 below*). Use this view to view, create or edit task information.

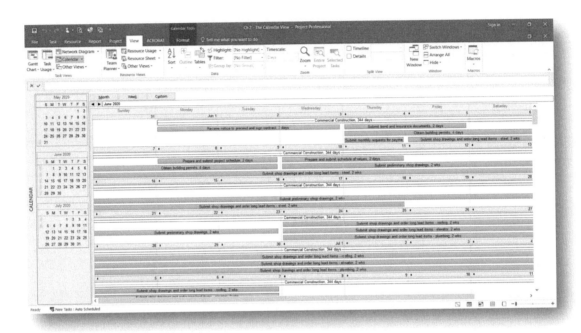

Figure 9 –Calendar View

- **Network Diagram View** – This view displays tasks and task dependencies in a flowchart format (*Figure 10 below*). Use this view to view, create or edit tasks and task dependencies.

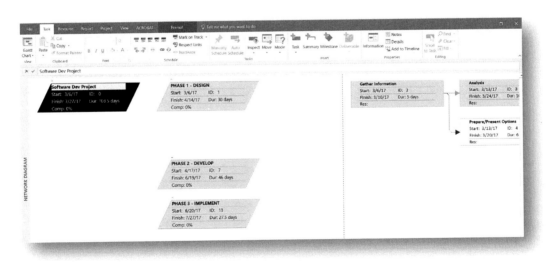

Figure 10 – Network Diagram View

21

■ **Resource Sheet View** – This view displays resource information for the entire project in a spreadsheet-like table (*Figure 11 below*). It includes resource information like pay rates and groups. Use this view, create or edit resource information.

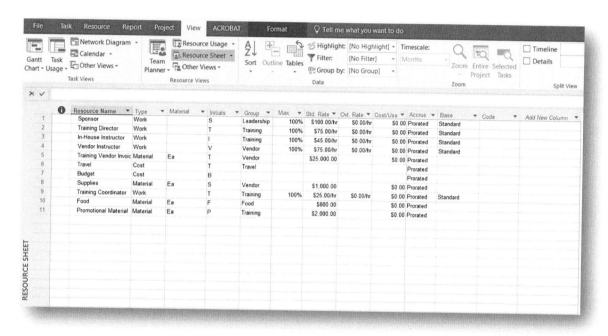

Figure 11 – Resource Sheet View

■ **Resource Usage View** – This view displays resource assignment information in a table (*Figure 12 below*). Resources, their task assignments, and cumulative work hours are listed on the left. On the right, information like work hours is displayed in the timescale increment that you choose. Use this view to view, enter or edit resource task assignment information. Over-allocated resources are conveniently highlighted in red font.

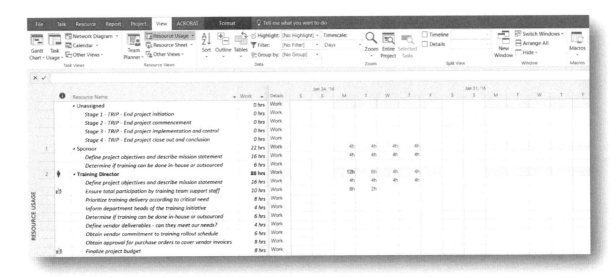

Figure 12 – Resource Usage View

- **Resource Form View** – This view displays resource information, one resource at time (*Figure 13 below).* The table on the left lists resource, task, and schedule information for a specific resource. Right-click anywhere in the gray area on the right to change the type of information shown in the fields on the left. Use this view to view, enter or edit information about a specific resource.

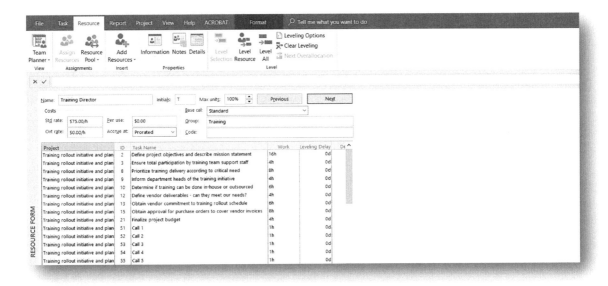

Figure 13 –Resource Form View

- **Resource Graph View** — This view displays a bar chart of an individual resource's workload and availability (*Figure 14 below*). It contains resource allocation, cost, or work for a single resource or group of resources in a graph format. Right-click anywhere in the bar chart to change the type of information shown. Use this view to quickly find over-allocated resources.

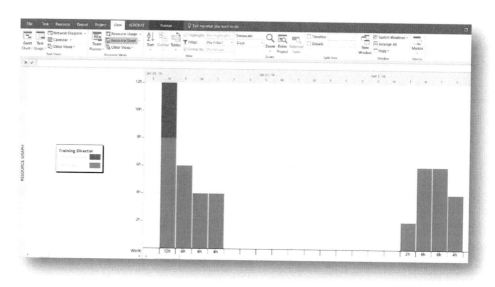

Figure 14 – Resource Graph View

- **Task Usage View** — This view displays task assignment information in a table (*Figure 15 below*). Tasks and the resources assigned to them are listed on the left. On the right, information about the task, such as work hours, is displayed in the timescale increment that you choose. Use this view to view, enter or edit task assignment information.

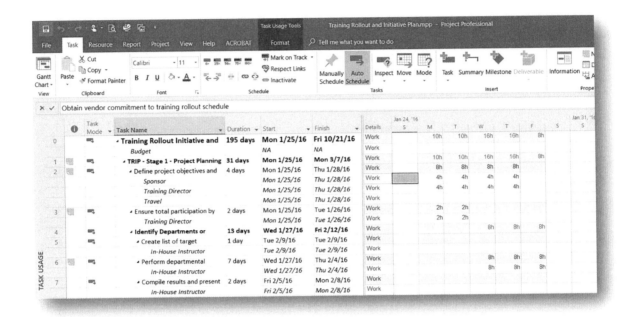

Figure 15 – Task Usage View

- **Task Form View** – This view displays task information one task at time. The table on the left lists resource, assignment, and schedule information for a specific task (*Figure 16 below*). Right-click anywhere in the gray area on the right to change the information shown in the fields on the left. Use this view to view, enter or edit information about a specific task.

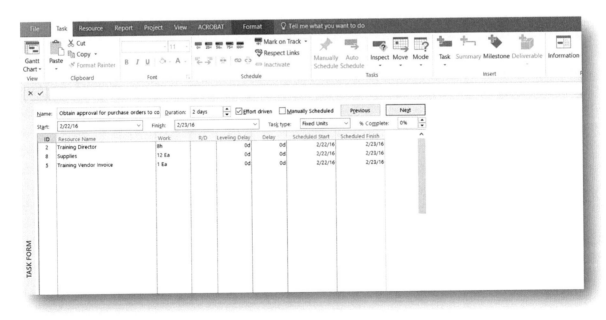

Figure 16 – Task Form View

- **Task Sheet View** – This view displays task information for the entire project in a spreadsheet-like table (*Figure 17 below*). Use this view to view, enter or edit task information, like cost and dependencies.

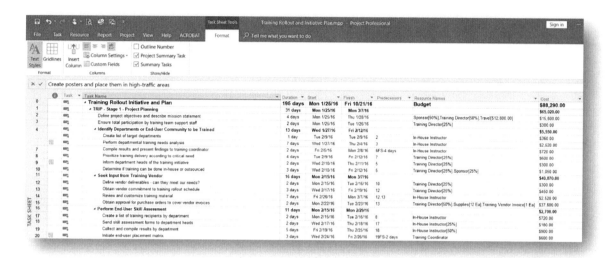

Figure 17 – Task Sheet View

- **Team Planner View** – Like the Resource Usage View, the Team Planner View displays resources, and their task assignments (*Figure 18 below*). Resource names and unassigned tasks are listed on the left. Resource task assignments are listed on the same row in the blue boxes on the right. Over-allocations are outlined in red. What this view offers that the Resource Usage View doesn't, is a drag and drop feature that allows you to reassign resources directly in the view. Use this view to quickly view and reassign tasks to resources.

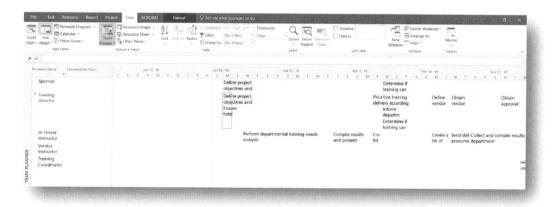

Figure 18 – Team Planner View

- **Timeline View** – This view displays your customized summary of the project timeline (*Figure 19 below*). This is the same timeline that can be toggled on and off in the Gantt Chart view. This view is useful for sharing an at-a-glance view of the project timeline.

Figure 19 – Timeline View

- **Tracking Gantt View** – Like the Gantt Chart view, this view displays task information in a table on the left, and a Gantt chart on the right (*Figure 20 below*). In the Tracking Gantt view, Project displays two sets of Gantt bars. The top task bars represent tasks as they are currently scheduled (tasks with red task bars are critical path tasks). The bottom gray task bars represent the original, baselined values. Use this view to compare baseline values with actual values.

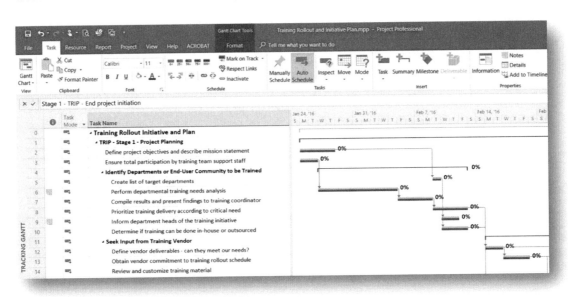

Figure 20 – Tracking Gantt View

In addition to using the Gantt Chart icon pick-list on the Task tab to change views, you can use the **View** tab. Simply select a view from the *Task Views* or *Resource Views* groups. Select "More Views" from any pick-list to see all the available views. Select "Save View" from any pick-list to save the current view so it can be used later. The look of the view and any fields, filters or groups will be saved.

Changing the Table

You can also change the table in any view to display different project information, such as cost or tracking information.

To Change the Table in a view:

1. Select the **View** tab.
2. In the **Data** group, select the table you want from the **Tables** pick-list (*Figure 21 below*).
3. Select "More tables" to view all task or resource tables.

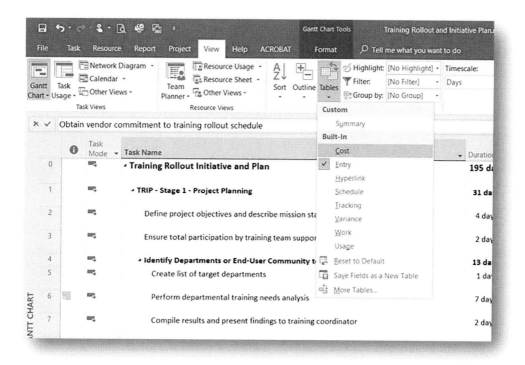

Figure 21 – Changing the Table

Displaying a Combination View for More Detail

If a single view doesn't provide enough detail, you can display a **Combination View**. Combination views display two views at the same time – one view in the top pane and another view in the bottom pane. To display a combination view, split the screen in any view as follows:

1. Select the **View** tab.

2. In the **Split View** group, select the "Details" checkbox.

When you select a task or resource in the top pane of a combination view, the view in the bottom pane shows detailed information about the selected task or resource. Also, the two views don't have to be the same type of view.

For example, you can display a *task* view like the Gantt chart view in the top pane and a *Resource* view, like the Resource Sheet view in the bottom pane. To change one of the views, click anywhere in the top or bottom pane, then use the View tab to select the view you want in that pane.

Choosing the Right View

Not sure which view to choose? To help determine the view you need, first decide which type of information you want to view (task, resource, or assignments). Then decide which format you want to view it in (E.g. chart, table, or diagram). You can also hover over any view's icon to get a description of the view. We'll look at project information in several views throughout the book.

The Backstage View

If you've used other Microsoft Office applications, you may be familiar with the **Backstage View**. Select the **File** tab to access the Backstage view. *Figure 22* below shows the Backstage view and the available options. This is where you manage files and adjust settings. The green pane on the left lists the available tabs. The panel on the right displays the details and options for the selected tab.

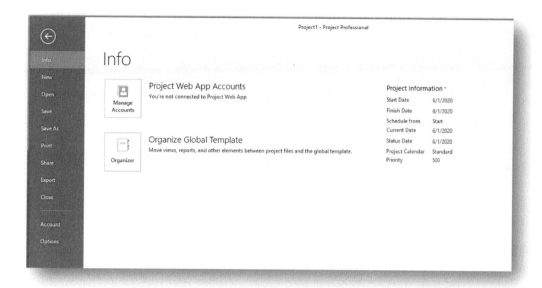

Figure 22 – The Backstage View

Here's a summary of the options on each tab:

- **Info** – Use this tab to manage Project Web App accounts (Project Professional only) and access the Organizer, a tool you can use to copy reports, calendars, and other elements to other projects, or to the Global template (Global.MPT). Copying an element to the Global template makes it available to all your projects. The Info tab also allows you to view project information for the current project, such as the start and finish date and project statistics.

- **New** – Use this tab to start a new project. You can create a project from scratch, using the "Blank Project" option or use one of the starter templates.

- **Open** – Use this tab to open saved project files.

- **Save, Save As, Save as Adobe PDF** – Use these tabs to save Project files.

- **Print** – Use this tab to access the printing options for Project files.

- **Share** – Use this tab to share Project files. Email files or sync with a SharePoint Tasks List.

- **Export** – Use this tab to export Project files as Abode Portable Document Format (PDF) or XML Paper Specification (XPS) files. We'll demonstrate these features in Chapter 17, "Creating Project Status Reports".

- **Account** – Use this tab to sign in to your Microsoft Office account. You can also view product information and manage updates on this tab.

- **Feedback** – Use this tab to provide feedback and make suggestions to Microsoft about Microsoft Project.

- **Options** – Use this tab to access the *Project Options* dialogue box, where you can customize Project and adjust various settings like, Display and Language.

To exit the Backstage view, select the back arrow in the top left corner of the screen or press the Escape key. We've now toured the Project 2019 interface!

Now You Can

- Navigate the Project 2019 Interface

- Navigate the Ribbon to find features and commands

- Change Views

- Choose the Right View

- Access the Backstage View

Chapter 3 Understanding the Work Breakdown Structure

IN THIS CHAPTER:

- Defining the Work Breakdown Structure

- Building the Work Breakdown Structure

- Top-Down & Bottom-Up Planning

- The "100% Rule"

- The WBS Coding Scheme

In the last chapter, you learned to navigate the Project 2019 interface. We reviewed the ribbon, views, and the commands you'll need to build a schedule. In this chapter, you'll learn one of the fundamental concepts for building a schedule – the **Work Breakdown Structure**. When you're done, you'll be able to define and create a Work Breakdown Structure, explain Top-Down and Bottom-Up Planning, and describe the Work Breakdown Structure Coding Scheme.

Unlike other Microsoft products, Microsoft Project is not a turnkey solution. You must do some pre-work to build a schedule. This pre-work includes developing a project outline and gathering task duration estimates. The best way to gather that information is to develop a **Work Breakdown Structure (or WBS)**. The Work Breakdown Structure is the chief prerequisite for using Microsoft Project.

Defining the WBS

The Project Management Institute (PMI®) defines a Work Breakdown Structure as a "deliverable-oriented hierarchical decomposition of the work to be executed by the project team..." A WBS is essentially a break-down of the project scope into manageable parts. This break-down of the work gets entered into Project and ultimately becomes your schedule. Next, we'll demonstrate the process of developing a WBS.

Building the WBS

Figure 23 below shows the finished "House Painting" schedule we looked at in Chapter 1. To get an idea of how the Work Breakdown Structure was developed, we'll reverse engineer this schedule back to the original WBS.

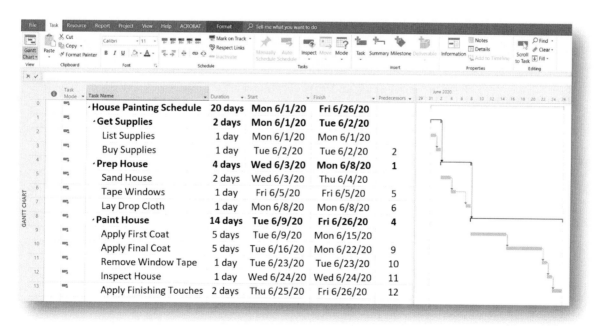

Figure 23 – *House Painting Schedule*

BEFORE THE WBS WAS ENTERED INTO PROJECT, the tasks were organized into a table, like the one shown below. As you can see, the project consists of 10 tasks organized into three phases.

GET SUPPLIES	PREP HOUSE	PAINT HOUSE
List Supplies	Sand House	Apply First Coat
Buy Supplies	Tape Windows	Apply Final Coat
	Lay Drop Cloth	Remove Window Tape
		Inspect House
		Apply Final Touches

BEFORE THE TASK LIST WAS ORGANIZED INTO PHASES, it was a disorganized task list, like the one shown below.

House Painting Project

Sand House

Tape Windows

Inspect House

Apply Final Touches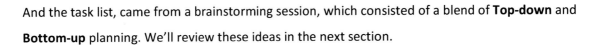

Apply Final Coat

Buy Supplies

Lay Drop Cloth

Apply First Coat

Remove Window Tape

List Supplies

And the task list, came from a brainstorming session, which consisted of a blend of **Top-down** and **Bottom-up** planning. We'll review these ideas in the next section.

By reverse engineering the House Painting schedule, we've demonstrated that projects begin by breaking down the work into manageable parts. And then, breaking down those manageable parts further to the specific tasks required to deliver an aspect of the project, and ultimately the entire project. Every project seems daunting until you break down the work.

Next, we'll review a methodology for building a schedule from the ground up.

Top-down and Bottom-up Planning

Top-Down and Bottom-up Planning is a well-documented methodology for planning any project. If you're planning a project that your team has little to no experience with, brainstorm to capture what the team already knows about the work required to deliver the project. It's a simple process. Gather your team, appoint a note-taker and start brainstorming. You may be able to develop a decent task list. This is the essence of **Bottom-up planning**.

Here are my four ground rules for conducting a Bottom-up Planning session. The goal of each rule is to extract every idea the team has to offer. A good brainstorming session will remind you of making popcorn – many ideas in rapid succession at the beginning, few ideas at the end.

1. Use at least two note-takers.
2. Capture everything!
3. Resist the urge to edit (you can do that later!).
4. Never say or imply that someone's idea is silly.

After you've exhausted your team's ideas, organize the list into phases. This list will become your project outline. If your team already has experience with the type of project you're planning, then you can incorporate **Top-down planning**. Using this method, the major categories (or phases) can be provided up front. The brainstorming would then occur within each phase.

Next, we'll review some important points about the Work Breakdown Structure.

Important Points about the WBS

The 100% Rule

Gregory T. Haugan describes the "100% Rule" in his book, "Effective Work Breakdown Structures" published by Management Concepts in 2001. The WBS must include 100% of the work described by the project scope. The sum of the work at the "child" level must equal 100% of the work represented by the "parent". Here's an example. Referencing the WBS for the House Painting project (*Figure 24* below), if the "List Supplies" and "Buy Supplies" tasks are complete, but some of the required supplies are missing, the 100% rule has not been followed. When the rule has been followed, since the "parent" involves getting supplies, the work performed at the "child" level will result in 100% of the supplies being gotten.

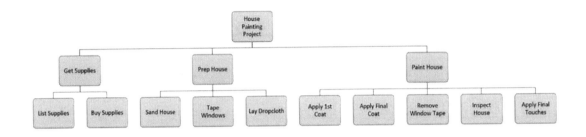

Figure 24 – WBS for House Painting Project

The Work Breakdown Structure Coding Scheme

Another important aspect of the Work Breakdown Structure is the **WBS Coding Scheme**. When placed in outline form, tasks in the work breakdown structure are commonly numbered with a coding scheme that shows each task's position in the hierarchy of the project outline.

Figure 25 shows the "House Painting" project, outlined with the WBS coding scheme.

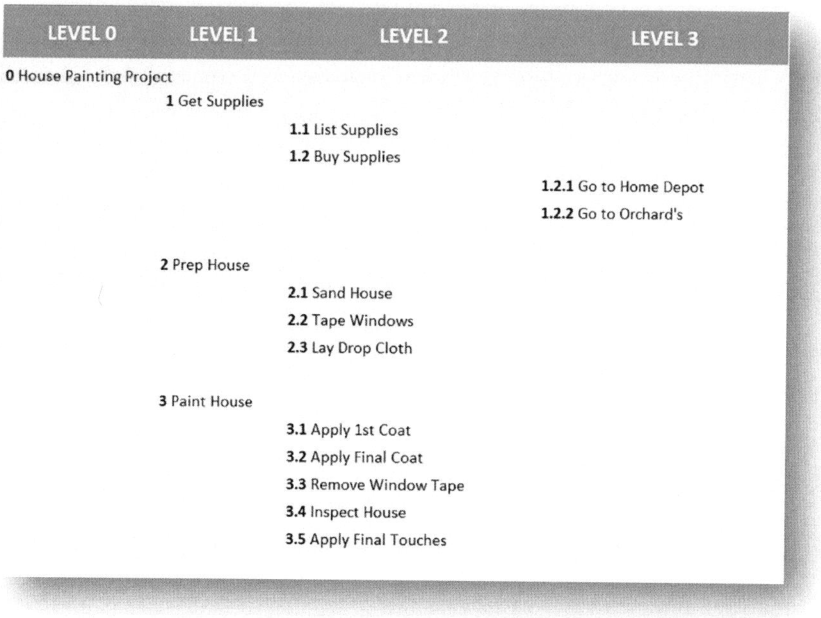

LEVEL 0	LEVEL 1	LEVEL 2	LEVEL 3
0 House Painting Project			
	1 Get Supplies		
		1.1 List Supplies	
		1.2 Buy Supplies	
			1.2.1 Go to Home Depot
			1.2.2 Go to Orchard's
	2 Prep House		
		2.1 Sand House	
		2.2 Tape Windows	
		2.3 Lay Drop Cloth	
	3 Paint House		
		3.1 Apply 1st Coat	
		3.2 Apply Final Coat	
		3.3 Remove Window Tape	
		3.4 Inspect House	
		3.5 Apply Final Touches	

Figure 25 – WBS Coding Scheme

The tasks are organized into levels that descend into greater detail. Each task has an identifier (or code) that shows its place within the hierarchy of the project outline. The tasks that represent the major phases of the project are **Level 1** tasks. Level 1 tasks are coded with 1 digit. For example, the code for the "Get Supplies" phase is "1". **Level 2** tasks are coded with two digits, separated by a decimal. For example, the code for the "List Supplies" task is 1.1. The next level 2 task in this phase, "Buy Supplies" is coded 1.2. If there were a 3rd task, its code would be 1.3 and so forth. **Level 3** tasks are coded with three digits separated by decimals. For example, the code for the "Go to Home Depot" task is 1.2.1. This pattern continues the further the project is broken down.

The WBS code given to a task not only identifies where the task fits in the outline, it also provides additional information about the project. For example, task identifier 3.5 tells us that the project has at least three Level 1 tasks (or phases) and at least 5 tasks in the 3rd phase.

Once you enter your task list into Project, you can add the WBS field to the Entry table in the Gantt Chart view. This is a handy way to check your project outline. We'll learn how to add fields like the WBS field as we progress through the book.

We've now reviewed the Work Breakdown Structure, which is the chief prerequisite for building a schedule in Microsoft Project. Once you've developed your WBS, you'll use it to create your task outline. In the next chapter, you'll learn how to do that.

DID YOU KNOW?

A key benefit of the starter templates included in Project is that the WBS, typical task durations and typical task relationships are already provided.

CHALLENGE – Practice Exercise

Develop a Work Breakdown Structure (WBS)

Instructions: In this practice exercise, you will develop a Work Breakdown Structure (WBS) for a project of your choice. Follow the steps below to complete this exercise:

1. Conduct a brainstorming session to develop a task list for the project.

2. Organize the tasks into categories. These categories will become your Level 1 tasks.

3. Review your Level 1 tasks and develop Level 2 tasks where appropriate.

4. Review your Level 2 tasks and develop Level 3 tasks where appropriate.

5. Review your Level 3 tasks and develop Level 4 tasks where appropriate.

6. Continue this process and develop as many levels as needed for your project.

SEE EXAMPLES

To see WBS examples, go to the companion website www.mspbasics.com. Select "Practice Exercise Solutions" from the menu, then select Chapter 3.

Now You Can

- Define and Build a Work Breakdown Structure

- Explain Top-Down and Bottom-Up planning

- Explain the "100% Rule"

- Explain the WBS Coding Scheme

Chapter 4 Understanding Tasks

IN THIS CHAPTER:

- Summary Tasks and Task Structure

- Milestones

- The Project Summary Task

- Task Relationships

- Predecessors and Successors

- Leads and Lags

In the last chapter, we discussed the Work Breakdown structure and the pre-work needed to build a schedule. In this chapter, we'll explain tasks – the key elements of a schedule. This is the most important chapter in the book. It explains the most fundamental aspects of building a schedule – creating tasks, outlining them, and establishing relationships between them. If you were constructing a new office building, completing this chapter would be comparable to completing the frame of the building. When you're done, you'll be able to outline your project plan using summary tasks, subtasks, and milestones. You'll be able to display the project summary task, create task relationships and use lead and lag time.

What is a Task?

A **Task** is an activity with a unique task ID, indicated numerically in the Entry table of the Gantt chart view (*Figure 26* below). It has a duration, a start date, and a finish date. Task durations and task relationships determine the project schedule. Project plans consist of three types of tasks – Summary tasks, Subtasks, and Milestones. We'll explain each, and their function in a project plan.

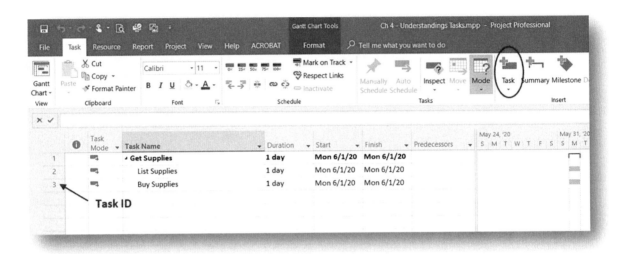

Figure 26 – Tasks in Microsoft Project

Creating Tasks

To create a task, simply type a task name into the **Task Name** field of the Entry table in the Gantt Chart view. You can also create a task by using the **Insert Task** command, located on the **Task** tab, in the **Insert** group (*Figure 26* above – red circle).

Naming Tasks

Task names should describe the activities they represent. They should be as concise as possible and follow a noun-verb pattern, such as "Paint House" or "Tape Windows". Extra details about the task shouldn't be included in the task name. Task names should simply describe the work to those completing it.

Task Duration

As mentioned earlier, tasks have a start date, a finish date and a duration. A task's **Duration** is the number of working days required to complete the task. Task duration is indicated in the "Duration" field of the Entry table in the Gantt Chart view. Duration can be expressed in increments ranging from minutes to months.

For example:

- 1m = 1 minute
- 1h = 1 hour
- 1d = 1 day
- 1w = 1 week
- 1mo = 1 month

By default, Project assigns all new tasks a 1-day duration. Depending on the type of schedule you're building, you can manually enter the correct duration or Project can calculate it for you. We'll discuss task duration further in upcoming chapters.

Scheduling Mode

New tasks are also given a **Scheduling Mode**, which is indicated in the **Task Mode** field of the Entry table. Tasks can be Manually or Automatically scheduled. By default, Project schedules new tasks in the Manual scheduling mode. We'll explain the scheduling modes in Chapter 5 "Understanding Settings".

Understanding Summary Tasks

Task lists are organized in a project plan using **Summary Tasks**. A summary task (parent task) is a task with **subtasks** (children) demoted under it. Summary tasks, also known as "phases" are used to group tasks into categories and sub-categories. In Project, they are indicated in bold typeface.

In *Figure 27* below, the "Get Supplies", "Prep House", and "Paint House" tasks are summary tasks and represent the major phases in the House Painting project. The tasks within each phase are subtasks (E.g. "List Supplies" and "Buy Supplies").

		Task Mode ▾	Task Name ▾	Duration ▾	Start ▾	Finish ▾	Predecessors ▾
1			⊿ **Get Supplies**	**2 days**	**Mon 6/1/20**	**Tue 6/2/20**	
2			List Supplies	1 day	Mon 6/1/20	Mon 6/1/20	
3			Buy Supplies	1 day	Tue 6/2/20	Tue 6/2/20	2
4			⊿ **Prep House**	**4 days**	**Wed 6/3/20**	**Mon 6/8/20**	1
5			Sand House	2 days	Wed 6/3/20	Thu 6/4/20	
6			Tape Windows	1 day	Fri 6/5/20	Fri 6/5/20	5
7			Lay Drop Cloth	1 day	Mon 6/8/20	Mon 6/8/20	6
8			⊿ **Paint House**	**14 days**	**Tue 6/9/20**	**Fri 6/26/20**	4
9			Apply 1st Coat	5 days	Tue 6/9/20	Mon 6/15/20	
10			Apply Final Coat	5 days	Tue 6/16/20	Mon 6/22/20	9
11			Remove Window Tape	1 day	Tue 6/23/20	Tue 6/23/20	10
12			Inspect House	1 day	Wed 6/24/20	Wed 6/24/20	11
13			Apply Final Touches	2 days	Thu 6/25/20	Fri 6/26/20	12

GANTT CHART

Figure 27 – Summary Tasks

Creating Summary Tasks

Summary tasks can be created using the **Indent Task** and **Outdent Task** commands on the **Task** tab, in the **Schedule** group (*Figure 28* below – left red circle). Indent a task to demote it and make it a subtask to the task above it. This will make the task above it a summary task. Outdent a task to promote it to a summary task over the task(s) beneath it. Summary tasks can also be created using the "Summary" command on the **Task** tab, in the **Insert** group (*Figure 28* below – right red circle).

Figure 28 – Creating Summary Tasks

TIP: When creating your project outline, begin by entering your entire task list without structuring it. Then, structure the tasks using the Indent Task icon to create summary tasks and subtasks. This will lead to less re-work. To check the outline, you can use the **Show Outline** feature.

1. Select the **View** tab.
2. In the **Data** group, select **"Level 1"** from the **Outline** pick-list. If your outline is correct, only the Level 1 summary tasks will be displayed. Repeat this process for each level you want to confirm.

Here are some characteristics of Summary Tasks:

- A summary task's duration is automatically calculated from the durations, dependencies and outline level of its subtasks. *

- If a subtask is outdented, it will be promoted to the same level as its parent task.

- If a summary task is outdented, its subtasks will be outdented with it. Their parent-child relationship remains intact.

- If a summary task is deleted, its subtasks will also be deleted.

*****Note**: Since the duration of the summary task is automatically calculated from the durations, dependencies and outline level of its subtasks, its duration should not be manually entered. If the duration of the summary task is manually entered, Project will toggle the scheduling mode to Manual.

Using Milestones

Milestones signify the completion of significant project events. They are often used as predecessors because they can summarize significant project deliverables. Milestones generally don't include project work, so they have a zero duration. They're indicated in Project, in the Gantt chart with a diamond icon. When naming Milestones, use a noun, past-tense verb naming scheme. For example, "Supplies Gotten" or "House Prepped". In *Figure 29* below, the milestones in the House Painting schedule are highlighted in yellow.

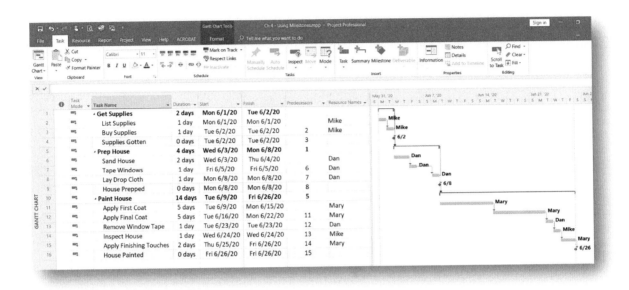

Figure 29 - Milestones

Using milestones in your project plan is optional, but they're useful because they mark completed deliverables. One key rule to follow when using milestones is to make sure that they are "true". Though milestones generally have no duration, they should be treated as other tasks. They should have dependencies and be linked to the schedule. They should complete when their predecessors complete. That's what makes them "true".

Creating Milestones

There are two ways to create a Milestone:

1. Give a task a zero duration OR

2. On the **Task** tab, in the **Insert** group, select the **Insert Milestone** command (*Figure 29* above – red circle). Then, rename the milestone appropriately.

Displaying the Project Summary Task

The **Project Summary Task** is the highest level of a project outline. Its task ID is zero. It summarizes the entire project and its duration is the duration of the entire project.

To display the Project Summary Task:

1. Select the **Format** tab.

2. In the **Show/Hide** group, check the "Project Summary Task" checkbox. The default Project Summary Task name will reflect the name of your saved project file (or "Project 1" if unsaved). Rename it as you wish.

In *Figure 30* below, the Project Summary Task for the House Painting project is highlighted in yellow. It tells us that the project has a 20-day duration, it starts on 6/1/20 and finishes on 6/26/20. The Project Summary Task will display cumulative values for any fields added to the active table.

Figure 30 – Project Summary Task

Mastering Task Relationships: Using the Predecessors Field

Predecessors and Successors

Understanding task relationships is essential for using Project. Tasks are linked together in a project plan by task relationships (or dependencies). These task relationships consist of **Predecessors** and **Successors**.

➢ A **Predecessor** is a task whose start or finish date determines the start or finish date of another task or tasks.

➢ A **Successor** is a task whose start or finish date is determined by the start or finish date of another task or tasks.

Task Relationship Types

There are four types of task relationships in Project – **Finish-to-Start**, **Start-to-Start**, **Finish-to-Finish**, and **Start-to-Finish**. The default task relationship type is *Finish-to-Start*. When tasks are linked, their Gantt bars on the Gantt chart will display connecting arrows that depict their task relationship type. Task relationship types are also indicated in the "Predecessors" field of the successor task with a two-letter acronym (SS, FF or SF). When the default *Finish-to-Start* type is used, the two-letter acronym (FS) is not shown. The table below includes a description of each task relationship type, how their Gantt bars appear in the Gantt chart and examples of how to use them in practice.

Task Relationship	Description	Gantt Chart Appearance	Example
Finish-to-Start (FS) (default)	The finish date of the predecessor task drives the start date of the successor task		The book must be written (predecessor) before it can be edited (sucessor)
Start-to-Start (SS)	The start date of the predecessor task drives the start date of the successor task		When the event starts (predecessor), live streaming must start (successor)
Finish-to-Finish (FF)	The finish date of the predecessor task drives the finish date of the successor task		To serve a hot breakfast, the bacon must finish cooking (predecessor) when the eggs finish cooking (successor) Note: The FF task relationship determines when to start cooking each item, working backward from the serving time
Start-to-Finish (SF)	The start date of the predecessor task drives the finish date of the successor task		Once the new email server is up and running (predecessor), the old server can be shut down (successor)

Creating Task Relationships

To create a *Finish-to-Start* task relationship between tasks, enter the task ID number of the predecessor task into the "Predecessors" field of the successor task. If a task has multiple predecessors, separate each task ID number with a comma.

A quick way to link tasks with the *Finish-to-Start* task relationship is to use the **Link the Selected Tasks** feature.

1. Select the tasks you want to link.

2. On the **Task** tab, in the **Schedule** group, select the "Link the Selected Tasks" command (*Figure 31* below).

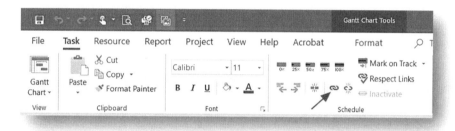

Figure 31 – Link Selected Tasks Feature

To create any of the other three task relationships, enter the task ID number of the predecessor task into the "Predecessors" field of the successor task, followed by the two-letter acronym for the task relationship type. *Figure 32* below shows the tasks relationship examples listed in the table above, entered into Project.

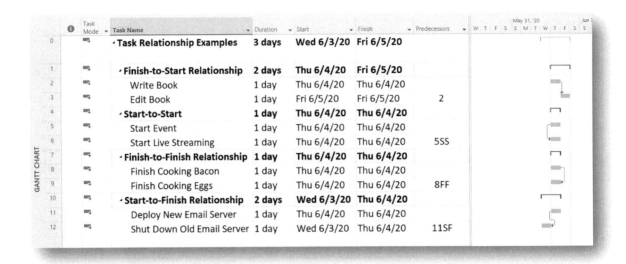

Figure 32 – Task Relationship Examples

Understanding Lag and Lead Time

Once task relationships have been established, you can apply **Lag** or **Lead** time to compress or delay the schedule.

➤ **LAG** – Use this when the successor task should be delayed after its predecessor finishes.

Example – In the *House Painting* schedule below, the "List Supplies" and "Buy Supplies" tasks have a Finish-to-Start task relationship. However, funding for the "Buy Supplies" task will not be available until 2 days after the "List Supplies" task is complete.

➤ **LEAD** – Use this when a successor task can start before its predecessor finishes.

Example – In the *House Painting* schedule in Figure 33 below, the "Apply First Coat" task and the "Apply Final Coat" task have a *Finish-to-Start* task relationship. The "Apply Final Coat" task can begin on the portions of the house that have dried, 2 days before the "Apply First Coat" task finishes (instead of waiting the entire 5 days).

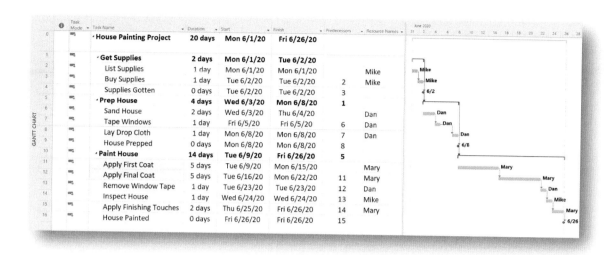

Figure 33 – House Painting Schedule

Creating Lag and Lead Time

Lag and Lead time are entered in the "Predecessors" field using the following syntax (don't include the brackets):

[Predecessor Task ID] [2-letter task relationship acronym] +/ - [Lag/Lead value, expressed in days or Lag/Lead value, expressed as a percentage of the Predecessor's duration]

For example, **4FS-2d** or **4FS + 50%**.

The **Lag** time value is entered with a plus sign (E.g. +2 days). The **Lead** time value is entered with a minus sign (E.g. -2 days). **Note**: In the case of lags and leads, the "FS" acronym for the *Finish-to-Start* relationship will be displayed.

Figure 34 below shows the lag and lead entries for the examples given earlier. When the 2-day Lag is applied, the "Buy Supplies" task will start 2 days after its predecessor "List Supplies" finishes. When the 2-day Lead is applied, the "Apply Final Coat" task will start 2 days before its predecessor "Apply First Coat" finishes. Lag and Lead time can also be expressed as a percentage.

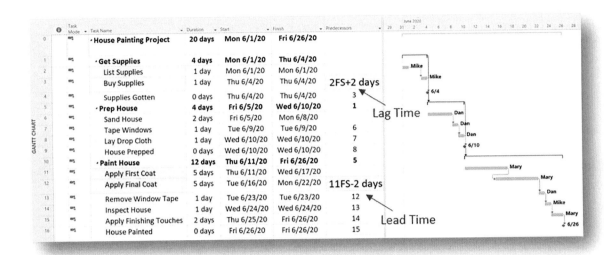

Figure 34 – Applying Lag and Lead Time

Here are more examples of Lead and Lag entries:

- 4FS – 2 days (the successor task will start 2 days before predecessor task 4 finishes)

- 4FS + 2 days (the successor task will start 2 days after predecessor task 4 finishes)

- 4FS – 50% (the successor task will start after predecessor task 4 is 50% done)

- 4FS + 50% (the successor task will start "X" days after predecessor task 4 is done; "where "X" = 50% of the duration of predecessor task 4)

We've now reviewed tasks the key elements of a schedule. Understanding how to create tasks, outline them, and establish relationships between them will benefit you greatly when building your schedule. In the next chapter, we'll go behind the scenes and look at the settings in Project 2019. We'll discover how settings affects the way Project schedules tasks.

Develop a Project Outline: Create Tasks and Task Relationships

Instructions: In this practice exercise, you will create the "House Painting" schedule we've referenced throughout the book. You'll develop the project outline by creating summary tasks, subtasks, and milestones. You will also create task relationships, apply lag time and display the project summary task. Follow the steps below to complete this exercise. Visit www.mspbasics.com for "checkpoint" images to check your work as you go along.

Start a New Project

1. From the opening view, select "Blank Project" to create a new project plan.

Adjust the Settings

Notice the *New Tasks: Manually Scheduled* message in the Status Bar (bottom left corner). This means that all new tasks will be scheduled in the "Manual" Task Mode. Next, you'll go to the *Backstage view* and adjust the settings so that new tasks are scheduled in the "Automatic" Task Mode.

1. Select the **File** tab to go *Backstage*, then select **Options** to open the *Project Options* dialog box. Select the **Schedule** tab on the left.

2. Under the "Scheduling options for this project" section, from the "New tasks created" pick-list, select **Auto Scheduled**. Click **OK** to close the *Project Options* dialog box. Notice the updated message in the Status Bar now reads *New Tasks: Auto Scheduled*.

3. If you'd like to check your results so far, visit www.mspbasics.com. Select "Practice Exercise Solutions" from the menu. Select "Chapter 4" and reference "Checkpoint Image #1".

Create a Task List

Next, you'll create the task list per the WBS below.

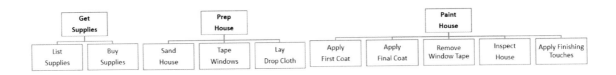

1. Enter the task names in the **Task Name** field of the Entry table. No tasks should be indented at this point. When you're done, you should have **13 tasks**. Each task should have a 1-day Duration. The Start and Finish dates should be the current date.

2. To check your results so far, visit www.mspbasics.com. Select "Practice Exercise Solutions" from the menu. Select "Chapter 4" and reference "Checkpoint Image #2".

Structure the Tasks: Create the Project Outline

Next, you'll structure the task list. You'll create summary tasks and subtasks using the **Indent Task** feature.

1. Select the "List Supplies" and "Buy Supplies" tasks.

2. On the **Task** tab, in the **Schedule** group, select the **Indent Task** command. The "Get Supplies" task is now a summary task. This represents the 1st phase of the project.

3. Select the "Sand House", "Tape Windows" and "Lay Drop Cloth" tasks. Indent the selected tasks to create the "Prep House" summary task. This represents the 2nd phase of the project.

4. Now, select the "Apply First Coat", "Apply Final Coat", "Remove Window Tape", "Inspect House" and "Apply Finishing Touches" tasks. Indent the selected tasks to create the "Paint House" summary task. This represents the 3rd phase of the project.

5. To check your results so far, visit www.mspbasics.com. Select "Practice Exercise Solutions" from the menu. Select "Chapter 4" and reference "Checkpoint Image #3".

Create Milestones

Next, you'll create Milestones, signifying the completion of each phase.

1. To create the milestone for the "Get Supplies" phase, select the "Prep House" task. **Note**: Inserted milestones and tasks appear above the selected task.

2. On the **Task** tab, in the **Insert** group, select the **Insert Milestone** command. Rename the milestone "Supplies Gotten". Notice the diamond icon in the Gantt chart, indicating the milestone.

3. Select the "Paint House" task. Then, select the **Insert Milestone** command to create the milestone for the *Prep House* phase. Rename the milestone "House Prepped".

4. You'll create the milestone for the "Paint House" phase a different way. In the row beneath the "Apply Final Touches" task, enter "House Painted" in the **Task Name** field.

5. In the **Duration** field, enter the number **0** for the duration value. Notice the task bar in the Gantt Chart became a diamond icon. This task is now a milestone.

6. To check your results so far, visit www.mspbasics.com. Select "Practice Exercise Solutions" from the menu. Select "Chapter 4" and reference "Checkpoint Image #4".

Enter Task Duration

Next, you'll give each task a Duration value.

1. In the **Duration** field, enter the duration value for each subtask, per the table below.

   Note: You will not enter a duration for the Summary tasks. Project will automatically calculate the summary task durations.

TASK	DURATION
List Supplies	1d
Buy Supplies	1d
Sand House	2d
Tape Windows	1d
Lay Drop Cloth	1d
Apply First Coat	5d
Apply Final Coat	5d
Remove Window Tape	1d
Inspect House	1d
Apply Finishing Touch	2d

2. To check your results so far, visit www.mspbasics.com. Select "Practice Exercise Solutions" from the menu. Select "Chapter 4" and reference "Checkpoint Image #5".

Connect the Tasks: Create Task Relationships

Next, you'll create task relationships. Since the tasks in this schedule occur in sequence, you'll give the tasks in each phase *Finish-to-Start* task relationships. Each task is the predecessor of the following task. For example, "List Supplies" is the predecessor of "Buy Supplies".

1. In the **Predecessors** field of each task, enter the predecessor task ID, per the table below:

    Note: After the tasks are connected, Project will re-calculate the summary task durations.

TASK	PREDECESSOR
Buy Supplies	2
Supplies Gotten	3
Sand House	4
Tape Windows	6
Lay Drop Cloth	7
House Prepped	8
Apply First Coat	9
Apply Final Coat	11
Remove Window Tape	12
Inspect House	13
Apply Finishing Touch	14
House Painted	15

2. To check your results so far, visit www.mspbasics.com. Select "Practice Exercise Solutions" from the menu. Select "Chapter 4" and reference "Checkpoint Image #6".

Create a Start-to-Start Task Relationship

Let's suppose you already have the sanding supplies for the "Sand House" task. This task can now start with the "List Supplies" task (instead of waiting for the "Supplies Gotten" milestone to finish). You'll give these tasks a *Start-to-Start* task relationship.

1. In the **Predecessors** field of the "Sand House" task, enter **2SS**.

Apply Lag Time

After the "Apply First Coat" task finishes, the paint must dry for 2 days before the "Apply Final Coat" task can begin. To account for this, you will apply a 2-day **Lag** to the "Apply Final Coat" task. This will delay the start of the task 2 days after its predecessor finishes.

1. In the **Predecessors** field of the "Apply Final Coat" task, enter **11FS+2d**.

Display the Project Summary Task

Last, you'll display the **Project Summary Task**, the highest level of the project outline.

1. Select the **Format** tab. In the **Show/Hide** group, select the **Project Summary Task** checkbox.

2. Rename the project summary task "House Painting Project".

Notice that the project summary task's ID is zero. It displays the overall project duration, which should be **20 days**.

YOU'VE NOW CREATED the *House Painting* schedule! You outlined the project by creating summary tasks, subtasks and milestones. You created task relationships, applied lag time and displayed the project summary task.

> ### CHECK YOUR FINAL RESULTS
>
> To check your final results, go to www.mspbasics.com.
>
> Select "Practice Exercise Solutions" from the menu. Select "Chapter 4" and reference "Checkpoint Image #7".

Now You Can

- Describe and Create Tasks

- Outline your Project Plan using Summary Tasks, Subtasks, and Milestones

- Display the Project Summary Task

- Create Task Relationships

- Use Lead and Lag Time

Chapter 5 Understanding Settings

IN THIS CHAPTER:

- The Manual Schedule Mode

- The Automatic Scheduling Mode

- The Duration Equation

- Effort-Driven Scheduling

- Task Type

In the last chapter, we covered the most important aspects of building a schedule – creating tasks, outlining them and establishing relationships between them. In this chapter, we'll review another fundamental topic – the settings in Microsoft Project 2019. A good understanding of settings can make the difference between a smooth and a frustrating experience using Microsoft Project. We'll start by reviewing the two scheduling modes. Then, we'll explore how Project's scheduling engine works by reviewing the Duration Equation, Effort-Driven Scheduling, and Task Type. We'll cover the details that you'll need to control how Project behaves and build the type of schedule you want to build!

Scheduling Modes

There are two scheduling modes in Project 2019 – the **Automatic** scheduling mode and the **Manual** scheduling mode. The scheduling mode determines how Project schedules tasks. By default, Project opens in the Manual scheduling mode. Let's review the aspects of each mode.

Using the Automatic Scheduling Mode

In the Automatic mode, Project schedules tasks using its powerful scheduling engine. Start dates, finish dates, and duration values are calculated based on task relationships and factors like constraints and calendars. By default, Project starts each task as soon as possible. If schedule changes are made (like increasing the duration of a task), Project will automatically update any impacted tasks.

In the Automatic mode:

- Numeric fields require numeric entries

- Task relationships are respected

- New tasks are automatically given a 1-day duration.

Figure 35 below shows tasks scheduled in the Automatic scheduling mode. The Automatic scheduling mode is indicated by a task bar icon in the **Task Mode** field and blue task bars in the Gannt Chart. The scheduling mode is also shown in the **Status Bar** in the bottom left corner.

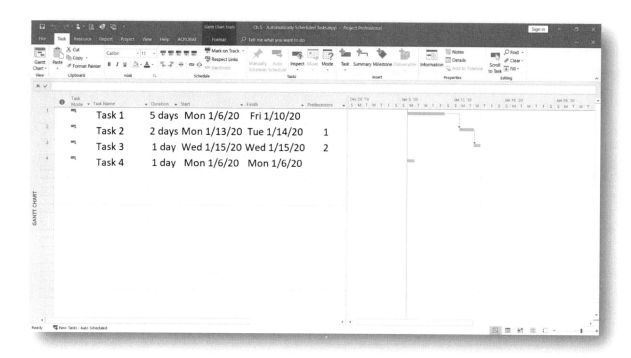

Figure 35 – Automatically Scheduled Tasks

Using the Manual Scheduling Mode

The Manual scheduling mode was added to the 2010 version of Microsoft Project. It was created to provide a middle-of-the-road scheduling environment for users who preferred more scheduling control. In the Manual scheduling mode, users have the option of scheduling tasks manually. The scheduling engine is still engaged, but users are less restricted. For example, text entries are allowed in numeric fields like the Duration field.

Manually scheduled tasks are not affected by:

➢ Changes in Duration

➢ Changes in Start Dates

➢ Changes in Finish Dates

➢ Changes in Task Relationships

➢ Occurrences that would normally cause Project to reschedule a task.

Figure 36 below shows tasks scheduled in the Manual scheduling mode. The Manual scheduling mode is indicated by a pushpin icon in the **Task Mode** field and teal task bars in the Gantt chart. The scheduling mode is also shown in the Status Bar in the bottom left corner.

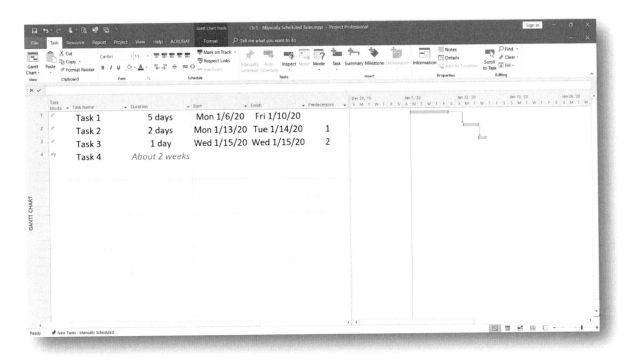

Figure 36 – Manually Scheduled Tasks

Comparing the Manual and the Automatic Scheduling Modes

Next, we'll take a closer look at how Project behaves in each scheduling mode. Using the figures below, we'll compare various entries in the two scheduling modes. *Figure 37* below shows five entries in the Manual mode. *Figure 38* below shows the same entries in the Automatic mode.

- **Entry #1** – A task name ("Task 1") was entered in the Task Name field of the Entry table.

  - **In the Manual mode** – Project did not assign a duration, determine a start or finish date or generate a task bar in the Gantt chart. The question mark next to the task mode icon is an alert that more scheduling information is needed.

  - **In the Automatic mode** – Project automatically assigned a 1-day duration and determined the start and finish dates. Also, a task bar was generated in the Gantt chart.

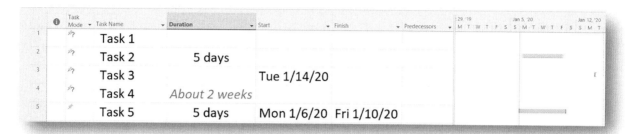

Figure 37 – Entries in the Manual Scheduling Mode

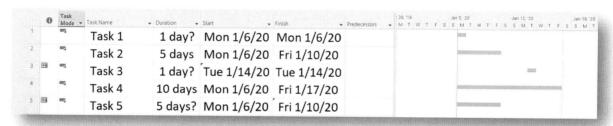

Figure 38 – Entries in the Automatic Scheduling Mode

- **Entry #2** – A task name ("Task 2") and a 5-day duration were entered.

  - **In the Manual Mode** – Project did not determine a start or finish date, but a task bar indicating the 5-day duration was generated in the Gantt chart.

  - **In the Automatic Mode** – Project automatically determined the start and finish dates based on the 5-day duration. Also, a task bar was generated in the Gantt chart.

- **Entry #3** – A task name ("Task 3"), and a start date of 1/14/20 were entered.

  - **In the Manual Mode** – Project did not assign a duration or determine a finish date. In the Gantt chart, Project generated an endcap, corresponding with the start date.

  - **In the Automatic Mode** – Project automatically assigned a 1-day duration and determined the finish date. Also, a task bar was generated in the Gantt chart. Because the start date was manually entered, Project applied a scheduling constraint (indicated by the calendar icon in the Indicators field). **Note:** Start dates should not be manually entered in the Automatic scheduling mode. This action causes Project to apply a *Start No Earlier Than* scheduling constraint, which limits scheduling flexibility. We'll discuss constraints further in Chapter 12 "Constraining Your Schedule".

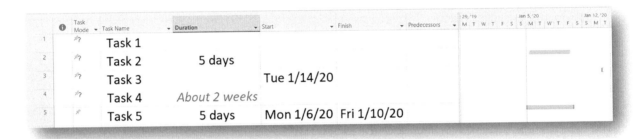

Figure 37 – Entries in the Manual Scheduling Mode

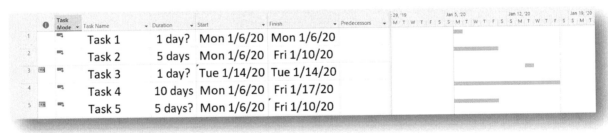

Figure 38 – Entries in the Automatic Scheduling Mode

- **Entry #4** – A task name ("Task4") was entered and the text "About 2 weeks" was entered into the Duration field.

  - **In the Manual Mode** – The text entry was allowed. Project did not determine a start or finish date and no task bar was generated in the Gantt chart.

  - **In the Automatic Mode** – The text entry was <u>not</u> allowed. Text is not supported in numeric fields in the Automatic mode. A numeric value (10d) was required for the 2-week duration. Project automatically determined the start and finish dates based on the 2-week duration. Also, a task bar was generated in the Gantt chart.

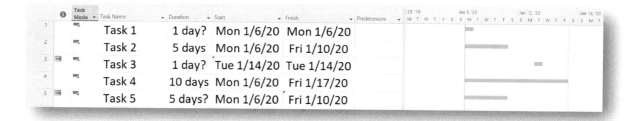

Figure 37 – Entries in the Manual Scheduling Mode

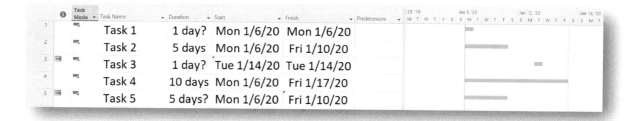

Figure 38 – Entries in the Automatic Scheduling Mode

- **Entry #5** – A task name ("Task 5"), a start date of 1/6/20 and a finish date of 1/10/20 were entered.

  - **In the Manual Mode** – Project assigned a 5-day duration from the start and finish dates. In the Gantt chart, a task bar was generated with end caps, representing the start and finish dates.

  - **In the Automatic Mode** – After the task name was entered, Project automatically assigned a 1-day duration and determined the start and finish dates. Also, a task bar was generated in the Gantt chart. After the start date was entered, Project applied a *Start No Earlier Than* scheduling constraint. After the finish date was entered, Project assigned a 5-day duration from the start and finish dates and extended the task bar in the Gantt chart to indicate the 5-day duration. Project also switched the scheduling constraint from *Start No Earlier Than* to *Finish No Earlier Than*.

    Note: Start and finish dates should not be manually entered in the Automatic scheduling mode. Manually entering these dates will cause Project to constrain the schedule. It's best to let Project automatically assign start and finish dates using its scheduling engine.

Figure 37 – Entries in the Manual Scheduling Mode

Figure 38 – Entries in the Automatic Scheduling Mode

In upcoming chapters, we'll discuss how resources, constraints and other factors determine how Project schedules tasks in the Automatic scheduling mode.

Scheduling modes and Task Relationships

Next, we'll review how task relationships are handled in the two scheduling modes. As reviewed in Chapter 4, in the Automatic scheduling mode, when tasks are linked, Project respects task relationships. Also, summary task durations are calculated from the durations, dependencies and outline levels of their subtasks (*Figure 39* below).

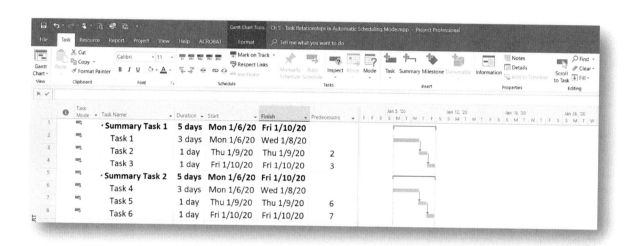

Figure 39 – Task Relationship in the Automatic Scheduling Mode

Figure 40 below shows task relationships in the Manual scheduling mode.

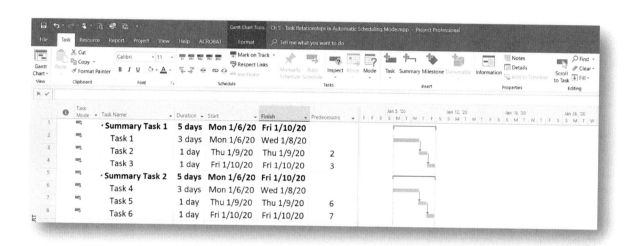

Figure 40 – Task Relationships in the Manual Scheduling Mode

Notice that the Task Mode for "Summary Task 1" is *Automatic* even though the tasks are scheduled in the Manual mode. This is because the default mode for summary tasks in either scheduling mode is *Automatic*. Since summary tasks are scheduled in the Automatic mode, Project calculates their durations per their subtasks. However, summary task durations can be overridden with manual entries in the Manual scheduling mode. In this case, Project will toggle the summary task to the *Manual* mode.

For example, in *Figure 40* above, the calculated 5-day duration for "Summary Task 2" was manually overridden with an 8-day duration entry and Project toggled the scheduling mode to *Manual*. This created a scheduling inconsistency; which Project indicates in the Gantt chart with two summary bars. The black summary bar reflects the 8-day duration. The teal summary bar reflects the 5-day duration (the sum of the subtasks). If you hover over the black summary bar, Project alerts you that the tasks will finish 3 days earlier than the finish date of the summary task.

Note: In the Manual mode, Project does not consistently respect task relationships. This may cause **scheduling conflicts**. When this occurs, Project will indicate the potential scheduling conflict with a red squiggly line under the conflicting date and dotted lines around the task bars in the Gantt chart. Hover over either to get a description of the conflict. Right-click for options to resolve the conflict.

For example, in *Figure 41* below, a start date of 1/7/20 was manually entered for "Task 5". Since this start date occurs before its predecessor finishes, Project alerts of a potential scheduling conflict.

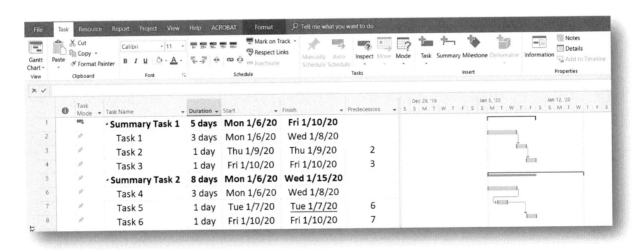

Figure 41 – Scheduling Conflicts in the Manual Scheduling Mode

You can cause Project to respect links in the *Manual* mode using the **Respect Links** feature. This will cause Project to schedule tasks per their task relationships.

To use the Respect Links feature:

1. Select the task(s) for which you want Project to respect the links.
2. On the **Task** tab, in the **Schedule** group, select the **Respect Links** icon.

Understanding the Duration Equation

The **Duration Equation** (also known as the Scheduling Formula) is the formula Project uses to calculate duration. The formula is expressed as:

$$DURATION = WORK/UNITS$$

When the scheduling engine is engaged, Project makes scheduling calculations using the three variables in the Duration Equation. The variables are defined as follows:

- **DURATION** – The number of working days required to complete a task.

- **WORK** – The number of hours required to complete a task.

- **UNITS** – The percentage an 8-hour work day a resource is assigned to work on a task. E.g. 2 hours per day = 25% Units (2 hours per day / 8-hour day = 25%).

Here's an example of how Project calculates duration using the Duration Equation:

A task requires 20 hours of *Work*. A resource is assigned to the task at 50% *Units* (4 hours per day). Project will calculate the *Duration* as 5 days (20 hours / 4 hours per day = **5 days**). *Figure 42* below shows this example in Project.

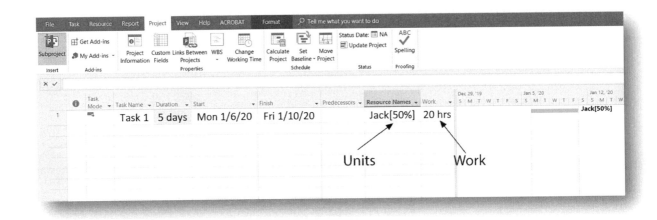

Figure 42 – The Duration Equation

In the next section, we'll review two of the most misunderstood (and underappreciated) aspects of the software – **Effort-driven Scheduling** and **Task Type**. Understanding these features will help you understand how the scheduling engine works and assist you with troubleshooting unexpected outcomes.

Understanding Effort-Driven Scheduling

Effort-Driven Scheduling is a Microsoft Project scheduling feature that keeps the work value constant (or fixed) and enables the duration value to increase or decrease as you assign resources to or remove resources from a task.

Here's an example of how the feature works. Task 1 has 40 hours of Work. One resource is assigned to work on the task at 100% units (8 hours per day). Using the Duration Equation, Project will calculate the task duration as 5 days (40 hours/**8 hours** = 5 days).

To expedite the schedule, a 2nd resource is assigned to the task at 100% units. When the effort-driven feature is enabled, Project will keep the work value constant at 40 hours and decrease the duration per the collective resources' units. Project will thus calculate the duration as 2.5 days (40 hours/**16 hours** = 2.5 days). If the additional resource is removed, Project will increase the duration.

Figure 43 below shows this scenario scheduled in Project with the effort-driven feature enabled.

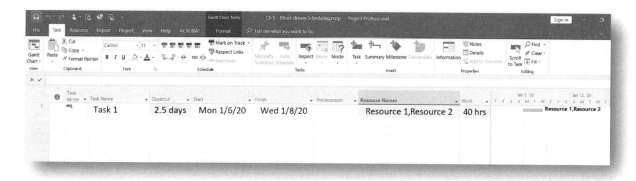

Figure 43 – Effort-driven Scheduling

Enabling Effort-Driven Scheduling

You can enable the effort-driven feature for specific tasks or the entire project.

To enable effort-driven scheduling for a specific task:

1. Double-click the task to open the *Task Information* dialogue box.

2. On the *Advanced* tab, select the *Effort-driven* checkbox.

To enable effort-driven scheduling for the entire project:

1. Select the *File* tab to go Backstage.

2. Select the *Options* tab to open the *Project Options* dialogue box.

3. Select the *Schedule* tab.

4. Under the "Scheduling options for this project" section, select the "New tasks are effort-driven" checkbox.

ACTION INDICATORS

When you add a second resource to a task that already has a resource assigned to it, Project will generate an **Action Indicator** indicated by a green triangle in the upper left corner of the **Task Name** field. If you click the alert icon, you'll be given options like those shown in *Figure 44* below. If you've already adjusted the settings, be sure to ignore this indicator. Selecting an option may override your settings.

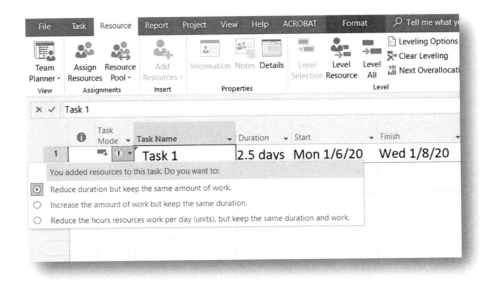

Figure 44 – Action Indicator

Understanding Task Type

Every task has a **Task Type**. Task Type works in conjunction with effort-driven scheduling to control the scheduling engine. It fixes the Work, Units or Duration value, depending on the Task Type you choose.

There are three Task Types:

- Fixed Units (default)
- Fixed Duration
- Fixed Work

The Task Type you select determines which variable in the Duration Equation will remain constant when the other variables are changed due to a scheduling event, such as adding or removing resources. Consider the following example.

A task requires 20 hours of work. A resource is assigned to the task at 2 hours per day (25% units). Per the Duration Equation, the task duration will be 10 days (20 hours / 2 hours per day = 10 days). To expedite the schedule, another resource is added to the task at 25% units. If the effort-driven feature is enabled, here's how Project will respond with each Task Type.

- If Task Type is **Fixed Units**, Project will adjust the Duration.
- If Task Type is **Fixed Duration**, Project will adjust the Work.

73

- If Task Type is **Fixed Work**, and the Units value has already been established, Project will adjust the Duration.

- If Task Type is **Fixed Work**, and the Duration value has already been established, Project will adjust the Units.

Changing the Task Type

Select the Task Type according to how you'd like Project to respond. You can change the Task Type for a specific task or for the entire project.

To change the Task Type for a specific task:

1. Double-click the task to open the *Task Information* dialogue box.

2. On the **Advanced** tab, select the **"Task Type"** you want from the respective pick-list.

To change the Task Type for the entire project:

1. Select the **File** tab to go Backstage.

2. Select the **Options** tab to access the *Project Options* dialogue box.

3. Select the **Schedule** tab.

4. Under the **"Scheduling options for this project"** section, select the **"Task Type"** from the **"Default task type"** pick-list.

We've now reviewed the science behind the settings in Microsoft Project. In the next chapter, we'll put these fundamental to use by applying them to one of two scheduling approaches. If you had difficulty conceptualizing some of the settings, don't worry. The next chapter will help by providing a practice context.

CHALLENGE – Practice Exercise

Adjust the Settings in Microsoft Project 2019

Instructions: In this practice exercise, you'll work with the settings in Microsoft Project 2019. You'll build a schedule and configure the settings using the features we reviewed throughout the chapter. You'll work with scheduling mode, task type, and effort-driven scheduling to observe how they function in a schedule. Visit www.mspbasics.com for "checkpoint" images to check your work as you go along.

Follow the steps below to complete this exercise:

Start a New Project

From the opening view, select "Blank Project" to create a new project plan.

Select the Scheduling Mode

Adjust the settings so that all new tasks are scheduled in the **Automatic** scheduling mode:

1. Select the **File** tab to go *Backstage*, then select **Options** to open the *Project Options* dialog box. Select the **Schedule** tab on the left to adjust the project settings.

2. Under the "Scheduling options for this project" section, from the "New tasks created" pick-list, select "Auto Scheduled". **Do not click OK**. Remain in the *Project Options* dialog box.

Select the Task Type

Next, you'll configure Project so that all new tasks are given the **Fixed Duration** Task Type. This Task Type will cause Project to fix the duration values. The task durations will remain constant when scheduling changes are made.

1. Under the "Scheduling options for this project" section, select "Fixed Duration" from the "Default task type" pick-list.

2. Under the same section, be sure the "New tasks are effort-driven" feature is <u>unchecked</u>. The effort-driven feature should be disabled.

3. Click OK to close the *Project options* dialogue box.

4. To check your results so far, visit www.mspbasics.com. Select "Practice Exercise Solutions" from the menu. Select "Chapter 5" and reference "Checkpoint Image #1".

Enter a Task List and Create a Project Outline

Next, you'll create the project outline for the *House Painting* project per the WBS below. If you need assistance completing the steps in this section, refer to the Chapter 4 practice exercise.

1. Enter the task list into the Entry table.

2. Structure the tasks using the Indent Task and Outdent Task commands.

3. Create a Milestone signifying the end of each phase. Rename the milestones "Supplies Gotten", "House Painted" and "House Painted" respectively.

4. Display the Project Summary Task. Rename it "House Painting Project".

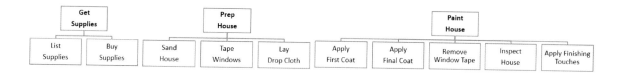

Confirm the Settings

Next, you'll add new fields to the Entry table to confirm the settings you applied earlier. You will use the **Add New Column** field.

1. If you don't see the "Add New Column" field in the Entry table, you'll need to drag the line that divides the Entry Table and the Gantt chart screen to the right until you see the "Add New Column" field.

2. Click on the "Add New Column" heading. This will display the available fields you can add to the table. Enter the word "Type" to display the **Type** field, then select it.

3. If the Task Type settings are correct, the "Type" field should be populated with "Fixed Duration".

4. Using the "Add New Column" field, add the "**Effort-Driven**" field to the Entry table. If the effort-driven settings are correct, "No" should be populated to the "Effort-Driven" field.

5. Using the "Add New Column" field, add the **"Work"** field to the table. Zero values should be populated to the field at this point.

6. To check your results so far, visit www.mspbasics.com. Select "Practice Exercise Solutions" from the menu. Select "Chapter 5 and reference "Checkpoint Image #2".

Create Task Relationships

Notice all tasks (including summary tasks) were given an estimated 1-day duration and a start and finish date. Notice the tasks all start and finish on the same date. This is because the tasks have not been given task relationships.

Next, you'll give the tasks, *Finish-to-Start* task relationships. Since the tasks in this schedule follow one after another, they can be quickly linked using a method I call "Lazy Linking".

1. Select the entire project plan by clicking on the empty gray cell above task ID 0.

2. On the **Task** tab, in the **Schedule** group, select the **Link the Selected Tasks** icon. The tasks are now linked with *Finish-to-Start* task relationships.

Here, you can see Project's scheduling engine at work in the Automatic scheduling mode. Each task now starts the next working day after its predecessor finishes. Project adjusted the start and finish dates respectively. The summary task durations were calculated according to the durations of their subtasks (using the 1-day estimates). The overall project duration (displayed in the "Duration" field of the Project Summary Task) is now 10 days, which is the sum of each summary task duration.

Enter Task Durations

1. Next, enter the duration values for each subtask, per the table below.

TASK	DURATION
List Supplies	1d
Buy Supplies	1d
Sand House	2d
Tape Windows	1d
Lay Drop Cloth	1d
Apply First Coat	10d
Apply Final Coat	5d
Remove Window Tape	1d
Inspect House	1d
Apply Finishing Touch	2d

2. When you're done, the summary task durations should be updated to 2, 4 & 19 days respectively. The project duration should be updated to **25 days**.

3. To check your results so far, visit www.mspbasics.com. Select "Practice Exercise Solutions" from the menu. Select "Chapter 5 and reference "Checkpoint Image #3".

Assign Resources to Tasks

To demonstrate the effect of the "Fixed Duration" Task Type, you'll assign 2 resources to the "Sand House" Task.

1. In the **Resource Names** field of the "Sand House" task, enter **Jack**. Jack is now assigned to the task. **Note**: Typing resource names directly into the Resource Names field quickly assigns resources to work on tasks 8 hours per day (100% Units). We'll discuss this further in Chapter 8, "Assigning Resources to Your Schedule".

    Notice Project populated **16 hours** of work into the "Work" field, which represents Jack working on the task for 8 hours per day for two days.

2. Next, you'll add a resource to the "Sand House" Task. In the **Resource Names** field, replace the "Jack" entry with **Jack,Jill** (Jack comma Jill). Two resources are now assigned to the task.

3. Since the Fixed Duration Task Type *fixes* the duration value, Project kept the duration at 2 days and adjusted the work value from 16 hours to **32 hours**. Each resource is working on the task 8 hours per day for two days.

   Notice Project generated an "Action Indicator" (indicated by the green triangle left of the resource names). Because you added a resource to the task, Project wants to know which variable to adjust in the Duration Equation. Click the alert icon to see the options. The options are, "Reduce duration but keep the same work", "Increase the amount of work but keep the same duration" or "Reduce the hours resources work per day (units) but keep the same duration and work". Since you've already adjusted the settings, leave option 2 selected. Selecting a different option would override your settings.

Enable Effort-Driven Scheduling and Change Task Type for a Specific Task

Next, you'll enable the **Effort-Driven scheduling** feature for the "Apply First Coat" task. To expedite the schedule, you'll decrease the duration for this task to 5 days by enabling effort driven scheduling and assigning 2 resources. Enabling this feature will cause Project to keep the work value fixed, and adjust the duration as you add resources to the task.

1. Double-click the "Apply First Coat" task name to open the *Task Information* dialogue box.

2. On the **Advanced** tab, select the **Effort-driven** checkbox. **Do not click OK**. Remain in the *Task Information* dialogue box.

This task currently has a "Fixed Duration" Task Type. Because you'd like Project to decrease the duration for this task, you'll change the Task Type from "Fixed Duration" to "Fixed Units". This will cause Project to keep the Work and Units values constant and adjust the Duration value.

1. Select "Fixed Units" from the "Task Type" pick-list. Click **OK** to close the *Task Information* dialogue box.

   Notice **Fixed Units** and **Yes** are now populated to the "Type" and "Effort-driven" fields respectively. Next, you'll assign resources to the task, to see the effect of effort-driven scheduling.

1. In the **Resource Names** field of the "Apply First Coat" task, enter **Jack**. Project kept the units value fixed (8 hours per day) and generated a work value of 80 hours (8 hours per day for 10 days). Next, you'll add a resource to the task.

2. In the **Resource Names** field of the "Apply First Coat" task, replace the "Jack" entry with **Jack,Jill**.

Notice, Project decreased the task's duration to **5 days**. Because the Task Type is "Fixed Units", Project kept the resources' hours at 8 hours per day each (16 hours collectively). Because the "effort-driven" feature is enabled, which fixes the work value, project kept the work value at 80 hours and adjusted the unfixed variable, which is Duration. Using the Duration Equation (D=W/U), the task duration was calculated at 5 days. You've expedited the schedule and the overall project duration is now **20 days**.

You've now worked with the scheduling mode, task type, and effort-driven scheduling features and observed how they function in a schedule.

CHECK YOUR FINAL RESULTS

To check your final results, visit www.mspbasics.com.

Select "Practice Exercise Solutions" from the menu. Select "Chapter 5" and reference "Checkpoint Image #4".

Now You Can

- Explain the Manual Scheduling Mode

- Explain the Automatic Scheduling Mode

- Explain the Duration Equation

- Explain Effort-Driven Scheduling

- Explain Task Type

Chapter 6 Selecting the Right Scheduling Method

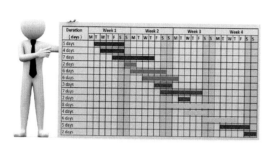 

IN THIS CHAPTER:

- The Simple Scheduling Method

- The Detailed Scheduling Method

- Comparing the Two Scheduling Methods

- Selecting the Right Scheduling Method

- Adjusting the Settings for Each Method

In the last chapter, we reviewed the settings in Microsoft Project 2019 and how they affect the way tasks are scheduled. In addition to understanding settings, you must understand the two basic ways to build a schedule. In this chapter, we'll review the **Simple Scheduling** method and the **Detailed Scheduling** method. When you're done, you'll be able to select the right scheduling method for your project and adjust the settings to support that method.

Understanding the Two Scheduling Methods

The two scheduling methods are often referred to as *Duration-based* and *Effort-based* scheduling. I don't prefer these labels because both scheduling approaches use duration to calculate the schedule. One approach simply requires more scheduling detail than the other. Also, users often confuse the Effort-based scheduling approach with the Effort-driven scheduling feature. In this book, we'll refer to the two ways to build a schedule as **Simple Scheduling** (Duration-based scheduling) and **Detailed Scheduling** (Effort-based scheduling).

The Simple Scheduling Method

A **Simple Schedule** is built by estimating the number of working days each task will take and entering those estimates directly into the Duration field of the Entry table in the Gantt Chart view (*Figure 45* below).

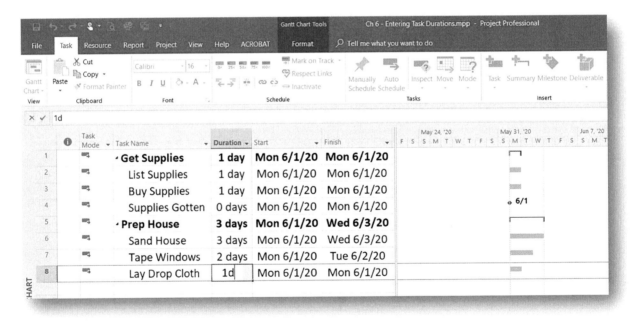

Figure 45 – Building a Simple Scheduling – Entering Duration

Once you've entered task durations and task dependencies, Project will calculate your finish date. There are a few more steps, but this is the basic idea. Using this approach, resources can simply provide you with a timeframe within which they'll complete a task (E.g. 2 days), rather than the specific number of hours the task requires (E.g. 4 hours) or the number of hours they'll work on it each day (E.g. 2 hours per day). Because of this flexibility, the Simple scheduling approach is used most often. The drawback, however, is this approach gives project stakeholders no visibility into the man-hours (Work), which are required to accurately generate project cost. Thus, the Simple scheduling approach is used to calculate schedules only and not project cost.

Some aspects of the auto repair process depict the Simple scheduling approach. You take your car in for repair and you're told your car will be repaired in 2 days. Only when you get the bill, do you discover that the repair required 4 hours of labor. And only after the mechanic assessed your car, did he determine the labor hours required to repair it. Therefore, the labor hours were not used to determine the 2-day estimate. This is the chief characteristic of the Simple scheduling approach. It allows resources to estimate task durations without providing details such as the man-hours required to complete them. In the case of the auto repair example, the 2-day estimate was a ballpark estimate and not a calculation based on man-hours or the mechanic's availability. Similarly, in the Simple scheduling approach, the schedule is based on task durations and not on the details that make up task durations, namely man-hours (Work) and resource availability (Units).

Assigning Resources in a Simple Schedule

In a Simple schedule, resources can be assigned by entering resource names directly into the **Resource Names** field of the Entry table (*Figure 46* below).

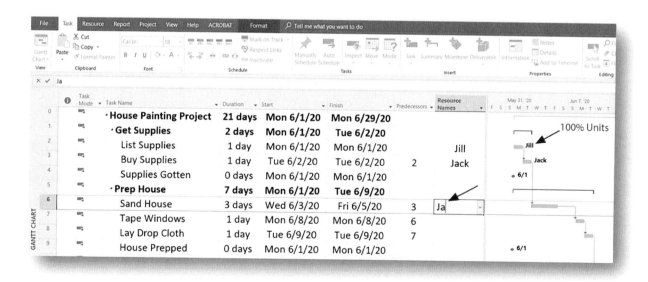

Figure 46 – Assigning Resources in the Resource Names Field

This method will result in resources being assigned to tasks at 100% Units (8 hour per day). Although resources will rarely work on tasks 8 hours per day, this exaggeration is perfectly acceptable in a Simple schedule. This is because resource Units do not affect task duration in a Simple schedule. As discussed in the auto repair example, the task duration is not derived from the units or work values. It's a ballpark estimate of how many days it will take to complete a task. For this reason, resource pay rates should not be added to a Simple schedule. Task cost equals resource pay rates multiplied by task work. Therefore, if pay rates are added, the exaggerated work values will be multiplied by resource pay rates, resulting in exaggerated cost.

For example, a resource has a pay rate of $50 per hour. The resource is assigned at 100% Units to a task with a 3-day duration. He finished the task in 9 hours, spread evenly across the 3 days. If pay rates were added to a Simple schedule, the task cost would be calculated as $1,200 ($50 per hour x 24 hours of work) instead of $450 ($50 per hour x 9 hours of work). This exaggerated cost calculation demonstrates that since the specific work hours are not used to calculate the schedule, resource pay rates should be excluded from a Simple schedule.

The Detailed Scheduling Method

If you're only tracking task durations and the project schedule, the Simple scheduling approach will work fine. If you're tracking cost, man-hours and resource allocation, then you must build a **Detailed Schedule**.

When building a Detailed schedule, task durations should not be entered directly into the Duration field. Project will <u>calculate</u> task durations from the Work and Units values. Resources must provide you with the specific number of hours each task requires (Work) and the number of hours they'll work on the tasks each day (Units).

Establishing the Work Values

Work values are entered into the "Work" field of the Entry table (*Figure 47* below). The "Work" field must be added to the Entry table in the Gantt chart view, using the "Add New Column" field.

To add the Work field:

1. Select the pick-list arrow to the right of the "Add New Column" field's title. This will display the available fields you can add to the table.

2. Scroll down the list until you find the **"Work"** field, then select it. You can also type the name of the field you want.

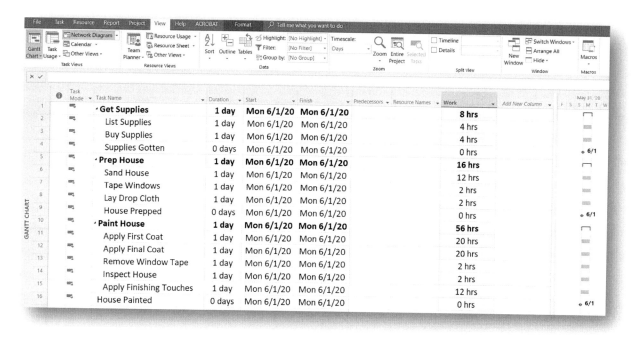

Figure 47 – Building a Detailed Schedule – Entering Work

Establishing the Units Values: Assigning Resources in a Detailed Schedule

Units values are established when resources are assigned to tasks. In a Detailed schedule, resources are assigned to tasks according to their precise availability. They are assigned with a Units value equal to the percentage of an 8-hour day they are available to work on the task. If more than one resource is assigned to a task, the Units value for the task will equal the collective Units of the resources assigned to it. For example, if Jack is assigned to a task at 25% Units, and Jill is assigned to the same task at 25% Units, the task will have a Units value of 50%. Because resources are assigned with specific Units, they should not be assigned by entering their names directly into the Resource Names field. If you recall, this approach results in resources being assigned at 100% Units. In a Detailed schedule, resources should be assigned using the *Assign Resources* dialogue box. We'll review this process in Chapter 8 "Adding Resources to Your Schedule".

Once the Work and Units values are set, Project will calculate the Duration using the Duration Equation. After the task dependencies are entered, Project will calculate the project finish date. There are few more steps to this scheduling approach, but this is the basic idea.

Comparing the Two Scheduling Methods

Figures 48 & 49 below show a comparison of the *House Painting* schedule using the two scheduling approaches. Let's review the similarities and differences.

Figure 48 – House Painting Project – Simple Schedule

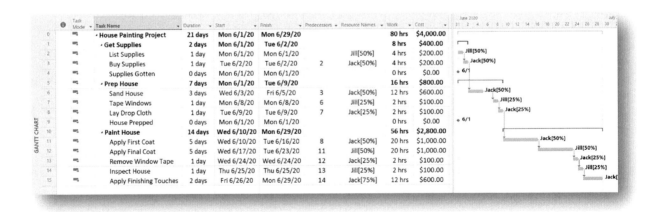

Figure 49 – House Painting Project – Detailed Schedule

Both schedules have a project duration of 21 days, beginning on 6/1/20 and ending on 6/29/20. Both schedules include tasks, durations, predecessors, and resources. These similarities demonstrate that scheduling calculations can be just as accurate in a Simple schedule as in a Detailed schedule. The key difference is the wealth of additional information provided in the Detailed schedule, namely cost and resource allocation information. For example, in the Simple schedule, we see that Jack is assigned to the "Sand House" task, which will take 3 days to complete. In the Detailed schedule, we're provided more detail. We see that the task requires 12 hours of Work. We also see that Jack is assigned to the task at 50% Units, which means he will be working on it 4 hours per day. In short, we see *why* the duration is 3 days. Since Jack's pay rate is $50 per hour, we also know that the task will cost $600.

Although, the Detailed scheduling method involves more upfront planning, it delivers more project intelligence. Advanced features such as Earned Value Analysis and Resource Leveling require a Detailed schedule. Also, most of the reports included in Project contain data such as Work and Cost, which will only be accurate in a Detailed schedule. The extra details involved in the Detailed scheduling method allow you to exploit the full capability of the Microsoft Project scheduling engine. By contrast, the Simple scheduling method uses the scheduling engine primarily to calculate the schedule.

Selecting the Right Scheduling Method

It's important to determine your scheduling approach at the beginning of the schedule building process. You'll learn throughout this book that your scheduling approach will impact how you initialize your schedule, assign resources, configure Project, and execute your schedule. Consider your project environment and determine what type of schedule is best. Because of its flexibility, the Simple scheduling approach is used most often. The Detailed approach is a good approach when cost information and more visibility into the plan is needed.

The following table can help you select the right scheduling method for your project.

WORKPLACE REALITIES	SIMPLE	DETAILED
My resources only provide duration estimates because they work on many other projects.	X	
My resource can provide Work and Availability estimates.		X
Work is impossible to determine because the project is new.	X	
If I asked for Work and Availability estimates, resources would feel micro-managed.	X	
My stakeholders expect me to provide Earned Value metrics.		X
I would like for Project to calculate the total cost of my project in addition to the project schedule.		X

Adjusting the Settings

After you determine which scheduling approach is best for your project, you'll need to adjust the settings to support that method. As discussed in Chapter 5, project settings are adjusted in the *Project Options* dialogue box.

Adjusting the Settings for a Simple Schedule

To configure Project for a **Simple Schedule**, adjust the settings as follows (*Figure 50* below):

1. Select the **File** tab to go *Backstage*.

2. Select **Options**, then select **Schedule** to access the *Project Options* dialogue box.

3. Under the "Scheduling options for this project" section, select **Auto Scheduled** from the "New tasks created" pick-list. This will enable Project to calculate the finish date from the task durations and task dependencies.

4. Select **Fixed Duration** from the "Default task type" pick-list. This will fix your initial Duration estimate if Work or resource Units are adjusted.

5. Uncheck the "New tasks are effort-driven" checkbox. This will <u>disable</u> the Effort-driven scheduling feature.

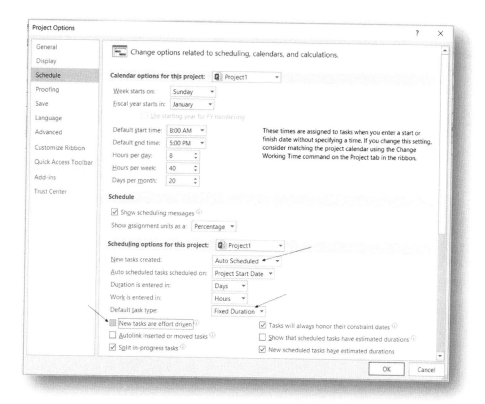

Figure 50 – Settings for a Simple Schedule

Adjusting the Settings for a Detailed Schedule

To configure Project for a **Detailed Schedule**, adjust the settings as follows (*Figure 51* below):

1. Select the **File** tab to go *Backstage*.

2. Select **Options**, then select **Schedule** to access the *Project Options* dialogue box.

3. Under the "Scheduling options for this project" section, select **Auto Scheduled** from the "New tasks created" pick-list. This will enable Project to calculate the finish date from the task durations and task dependencies.

4. Set the **Default task type** to "Fixed Units". This will allow your resource Units to remain fixed if changes are made to the Work or Duration values.

5. Check the "New tasks are effort-driven" checkbox to <u>enable</u> Effort-driven scheduling. This will fix your initial Work values and cause Project to increase or decrease task Duration as resources are added to or removed from tasks.

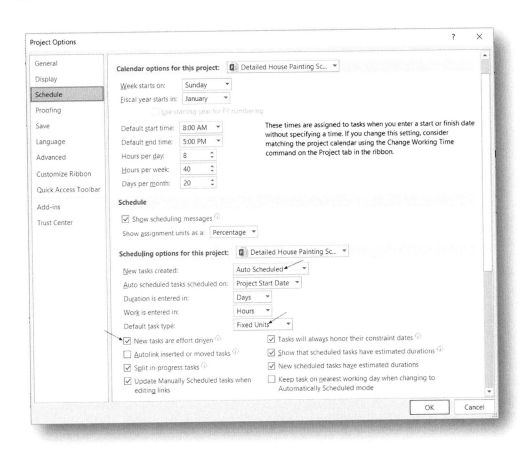

<u>Figure 51 – Settings for a Detailed Schedule</u>

We've now reviewed the two ways to build a schedule, how to adjust project settings to support either method and the use cases and benefits of using either approach.

CHALLENGE – Practice Exercise

Select the Scheduling Method

Instructions: In this practice exercise, you'll answer questions concerning the two scheduling methods discussed in this chapter. Visit www.mspbasics.com to check your answers. Select "Practice Exercise Solutions" from the menu, then select "Chapter 6".

Part One: Select the Right Scheduling Method

Consider the following scenarios and select the most appropriate scheduling method:

Scenario #1

The resources assigned to your project are scarce. Because of the demand for their skills, they are often overbooked. As a result, they provide duration estimates within which to complete their tasks. They do not provide work and availability estimates.

    a. Simple Scheduling

    b. Detailed Scheduling

Scenario #2

Senior leadership has asked you to provide a monthly cost overview report to the stakeholders funding your project. They would also like to view quarterly Earned Value metrics.

    a. Simple Scheduling

    b. Detailed Scheduling

Part Two: Identify the Scheduling Method

Refer to the images below and identify the scheduling method:

Image #1

    a. Simple

    b. Detailed

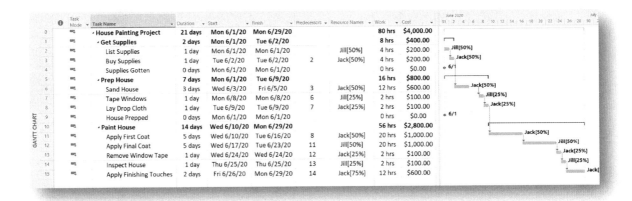

Image #1

Image #2

    a. Simple

    b. Detailed

Image #2

93

Now You Can

- Explain the Simple Scheduling Method

- Explain the Detailed Scheduling Method

- Select the Right Scheduling Method

- Adjust the Settings for Simple or Detailed Scheduling

Part One Summary

This concludes Part One – Laying the Foundation. You've learned the fundamental concepts for building a schedule with Microsoft Project, including a comparison of Excel to Project as a scheduling solution, an overview of the software, instructions for preparing a Work Breakdown Structure, an overview of tasks, milestones and task relationships, an overview of Project 2019 settings, an overview of the two scheduling approaches and guidance on selecting the right approach for your project. In Part Two – Building the Schedule, we'll put these fundamentals into practice.

PART TWO: Building Your Schedule

In PART TWO, you'll learn to apply the B.A.S.I.C.S. acronym to consistently build reliable schedules. You'll also learn to add resources, calendars and documentation to your schedule. You'll learn to compress your schedule, constrain it, level resources and perform an in-depth inspection before beginning the execution phase. This section covers many of the skills measured by Microsoft Project Exam 74-343.

Chapter 7 Building Your Schedule

IN THIS CHAPTER:

- Building a Simple Schedule

- Building a Detailed Schedule

- Using the **B.A.S.I.C.S.** Approach

- Initializing Durations

In the last chapter, we reviewed the two ways to build a schedule. In this chapter, we'll use the B.A.S.I.C.S acronym to walk through each step of the schedule building process. Along the way, we'll apply many of the concepts we've covered in Part One and explore exciting software features.

Now that we've reviewed the fundamentals, we're ready to build a schedule! To begin, you'll need to gather some initial scheduling information about your project.

Here's some information you'll need as you build your schedule:

- WBS
- The Project Start Date
- Vacation Schedules and other Non-Working Days
- Work or Duration estimates for each task
- Resource Availability (Units) – Detailed schedule only
- Resource Pay Rates – Detailed schedule only

Using the B.A.S.I.C.S Acronym

The **B.A.S.I.C.S.** acronym includes all the steps you'll need to build and execute a schedule. By building your schedule in the order prescribed, your scheduling calculations will be made *after* you configure Project for the type of schedule you're building. This will lead to less re-work and consistent results. Let's review the B.A.S.I.C.S. approach, step by step.

Break Down the Project

The first step is to **Break Down the Project**. Gather your team (or yourself!) and create a Work Breakdown Structure. Conduct a brainstorming session, use Top-down and Bottom-up planning and be sure to follow the 100% Rule. See Chapter 3 for a refresher.

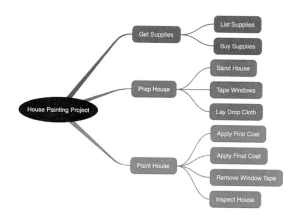

Work Breakdown Structure

Adjust the Settings

After you've broken down the project, you're ready to enter scheduling details into Microsoft Project. Before you enter tasks and other scheduling information, you must **Adjust the Settings** to support either a Simple or a Detailed schedule (Chapter 6). The settings are adjusted in the *Project Options* dialogue box.

To adjust the settings for a Simple schedule:

1. Select the **File** tab to go *Backstage*.

2. Select **Options**, then select **Schedule** to access the *Project Options* dialogue box (*Figure 52a* below)*.

3. Under the "Scheduling options for this project" section, select **Auto Scheduled** from the "New tasks created" pick-list. This will enable Project to calculate the finish date from the task durations and task dependencies.

4. Select **Fixed Duration** from the "Default task type" pick-list. This will fix your initial Duration estimate if Work or resource Units are adjusted.

5. Uncheck the "New tasks are effort-driven" checkbox. This will <u>disable</u> the Effort-driven scheduling feature.

To adjust the settings for a Detailed schedule:

1. Select the **File** tab to go *Backstage*.

2. Select **Options**, then select **Schedule** to access the *Project Options* dialogue box (*Figure 52b* below).

3. Under the "Scheduling options for this project" section, select **Auto Scheduled** from the "New tasks created" pick-list. This will enable Project to calculate the finish date from the task durations and task dependencies.

4. Set the **Default task type** to "Fixed Units". This will allow your resource Units to remain fixed if changes are made to the Work or Duration values.

5. Check the "New tasks are effort-driven" checkbox to <u>enable</u> Effort-driven scheduling. This will fix your initial Work values and cause Project to increase or decrease task Duration as resources are added to or removed from tasks.

Figure 52a
Settings for a Simple Schedule

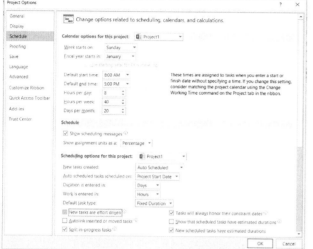

Figure 52b
Settings for a Detailed Schedule

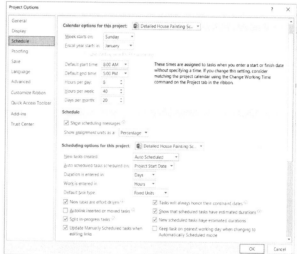

<u>Figure 52a and 52b – Adjust the Settings</u>

Note: The settings should always be adjusted <u>before</u> you assign resources, work, or durations to tasks. Performing this step out of sequence could result in scheduling calculations which are inconsistent with the scheduling method you've chosen. For more information about settings, review Chapter 5.

Setting the Project Start Date

It's important to use the proper method to set the **Project Start Date**. A common (and incorrect) approach is to enter the start date in the "Start" field of the first task. As discussed in Chapter 5, this approach creates scheduling constraints that override Project's default scheduling behavior, which efficiently begins all tasks as soon as possible.

To set the Project Start Date:

1. On the **Project** tab, in the **Properties** group, select the **Project Information** command to open the *Project Information* dialogue box.

2. Enter the date in the **Start date** field. Click **OK** to close the dialogue box.

Structure the Tasks

After you've adjusted the settings, you're ready to **Structure the Tasks**. Begin by entering the tasks in the **Task Name** field of the Entry table in the Gantt Chart view. No task should be indented at this point. Next, structure the tasks using the **Indent Task** and **Outdent Task** commands on the **Task** tab, in the **Schedule** group. Promote tasks to create Summary tasks and demote tasks to create subtasks (*Figure 53* below). Add Milestones to signify important project events, such as the end of a phase. For a refresher on summary task and subtask behaviors, review Chapter 4.

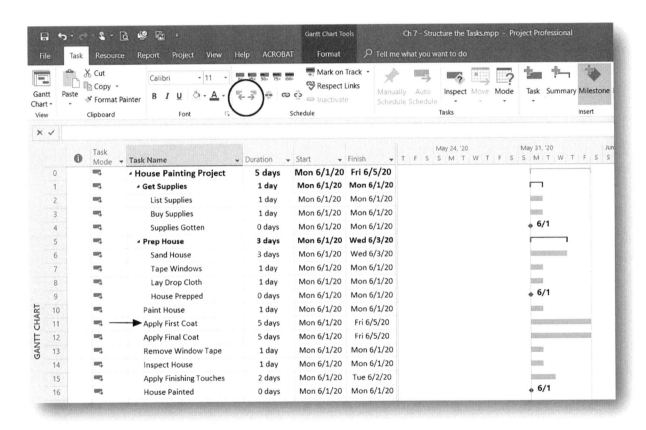

Figure 53 – Structure the Tasks

Show Outline Feature

As you structure the tasks, it's a good idea to check your project outline to ensure that summary tasks and subtasks are properly aligned. A handy way to check the outline is to use the **Show Outline** feature. This feature allows you to specify the outline level of the plan you want to view (*Figure 54* below*). Also, with larger projects, you can use this feature to collapse the plan to levels 1 or 2, then expand only the sections that you want to see.

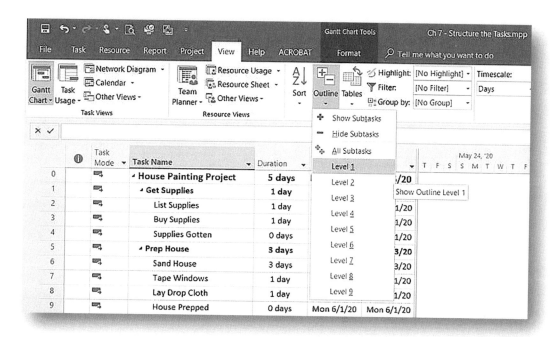

Figure 54 – Show Outline Feature

To use the **Show Outline** feature:

1. On the **View** tab, in the **Data** group, select the outline level you want to view from the **Outline** pick-list.

Initialize the Durations

After you've structured the tasks, you'll need to **Initialize the Task Durations**. Duration is the number of working days it takes to complete a task. Task duration is *Initialized* after each of the three variables in the Duration Equation is assigned a value. How these values are assigned will depend on whether you're building a Simple or Detailed schedule.

Initialize Durations for a Simple Schedule

As explained in Chapter 6, in a Simple schedule, task durations can be entered directly into the Duration field. This will establish duration values, but these values will not be <u>initialized</u> until resources are assigned to tasks (which will establish the Units and Work values).

To assign resources to tasks, you can enter resource names directly into the **Resource Names** field (*Figure 55* below).

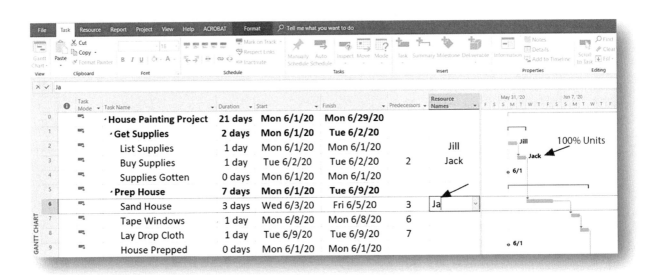

Figure 55 – Assigning Resources in a Simple Schedule

When you enter resource names into the Resource Names field, two events will occur in the background:

1. Project will establish the resource assignment Units values at 100%.

2. The Work values will be calculated from the Duration and Units values per the Duration Equation.

Once the Units and Work values have been established, the task durations will be initialized.

Initialize Durations for a Detailed Schedule

As discussed in Chapter 6, in a Detailed schedule, task duration should not be entered directly into the Duration field. Project will <u>calculate</u> task durations from the Work and Units values.

Work values are entered directly into the "Work" field of the Entry table (remember this field must be added). Units values are established when resources are assigned to tasks. Using the *Assign Resources* dialogue box, they are assigned with a Units value equal to the percentage of an 8-hour day they are available to work on tasks.

Note: In a Detailed schedule, before resources can be assigned to tasks, their information must be added to the schedule in the Resource Sheet view. Until they are added, they will not be available for assignment using the *Assign Resources* dialogue box. We'll review this process in the next chapter, "Adding Resources to Your Schedule".

Assign resources to tasks using the *Assign Resources* dialogue box as follows (*Figure 56* below):

1. Select the task name in the Entry table that you want to assign the resource(s) to.

2. On the **Resource** tab, in the **Assignments** group, select **Assign Resources** to open the *Assign Resources* dialogue box.

3. In the **Units** field for the resource you want to assign, type the Units value, then click **Assign** (or press Enter).

4. Repeat steps 1 thru 3 to assign additional resources to tasks.

5. Once all resources are assigned, select **Close** to close the *Assign Resources* dialogue box.

Once the Work and Units values have been established, the task durations will be initialized.

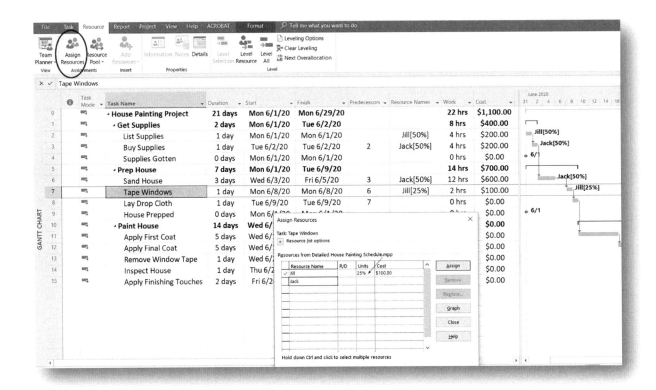

Figure 56 – Assigning Resources in a Detailed Schedule

Connect the Tasks

After you've initialized task durations, **Connect the Tasks** using the task relationships discussed in Chapter 4. Enter predecessors directly into the Predecessors field to create dependencies and apply lead and lag time as appropriate for your project.

You can create task relationships and apply lead and lag time using the *Task Information* dialogue box (*Figure 57* below). In Chapter 18, we'll use this method to create dependencies between projects.

1. Double-click the task to open the *Task Information* dialogue box.
2. Select the **Predecessors** tab.
3. Enter the predecessor's task ID in the **Task ID** field **OR**
4. Select the predecessor's task name from **Task Name** field pick-list.
5. Select the task relationship type from the **Type** field pick-list. Use the **Lag** field to apply lag or lead time (to enter lead time, enter a negative value).

6. Click **OK** to close the *Task Information* dialogue box.

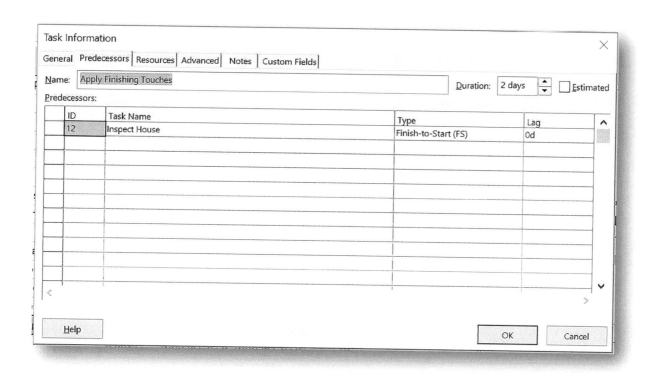

Figure 57 – Task Information Dialogue Box

Start the Project

After completing the first 5 steps, you're ready to **Start the Project**. We'll cover this step in Chapter 15 "Executing your Schedule". There are a lot of exciting things to learn before we get there, including adding resources, adding calendars, displaying the critical path and compressing the schedule to meet a deadline!

We have now reviewed the B.A.S.I.C.S. scheduling approach. This approach will yield more consistent scheduling results by ensuring that scheduling calculations occur after you've properly configured the software.

CHALLENGE – Practice Exercise

Build a Simple Schedule using the B.A.S.I.C.S.

Instructions: In this practice exercise, you'll build a Simple schedule using the **B.A.S.I.C.S.** scheduling approach. Visit www.mspbasics.com for "checkpoint" images to check your work as you go along.

Follow the steps below to complete this exercise:

Start a New Project

From the opening view, select "Blank Project" to create a new project plan. **Note**: It's important to start this exercise with a blank project. Do not use a saved project file from a previous practice exercise.

Depending on how your version of Project is configured, the **Timeline View** may be displayed. Since it is currently empty, close the panel to see more of the Gantt Chart view.

1. Select the **View** tab.

2. In the **Split View** group, uncheck the **Timeline** checkbox.

Breakdown the Project

Step 1, "**B**reakdown the Project" has already been done and is represented by the WBS included in this exercise.

Adjust the Settings

Adjust the settings to support a **Simple** schedule:

1. Select the **File** tab to go *Backstage*.

2. Select **Options**, then select **Schedule** to access the *Project Options* dialogue box.

3. Under the "Scheduling options for this project" section, select **Auto Scheduled** from the "New tasks created" pick-list. This will enable Project to calculate the finish date from the task durations and task dependencies.

4. Select **Fixed Duration** from the "Default task type" pick-list. This will fix your initial Duration estimate if Work or resource Units are adjusted.

5. Uncheck the "New tasks are effort-driven" checkbox. This will <u>disable</u> the Effort-driven scheduling feature.

6. To check your results so far, visit www.mspbasics.com. Select "Practice Exercise Solutions" from the menu. Select "Chapter 7" and reference "Checkpoint Image #1".

Set the Project Start Date

Set the Project Start Date to **June 1, 2020**:

1. On the **Project** tab, in the **Properties** group, select the **Project Information** command to open the *Project Information* dialogue box.

2. Enter the project start date in the **Start date** field. Click **OK** to close the *Project Information* dialogue box.

Enter the Task List and Structure the Tasks

Enter the project outline for the *House Painting* project per the WBS below. If you need assistance completing the steps in this section, refer to the Chapter 4 practice exercise.

1. Enter the task list into the Entry table in the Gantt Chart view.

2. Create summary tasks and subtasks to outline the project plan. Structure the tasks using the **Indent Task** and **Outdent Task** commands, located on the **Task** tab, in the **Schedule** group.

3. Create milestones signifying the end of each phase. Rename the milestones "Supplies Bought", "House Prepped" and "House Painted" respectively.

4. Display the Project Summary Task. On the **Format** tab, in the **Show/Hide** group, check the **Project Summary Task** checkbox. Rename it "House Painting Project".

5. To check your results so far, visit www.mspbasics.com. Select "Practice Exercise Solutions" from the menu. Select "Chapter 7" and reference "Checkpoint Image #2".

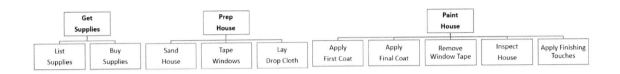

WBS for House Painting Project

Initialize the Task Durations – Enter Durations and Assign Resources

Enter the duration values for each subtask into the Duration field, per the table below.

TASK	DURATION
List Supplies	1d
Buy Supplies	1d
Sand House	2d
Tape Windows	1d
Lay Drop Cloth	1d
Apply First Coat	5d
Apply Final Coat	5d
Remove Window Tape	1d
Inspect House	1d
Apply Finishing Touch	2d

Next, you'll initialize the duration values by assigning resources to the tasks to establish the Units values (Work will be assigned in the background).

Assign the resources per the table below.

TASK	RESOURCE
List Supplies	Jill
Buy Supplies	Jack
Sand House	Jack
Tape Windows	Jill
Lay Drop Cloth	Jack
Apply First Coat	Contractor, Jack
Apply Final Coat	Contractor, Jill
Remove Tape	Jack
Inspect House	Jill
Apply Finishing Touches	Jack

1. Enter resource names into the **Resources Names** field to assign resources at 100% Units.

   Note: As the resources are assigned to the tasks, they will become over-allocated (indicated by the red man icons in the Indicators field). This is because the tasks are not yet connected and are all starting on the same date. We'll discuss resource over-allocation in Chapter 13, "Leveling Your Resources".

2. To check your results so far, visit www.mspbasics.com. Select "Practice Exercise Solutions" from the menu. Select "Chapter 7" and reference "Checkpoint Image #3".

Connect the Tasks: Create Task Relationships

Give the tasks, *Finish-to-Start* task relationships. Since the tasks in this schedule follow one after another, they can be quickly linked using the "Lazy Linking" method.

1. Select the entire project plan by clicking on the empty gray cell above task ID 0.

2. On the **Task** tab, in the **Schedule** group, select the **Link the Selected Tasks** command.

Notice that the resources are no longer over-allocated. Project rescheduled the tasks according to their Finish-to-Start task relationships. Each task now starts after its predecessor finishes. Project has also calculated the project duration as **20 days** and the project finish date as **6/26/20**.

You have now built a Simple schedule using the first 5 steps of the **B.A.S.I.C.S.** scheduling approach.

We'll review the last step, "Start the Project", in Chapter 15 "Executing your Schedule".

SAVE THIS PROJECT FILE. You will use this file to complete the Chapter 15 practice exercise.

CHECK YOUR FINAL RESULTS

To check your final results, go to www.mspbasics.com.

Select "Practice Exercise Solutions" from the menu. Select "Chapter 7" and reference "Checkpoint Image #4".

Now You Can

- Build a Simple Schedule
- Build a Detailed Schedule
- Use the **B.A.S.I.C.S.** Approach
- Initialize Durations

Chapter 8 Adding Resources to Your Schedule

IN THIS CHAPTER:

- Understanding Resource Types

- Creating Resources

- Adding Resource Information

- Assigning Resources to Tasks

In the last chapter, we learned to build a Simple and a Detailed schedule using the **B.A.S.I.C.S.** scheduling method. In this chapter, we'll review resources – the primary way that cost accrues on a project. When you're done, you'll be able to describe the three resource types, create resources, add resource information to the schedule and assign resources to tasks.

Understanding Resource Types

Resources are the people and things required to complete a project. In Microsoft Project, there are three types of resources – Work, Material and Cost. Let's review the characteristics of each.

Work Resources are resources that have an hourly rate and a calendar. They can be people, equipment, or rentals, such as a conference room, a crane or a lighting boom. They can also be generic, representing a trade or professional group, such as Engineers or Architects.

Material Resources are consumable supplies that are priced by the amount consumed. For example, if you're painting a house, the paint would be a material resource. Material resources can be assigned using a **Fixed Consumption Rate** or a **Variable Consumption Rate**.

If the consumption rate is Fixed, Project calculates cost by multiplying the cost per units value by the number of units assigned. For example, if paint costs $50.00 per gallon, and 5 gallons are assigned, the cost will be $250. If the consumption rate is Variable, Project calculates cost by multiplying the cost per units value by the number of gallons consumed within a specified time increment (E.g. 1 gallon per hour). For example, if paint cost $50 per gallon and 1 gallon is consumed per hour, then after 5 hours, 5 gallons would be consumed at a cost of $250. The difference is, with a Fixed rate, the amount consumed is *fixed*, irrespective of task duration. With a Variable rate, the amount consumed *varies* with task duration.

When assigning material resources to tasks, the consumption rate is entered in the Units field of the *Assign Resources* dialogue box. For a Fixed consumption rate, enter the quantity being assigned in the Units field (E.g. **5**). For a Variable consumption rate, enter the Unit per time increment (E.g. **1/h**).

Cost Resources are used to capture non-recurring cost items that don't accrue via an hourly rate, and cannot be classified as consumable. There are two types of Cost resources – **Budget** and **Expense**. Budget cost resources are used as a placeholder for the Project Budget. Expense cost resources, capture non-recurring expenses like food, travel, or speaker fees. We'll work with Budget cost resources in Chapter 18, "Tracking Project Cost".

Creating Resources and Adding Resource Information

In a Simple schedule, resources can be assigned to tasks by entering their names into the Resource Names field of the Entry table. When this is done, resources are added to the project plan in the background. They are populated to the **Resource Sheet** view with a Max. Units value of 100% and are assigned as Work resources by default. We'll explain Max. Units later in the chapter. In a Detailed schedule, resources and their information must be added to the Resource Sheet view *before* they can be assigned to tasks. The Resource Sheet view displays resource information for the entire project in a spreadsheet-like table.

To access the Resource Sheet view:

1. Select the **View** tab.

2. In the **Resource Views** group, select **Resource Sheet**.

Using *Figure 58* below, let's review the fields in the Resource Sheet.

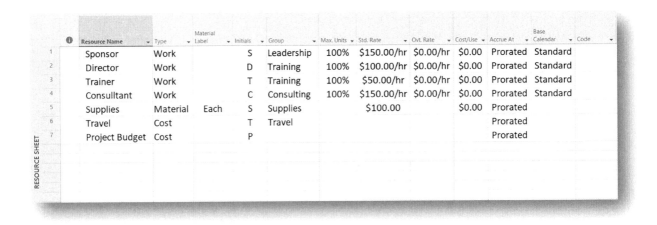

	Resource Name	Type	Material Label	Initials	Group	Max. Units	Std. Rate	Ovt. Rate	Cost/Use	Accrue At	Base Calendar	Code
1	Sponsor	Work		S	Leadership	100%	$150.00/hr	$0.00/hr	$0.00	Prorated	Standard	
2	Director	Work		D	Training	100%	$100.00/hr	$0.00/hr	$0.00	Prorated	Standard	
3	Trainer	Work		T	Training	100%	$50.00/hr	$0.00/hr	$0.00	Prorated	Standard	
4	Consulltant	Work		C	Consulting	100%	$150.00/hr	$0.00/hr	$0.00	Prorated	Standard	
5	Supplies	Material	Each	S	Supplies		$100.00		$0.00	Prorated		
6	Travel	Cost		T	Travel					Prorated		
7	Project Budget	Cost		P						Prorated		

Figure 58 – Creating Resources in the Resource Sheet View

Fields in the Resource Sheet

-   Resource names are entered in the **Resource Name** field.

-   Select the type of resource (Work, Material or Cost) from the pick-list in the **Type** field.

-   Enter the unit of measurement for a <u>material</u> resource in the **Material** field.

- Enter the abbreviation for the resource name in the **Initials** field. By default, Project enters the first initial of the resource name.

- Enter the name of the group that the resource belongs to in the **Group** field. This field is handy when sorting and grouping resource data, which we'll cover in Chapter 14, "Inspecting Your Schedule".

- Enter the resource's Max Units in the **Max.** field. **Max Units** is the maximum capacity a resource(s) is available to work on any given day. It is expressed as a percentage of an 8-hour day. By default, Project assigns 100% Max Units to new resources. This means that the resource is available to work on tasks the full eight-hour day. If the resource is only available 4 hours per day, their Max Units would be 50%.

- For Work resources, enter the pay rate in the **Std. Rate** (Standard Rate) field. For Material resources, if using a fixed consumption rate, enter the cost per unit (E.g. $50.00). If using a variable consumption rate, enter the unit per time increment (E.g. 1/h). **Note:** The cost for Cost resources is not entered in the Std. Rate field. Cost values for Cost resources are entered in the "Units" field of the *Assign Resources* dialogue box.

- Enter the resource's overtime pay rate in the in the **Ovt.** (Overtime Rate) field.

- The **Cost/Use** (Cost Per Use) field pertains to Work and Material resources. For a Work resource, enter the cost that accrues every time the resource is used. For example, a plumber's "trip charge" would be entered here. For Material resources, enter a charge that is assessed in addition to the cost per unit.

- The **Accrue** (Accrue At) field is where you determine how cost should be dispensed throughout your project. The choices are Start, End or Prorated (default).

  o "Start" means pay up-front, meaning the entire cost of the task will accrue when the task starts.

  o "End" means pay at the end, meaning the entire cost of the task will accrue when the task completes.

  o "Prorated" means pay as you go, meaning cost accrues evenly as task work is completed.

- Select the base calendar you want for Work resources in the **Base** (Base Calendar) field. The base calendar options are Standard (default), 24 hours, and Nightshift. We'll review calendars in Chapter 9, "Adding Calendars to Your Schedule".

- Enter any code, abbreviation, or number you want to associate with a resource in the **Code** field. For example, you might use this field to designate the cost code for a resource.

Important Information about Max Units

Generic Resources and Max Units

As mentioned earlier, resources can be generic, representing a trade or professional group, such as Engineers or Architects. If 4 Engineers are assigned to the project and each is available to work on tasks 8 hours per day (100% Max Units each), then their collective Max Units would be 400%. This means that up to 32 engineering hours are available each day for task work.

Over-Allocated Resources

If a resource's Max Units are exceeded, meaning they're assigned to tasks beyond their capacity, then the resource becomes over-allocated. Project creates an alert of the overallocation with a "red man" icon in the Indicators field.

Max Units vs. Assignment Units

It's important not to confuse **Max Units** with resource **Assignment Units**. Max Units is the maximum capacity a resource(s) is available to work on tasks on any given day. Assignment Units is the percentage of the day resources will work on specific tasks. For example, if a resource is available to work on tasks the entire day, their Max Units would be 100%. However, you may only need a portion of that time to perform your task. Though they're available 8 hours per day, your current task may only require 2 of those 8 hours per day. In this case, the Max Units would be 100% and the Assignment Units would be 25%. Stated differently, you only need them 2 hours per day, though they're available to you 8 hours per day. Here's a rule of thumb to distinguish Max Units from resource Assignment Units. Max Units are entered in the "Max." Field on the Resource Sheet. Resource Assignment Units are entered in the "Units" field in the *Assign Resources* dialogue box.

Adding Additional Resource Information

You can add additional information about a resource in the *Resource Information* dialogue box. On the Resource Sheet, double-click a resource's name to access the *Resource Information* dialogue box (*Figure 59* below).

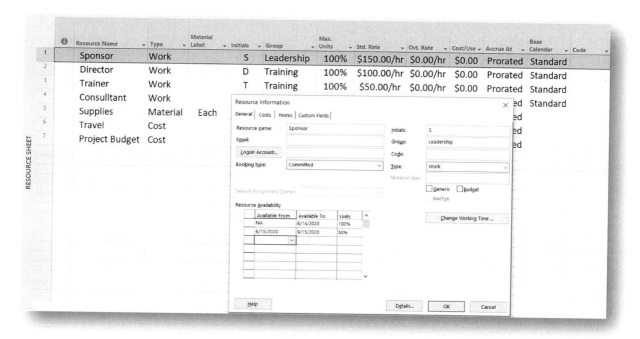

Figure 59 – Resource Information Dialogue Box

When you open the *Resource Information* dialogue box, the **General** tab is selected by default. On this tab, you can enter contact information for the resource such as an email address. You can also enter the resource's availability for different times of the year. *Figure 59* above shows that the Sponsor resource is available at 100% Max Units through 06/14/2020, but is only available at 25% Max Units from 6/15/2020 to 9/15/2020.

On the **Costs** tab, you can add additional pay rates for a resource. For example, a resource might be paid one rate for one type of task and another rate for a different type of task. Enter the additional pay rates on tabs B, C, D & E, as needed. A resource's overtime rate can also be entered on this tab.

On the **Notes** tab, you can add any notes about the resource. We will review Resource Notes further in the Chapter 10, "Documenting Your Schedule".

The **Custom Fields** tab is where you can access custom fields. Custom fields can be created to store additional information about a resource.

Assigning Resources

There are several ways to assign resources to tasks. As discussed in Chapter 6, in a Simple schedule, resources can be assigned by entering the resource names directly into the Resource Names field. This will result in resources being assigned to tasks at 100% Units (8 hour per day). In this chapter, we will assign resources to a Detailed schedule using the *Assign Resources* dialogue box and the Task Form.

Assigning Resources using the Assign Resources Dialogue Box.

To assign resources using the *Assign Resources* dialogue box:

1. In the Gantt Chart view, in the **Task Name** field of the Entry table, select the task you want to assign the resource(s) to.

2. On the **Resource** tab, in the **Assignments** group, select **Assign Resources** to open the *Assign Resources* dialogue box (*Figure 60* below).

   ➢ For a **Work** resource, enter the assignment Units in the **Units** field, then click **Assign** (or press Enter).

   ➢ For a **Material** resource, enter the quantity in the **Units** field, then click **Assign** (or press Enter).

   ➢ For a **Cost** resource, enter the cost value in the **Cost** field.

3. Repeat steps 1 & 2 to assign additional resources.

4. Select **Close** to close the *Assign Resources* dialogue box.

When a resource is assigned to a task, the resource's name and units will populate in the Resource Names field and in the Gantt chart. As mentioned earlier, resources are the primary way that cost accrues on a project. When resource pay rates have been added to the Resource Sheet, Project will automatically calculate cost as resources are assigned to tasks. Cost will appear in the Cost field of the *Assign Resources* dialogue box. The Cost field can also be added to any table using the Add New Column field (*Figure 60* below).

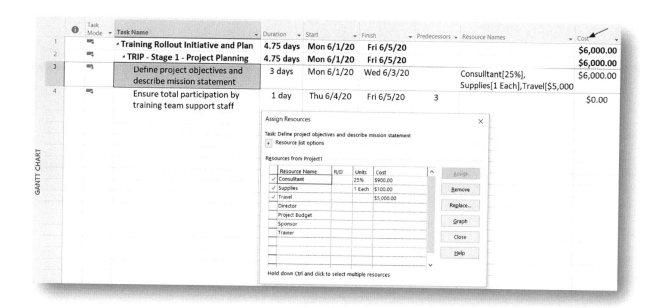

Figure 60 – Assign Resources Dialogue Box

Assign Resources using the Task Form

As reviewed in Chapter 2, the active view can be split to show additional details for a task or resource in the bottom pane.

To Split the View:

1. On the **View** tab, in the **Split View** group, check the **Details** checkbox.

When the view is split in the Gantt Chart view, the **Task Form** appears in the bottom pane by default (*Figure 61* below).

To assign resources using the Task Form:

1. In the Gantt Chart view, in the **Task Name** field of the Entry table, select the task that you want to assign the resource(s) to.

2. Split the view to display the **Task Form** in the bottom pane.

3. In the Task Form, place your cursor in the **Resource Name** field, then select the resource you want to assign to the task from the pick-list (*Figure 61* below).

> ➢ For a **Work** resource, enter the assignment Units in the Units field.

> ➢ For a **Material** resource, enter the quantity in the Units field.

4. Repeat steps 1 thru 3 for each task you want to assign resources to, then Select **OK**.

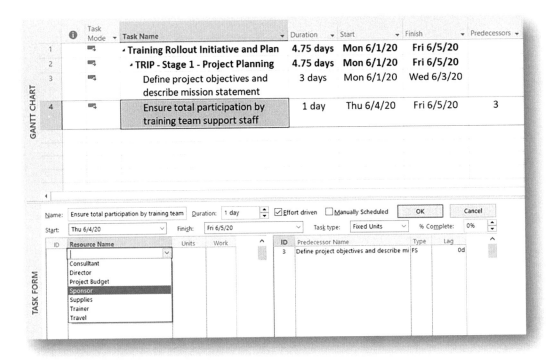

<u>Figure 61 – Assign Resources in the Task Form View</u>

Note: Cost resources cannot be assigned using the Task Form view. Cost resources should be assigned using the *Assign Resources* dialogue box, where the Cost field is available.

One advantage of assigning resources in this Task Form is that the "Work" field is provided, which means you don't have to add a Work column in the Gantt chart view to enter the work values. You can enter it directly in the Task Form.

We have now reviewed resources – the primary way that cost accrues on a project. We've explained the three resource types, how to create resources and add their information to the schedule and how to assign resources to tasks.

CHALLENGE – Practice Exercise

Build a Detailed Schedule Using the B.A.S.I.C.S.

Instructions: In this practice exercise, you'll build a Detailed schedule using the B.A.S.I.C.S. scheduling approach. Visit www.mspbasics.com for "checkpoint" images to check your work as you go along.

Follow the steps below to complete this exercise:

Start a New Project

From the opening view, select "Blank Project" to create a new project plan. **Note**: It's important to start this exercise with a blank project. Do not use a saved project file from a previous practice exercise.

Depending on how your version of Project is configured, the **Timeline View** may be displayed. Since it is currently empty, close the panel to see more of the Gantt Chart view.

1. Select the **View** tab.

2. In the **Split View** group, uncheck the **Timeline** checkbox.

Breakdown the Project

Step 1, "**B**reakdown the Project" has already been done and is represented by the WBS included in this exercise.

Adjust the Settings and Set the Project Start Date

Adjust the settings to support a **Detailed** schedule:

1. Select the **File** tab to go *Backstage*.

2. Select **Options**, then select **Schedule** to access the *Project Options* dialogue box.

3. Under the "Scheduling options for this project" section, select **Auto Scheduled** from the "New tasks created" pick-list. This will enable Project to calculate the finish date from the task durations and task dependencies.

4. Select **Fixed Units** from the "Default task type" pick-list. This will cause Project to keep the Units values constant.

5. Check the "New tasks are effort-driven" checkbox. This will <u>enable</u> the Effort-driven scheduling feature.

6. To check your results so far, visit www.mspbasics.com. Select "Practice Exercise Solutions" from the menu. Select "Chapter 8" and reference "Checkpoint Image #1".

Set the Project Start Date

Set the Project Start Date to **June 1, 2020**:

1. Select the **Project** tab.

2. In the **Properties** group, select the **Project Information** command to open the *Project Information* dialogue box.

3. Enter the project start date in the **Start date** field.

4. Click **OK** to close the *Project Information* dialogue box.

Enter the Task List and Structure the Tasks

Create the project outline for the *House Painting* project per the WBS below. If you need assistance completing the steps in this section, refer to the Chapter 4 practice exercise.

1. Enter the task list into the Entry table of the Gantt Chart view. No task should be indented at this point.

2. Create summary tasks and subtasks to outline the project plan. Structure the tasks using the **Indent Task** and **Outdent Task** commands, located on the **Task** tab, in the **Schedule** group.

3. Create milestones signifying the end of each phase. Rename the milestones "Supplies Bought", "House Prepped" and "House Painted" respectively.

4. Display the Project Summary Task. On the **Format** tab, in the **Show/Hide** group, check the **Project Summary Task** checkbox. Rename it "House Painting Project".

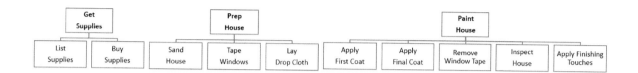

House Painting Project WBS

Initialize the Task Durations – Enter Work and Assign Resources

Next, you'll initialize the duration values by establishing the Work and Units values. Project will calculate (and initialize) the durations from the Work and Units values.

Enter Work Estimates

To enter the Work estimates, the "Work" field must be added to the Entry table using the "**Add New Column**" field. If you don't see the "Add New Column" field in the Entry table, you'll need to drag the line that divides the Entry table from the Gantt Chart to the right until you see the "Add New Column" field.

1. Click on the "Add New Column" heading. This will display the fields you can add to the table. Enter the word "Work" to display the **Work** field, then select it.

2. In the "Work" field for each task, enter the work values per the table below. Do not enter work values for summary tasks as Project will calculate work for the summary tasks per their subtasks. The total work for the project should be **80 hours**.

3. To check your results so far, visit www.mspbasics.com. Select "Practice Exercise Solutions" from the menu. Select "Chapter 8" and reference "Checkpoint Image #2".

Task	Work (Hours)
List Supplies	4h
Buy Supplies	4h
Sand House	12h
Tape Windows	2h
Lay Drop Cloth	2h
Apply 1st Coat	20h
Apply Final Coat	20h
Remove Window Tape	2h
Inspect House	2h
Apply Finishing Touches	12h

Create Resources

Next, you'll create Work, Material and Cost resources and add their resource information to the schedule. To create resources, switch to the **Resource Sheet View**.

1. On the **View** tab, in the **Resource Views** group, select **Resource Sheet**.

2. In the Resource Sheet table, enter the resource information per the table below.

3. To check your results so far, visit www.mspbasics.com. Select "Practice Exercise Solutions" from the menu. Select "Chapter 8" and reference "Checkpoint Image #3".

Resource Name	Type	Material Label	Group	Max. Units	Std. Rate
Jack	Work		Painters	100%	$75.00/Hour
Jill	Work		Painters	100%	$75.00/Hour
Contractor	Work		Contractors	100%	$150.00/Hour
Paint	Material	Gallons	Supplies		$50.00
Food	Cost		Food		

Assign Resources to Tasks

Next, you'll assign the resources to tasks using the *Assign Resources* dialogue box. This will establish the Units values. Return to the Gantt Chart view by selecting the **Gantt Chart** icon in the top left corner of the ribbon.

Since resource pay rates have been added to the schedule, Project will automatically calculate cost as resources are assigned. To view the cost, use the "Add New Column" field to add the **"Cost"** field to the Entry table.

Complete the following steps to assign resources to tasks per the table below:

TASK	RESOURCE(S)	ASSIGNMENT UNITS / QUANTITY	COST
List Supplies	Jill	50%	
Buy Supplies	Jack	50%	
Sand House	Jack	50%	
Tape Windows	Jill	25%	
Lay Drop Cloth	Jack	25%	
Apply 1st Coat	Contractor	50%	
	Jack	50%	
	Paint	10	
Apply Final Coat	Contractor	50%	
	Jill	50%	
	Paint	10	
Remove Window Tape	Jack	25%	
Inspect House	Jill	25%	
Apply Finishing Touches	Jack	75%	
	Paint	2	
	Food		$500

1. In the **Entry table**, in the **Task Name** field, select the task you want to assign the resource(s) to.

2. Select the **Resource** tab. In the **Assignments** group, select **Assign Resources** to open the *Assign Resources* dialogue box.

3. In the *Assign Resources* dialogue box:

   ➤ For a **Work** resource, enter the assignment Units in the **Units** field of the resource you're assigning, then click **Assign** (or press enter).

   ➤ For a **Material** resource, enter the quantity in the **Units** field of the resource you're assigning, then click **Assign** (or press enter).

   ➤ For a **Cost** resource, enter the cost value in the **Cost** field of the resource you're assigning.

4. Repeat steps 1 thru 3 for each task, then select **Close** to close the *Assign Resources* dialogue box. Notice the resource names and their units are populated in the **Resource Names** field and in the Gantt chart.

5. To check your results so far, visit www.mspbasics.com. Select "Practice Exercise Solutions" from the menu. Select "Chapter 8" and reference "Checkpoint Image #4".

The Work and Units values are now established, and the task durations are *Initialized*. Project calculated the task durations per the Work and Units values. Take note of the tasks with more than one resource assigned. Since the effort-driven feature is enabled, Project left the Work value constant and calculated the Duration by dividing the Work value by the collective resource Units value. Project also calculated the cost for each task and the overall project. The Total Cost should be **$9,100**.

Notice the resources are over-allocated (indicated by the red man icons in the Indicators field). This is because the tasks are not yet connected and are all starting on the project start date.

Connect the Tasks: Create Task Relationships

Next, you'll connect the tasks and give them *Finish-to-Start* task relationships. Since the tasks in this schedule follow one after another, they can be quickly linked using the "Lazy Linking" method.

1. Select the entire project plan by clicking the empty gray cell above task ID 0.

2. On the **Task** tab, in the **Schedule** group, select the **Link the Selected Tasks** command.

Notice the resources are no longer over-allocated. Project has rescheduled the tasks according to their Finish-to-Start task relationships. Each task now starts after its predecessor finishes. Project has also calculated the project duration as **16 days** and the project finish date as **6/22/20**.

Remove the Question Marks (Estimated Durations)

Notice the questions marks next to the task durations. By default, Project places a question mark next to durations to indicate that the durations are estimated. You'll now adjust the settings to remove the question marks for existing and new tasks. This will make for a cleaner looking schedule as we move into the execution phase.

1. Select the **File** tab to go *Backstage*.

2. Select **Options** to open the *Project Options* dialogue box, then select **Schedule**.

3. In the **Scheduling options for this project** section, uncheck the **"show that scheduled tasks have estimated durations"** checkbox. This will remove the question marks for the currently scheduled tasks.

4. Uncheck the **"New scheduled tasks have estimated durations"** checkbox. This will remove the question marks for new tasks added to the schedule.

5. Click **OK** to close the *Project Options* dialogue box. The question marks have been removed from the durations.

6. **SAVE THIS PROJECT FILE**. You will use this file to complete the Chapter 16 practice exercise.

You have now built a Detailed schedule using the first 5 steps of the **B.A.S.I.C.S.** scheduling approach. We'll review the last step, "Start the Project", in Chapter 15 "Executing your Schedule".

CHECK YOUR FINAL RESULTS

To check your final results, go to www.mspbasics.com.

Select "Practice Exercise Solutions" from the menu. Select "Chapter 8" and reference "Checkpoint Image #5".

Now You Can

- Explain Resource Types
- Create Resources
- Add Resource Information
- Assign Resources to Tasks

Chapter 9 Adding Calendars to Your Schedule

IN THIS CHAPTER:

- The Microsoft Project Work Week

- Base Calendars

- The Project Calendar

- Resource Calendars

- Task Calendars

- Calendar Precedence

- Elapsed Duration

In the last chapter, we added resources to the schedule. In this chapter, we'll add calendars to the schedule and observe how they affect the scheduling of tasks. When you're done, you'll be able to explain the Project calendar and use Task and Resource calendars to create exceptions for the tasks and resources. You'll also be able to explain Elapsed Duration.

In Microsoft Project, calendars are used to define working and non-working times and to create scheduling exceptions for tasks and resources. By default, Project only schedules work during business days. Business days are referred to as "working times" in Project. Non-business days are referred to as "non-working times".

Understanding the Microsoft Project Work Week

The default work week in Project is Monday through Friday, from 8:00 am to 5:00 pm, with a 1-hour lunch break from 12:00 pm to 1:00 pm. A "week" in Project is 5 business days. For example, if you enter a 1-week task duration (1w), this equates to 5 business days (and not 7 business days). Entering a 5-day duration (5d) will yield the same result as entering 1w. A "month" in Project is 4 weeks, or 20 business days.

It's important to distinguish calendar days from business days when using Project. Calendar days include weekends, whereas business days do not. As mentioned earlier, Project only schedules work during business days. For example, if a task with a 5-day duration begins on Thursday, its duration will span 7 calendar days, but task work will be scheduled across 5 business days (Thursday, Friday, Monday, Tuesday and Wednesday). In Project, task duration always refers to business days.

Base Calendars

Calendars are used to determine working times for tasks and resources. There are several calendar types in Microsoft Project. We'll start with what Project refers to as **Base Calendars**.

There are three Base calendars in Project:

> **Standard** (default) – Monday thru Friday; 8:00 am – 5:00 pm (1-hour lunch break from 12:00 pm to 1:00 pm)

> **Night Shift** – Monday night thru Saturday morning; 11:00 pm – 8:00 am (1-hour lunch break from 3:00 am to 4:00 am)

> **24-Hours** – No defined working times; Runs continuously

The Project Calendar

The **Project Calendar** defines the working and non-working times for the entire schedule. When you build your schedule, you'll need to designate one of the three Base calendars as the Project calendar.

Tasks will be scheduled per the days and hours of the Base calendar you select as the Project calendar. The default Base calendar (Standard) works for most projects. However, if none of the Base calendar options work for your schedule, you can create a custom Base calendar. We'll demonstrate how to do this later in the chapter.

To set the Project Calendar:

1. On the **Project** tab, in the **Properties** group, select **Project Information**. The *Project Information* dialogue box opens (*Figure 62* below).

2. From the **Calendar** pick-list, select the Base calendar you want as the Project calendar.

3. Click **OK** to close the *Project Information* dialogue box.

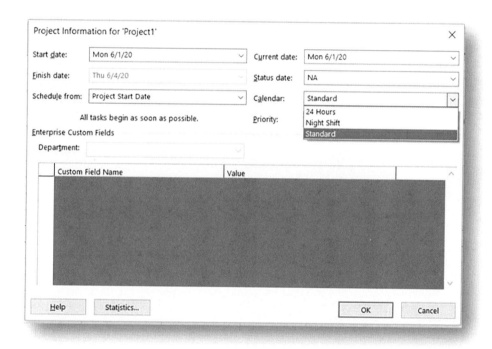

Figure 62 – Project Information Dialogue Box

Creating Exceptions to the Project Calendar

Once you set the Project calendar, you may need to create scheduling exceptions for times when work will not occur. For example, work may not occur during a training event or during a national holiday. Such exceptions to the Project calendar are created using the **Change Working Time** dialogue box.

To create an exception to the Project calendar for non-working time:

1. Select the **Project** tab.

2. In the **Properties** group, select **Change Working Time** to open the *Change Working Time* dialogue box.

3. In the **For calendar** field, be sure the Project calendar is selected. This will ensure the scheduling exception(s) apply to the entire project.

4. Select the **Exceptions** tab.

5. Enter the name of the exception in the **Name** field (E.g. "Training" or "Holiday").

6. Enter the non-working dates in the **Start** and **Finish** fields.

7. Click **OK** to close the *Change Working Time* dialogue box.

Resource Calendars

Resource Calendars set exceptions for *Work* resources. They can be used to schedule non-working days for a resource, such as vacation time. If the resource assigned to a task is on vacation, and a Resource calendar has been created for the vacation time, Project will not schedule work until the resource returns. Resource calendars can also be used to create a special work schedule for a resource. For example, a resource may only work Monday thru Thursday.

To create a Resource calendar for non-working times:

1. On the **Project** tab, in the **Properties** group, select **Change Working Time** to open the *Change Working Time* dialog box.

2. In the **For calendar** field, select the resource from the pick-list. This will ensure the scheduling exception(s) apply to the selected resource and not the entire project.

3. Select the **Exceptions** tab.

4. Enter the name of the exception in the **Name** field (E.g. "Vacation").

5. Enter the non-working dates in the **Start** and **Finish** fields. Click **OK** to close the *Change Working Time* dialogue box.

To create a Resource calendar for a special work schedule:

1. On the **Project** tab, in the **Properties** group, select **Change Working Time** to open the *Change Working Time* dialogue box.

2. In the **For calendar** field, select the resource from the pick-list.

3. Select the **Work Weeks** tab, then select the **[Default]** cell and then select **Details** to open the *Details* dialogue box.

4. In the **Select day(s)** field, press and hold the *Ctrl* key while selecting the resource's non-working day(s).

5. Select the **Set days to nonworking time** option (*Figure 63* below).

6. Click **OK** to close the *Details* dialog box.

7. Click **OK** again to close the *Change Working Time* dialog box.

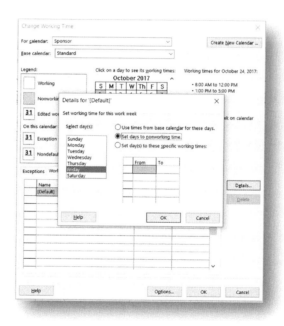

Figure 63 – Changing Working and Details dialogue boxes

Task Calendars

Task Calendars set exceptions for tasks. If work on a task needs to occur outside of normal business hours, you can use a Task calendar to create the exception. For example, if your Project calendar is the

Standard calendar and work needs to occur on the weekend, you can use a Task calendar to schedule the work. Any resources assigned to the task, will be scheduled to work through the weekend.

Task calendars are created by applying a Base calendar to a task. You can choose one of the three Base calendars in Project (Standard, 24-Hours, Nightshift) or you can create a custom Base calendar.

To create a Task calendar:

Step 1 – Create a custom Base calendar:

1. Select the **Project** tab.

2. In the **Properties** group, select **Change Working Time** to open the *Change Working Time* dialog box.

3. Select **Create New Calendar** to open the *Create New Base Calendar* dialogue box.

4. In the **Name** field, enter a name for the new Base calendar.

5. If you want to create the Base calendar from scratch, select the **Create new base calendar** option. If the working times you want are similar to those in an existing Base calendar, select the **Make a copy of** option, then select the Base calendar you want to copy from the pick-list in the **calendar** field.

6. Click **OK** to close the *Create New Base Calendar* dialogue box.

Step 2 – Enter the working times for the new Base calendar:

1. In the *Change Working Time* dialogue box, select the **Work Weeks** tab.

2. In the **Name** field, select the **[Default]** cell and then select **Details** to open the *Details* dialogue box.

3. In the **Select day(s)** field, press and hold the *Ctrl* key while selecting the non-working days for the new Base calendar.

4. Select the **Set days to non-working time** option.

5. Then click **OK** to close the *Details* dialogue box.

6. Click **OK** again to close the *Change Working Time* dialogue box.

Step 3 – Apply the custom Base calendar to the task as a Task Calendar:

1. In the Gantt Chart view, double-click the task to open the *Task Information* dialogue box.

2. Select the **Advanced** tab.

3. From the **Calendar** pick-list, select the new Base calendar.

4. Click **OK** to close the *Task Information* dialogue box. Project will generate an indicator, denoting that the task has a Task Calendar.

Create a Custom Base Calendar for the Project Calendar

As mentioned earlier, a custom Base calendar can also be created for the Project calendar if none of the existing Base calendars work for your schedule.

To create a custom Base calendar for your Project calendar:

1. Complete Step 1 and Step 2 above to create a new custom Base calendar.

2. On the **Project** tab, in the **Properties** group, select **Project Information**. The *Project Information* dialogue box opens.

3. From the **Calendar** pick-list, select the new custom Base calendar as the Project calendar.

4. Click **OK** to close the *Project Information* dialogue box.

Calendar Precedence

Since a schedule can contain several calendars, there are rules of precedence to govern how Project schedules tasks.

Here's the pecking order:

➤ If there is <u>no</u> Task or Resource calendar, then the Project calendar rules the day.

➤ If there is <u>either</u> a Resource or a Task calendar, then it is the boss.

➤ If there is <u>both</u> a Resource and a Task calendar, then Project will use the <u>common hours</u> between the two calendars.

Example: If the Task calendar hours are 8am to 5pm and the Resource calendar hours are 6am to 2pm, then Project will schedule the resource to work the common hours from 8am to 2pm.

Elapsed Duration

If you're using the *Standard* Project calendar and you need Project to schedule a task through the weekend, you can add an **Elapsed Duration** to a task. Elapsed durations cause Project to schedule work during the non-working times specified in the Project calendar. For example, if a 4-hour task begins on Friday at 4:00 pm, Project will schedule the task for 1 hour on Friday (4:00 pm – 5:00 pm) and 3 hours on the next working day (Monday, 8:00 am – 11:00 am). By contrast, using elapsed duration (E.g. 4eh), if the same 4-hour task began on Friday at 4:00 pm, Project would schedule the task for 1 hour on Friday and 3 hours on the following day (Saturday, 8:00 am – 11:00 am). Enter elapsed duration into the **Duration** field.

Examples of Elapsed Duration time entries:

➢ **1emo** (1 elapsed month)

➢ **1ew** (1 elapsed week)

➢ **1ed** (1 elapsed day)

➢ **1eh** (1 elapsed hour)

➢ **1emin** (1 elapsed minute)

We've now reviewed how to add calendars to the schedule and observed how they affect the scheduling of tasks. We've covered Base calendars, the Project calendar, Task and Resource calendars and Elapsed Duration.

CHALLENGE – Practice Exercise

Work with Calendars

Instructions: In this practice exercise, you'll work with the Project calendar, Resource calendar and Task calendar to observe how they function in a schedule. Visit www.mspbasics.com for "checkpoint" images to check your work as you go along.

Follow the steps below to complete this exercise:

Start a Project from a Template

You'll use a project template to complete this exercise. **Note**: The templates are hosted on a companion website. You'll need to be connected to the internet to access them.

1. From the opening view, double-click the "Software Development Plan" project template.
2. When the project plan opens, the view will be split. A custom report will be in the top pane and the Gantt Chart view will be in the bottom pane. Unsplit the view by selecting the **View** tab. Then, in the **Split View** group, uncheck the **Details** checkbox.
3. Select the **Gantt Chart** icon in the left corner of the ribbon to get back to the Gantt Chart view. The project plan will be collapsed, displaying only the Level 1 tasks in the outline.
4. To view the entire plan, display all subtasks using the **Show Outline** feature. On the **View** tab, in the **Data** group, select the **Outline** command and select **"All Subtasks"** from pick-list.

Set the Project Start Date & Set the Project Calendar

Set the Project Start Date to **January 6, 2020**.

1. On the **Project** tab, in the **Properties** group, select the **Project Information** command to open the *Project Information* dialogue box.

2. Enter the project start date in the **Start date** field. DO NOT CLICK **OK**. Remain in the *Project Information* dialogue box.

3. Be sure that **"Standard"** is selected in the **Calendar** field. This sets the *Standard* base calendar as the Project calendar. The working days for this project will be Monday thru Friday, from 8:00 am to 5:00 pm (1-hour lunch break from 12:00 pm to 1:00 pm).

4. Click **OK** to close the *Project Information* dialogue box.

Establish Non-Working Days

Your company is conducting a training event from 1/27/20 to 1/31/20. You'll establish these days as non-working days on the Project calendar and observe the impact on the schedule. Notice that the project is currently scheduled to finish on 5/18/20.

Set the non-working days as follows:

1. Select the **Project** tab.

2. In the **Properties** group, select the **Change Working Time** command to open the *Change Working Time* dialogue box.

3. Be sure that "Standard (Project Calendar)" is selected in the **For calendar** field. This will set the non-working days for the entire project.

4. Be sure the **Exceptions** tab is selected. In the **Name** field, enter "Training" as the name of the exception.

5. In the **Start** field, enter 1/27/20.

6. In the **Finish** field, enter 1/31/20.

7. Click **OK** to close the *Change Working Time* dialogue box.

8. To check your results so far, visit www.mspbasics.com. Select "Practice Exercise Solutions" from the menu. Select "Chapter 9" and reference "Checkpoint Image #1".

Notice several start and finish dates (including the project finish date) are now highlighted in blue. This feature is called **Change Highlighting**. Project rescheduled several tasks because of the non-working days and highlighted the schedule changes. The project finish date was also updated, it is now 5/25/20.

Create a Resource Calendar for Non-Working Day

Next, you'll create a Resource calendar to incorporate a resource's vacation time into the schedule. The "Analyst" resource is on vacation from 1/6/20 – 1/10/20.

1. Select the **Change Working Time** command to re-open the *Change Working Time* dialogue box.

2. In the **For calendar** field, select "Analyst" from the pick-list. Now, all changes will be made to the Analyst's calendar and not the Project calendar.

3. Be sure the **Exceptions** tab is selected. In the **Name** field, enter "Vacation".

4. In the **Start** field, enter 1/6/20.

5. In the **Finish** field, enter 1/10/20.

6. Click **OK** to close the *Change Working Time* dialogue box.

7. To check your results so far, visit www.mspbasics.com. Select "Practice Exercise Solutions" from the menu. Select "Chapter 9" and reference "Checkpoint Image #2".

Note the highlighted cells. Project rescheduled all tasks affected by the Analyst's vacation days. For example, the Analyst is assigned to task 8 *"Conduct needs analysis"*. Its predecessor, "Scope complete" (task 6) finishes on 1/9/20. Task 8 was originally scheduled to begin the next working day on 1/10/20. Because of the vacation days, the task has been rescheduled to begin the first working day the Analyst returns from vacation (Monday, 1/13/20). The project finish date has also been updated to 5/27/20.

Create a Resource Calendar for a Special Work Schedule

Next, you'll create a Resource calendar to incorporate a resource's special work schedule. The "Developer" resource works a Monday thru Thursday schedule. She doesn't work on Fridays.

1. Select the **Change Working Time** command to re-open the *Change Working Time* dialogue box.

2. In the **For calendar** field, select the "Developer" resource from the pick-list.

3. Select the **Work Weeks** tab. Then, select the **[Default]** cell in the **Name** field, then select **Details** to open the *Details* dialogue box.

4. In the **Select day(s)** field, select "Friday". Then, select the **set days to non-working time** option.

5. Click **OK** to close the *Details* dialog box. Notice that Fridays are now grayed out in the Developer's Resource calendar, indicating the non-working days.

6. Click **OK** again, to close the *Change Working Time* dialog box.

7. To check your results so far, visit www.mspbasics.com. Select "Practice Exercise Solutions" from the menu. Select "Chapter 9" and reference "Checkpoint Image #3".

Note the highlighted fields. Project rescheduled all tasks affected by the Developer's vacation days. The schedule updates begin with task 26 *"Review functional specifications"*, when the Developer's task assignments begin. The project finish date has also been updated to 6/8/20.

Create a Task Calendar

Last, you'll create a Task calendar. Recall that the Project calendar is set to the "Standard" work week of Monday through Friday, from 8:00 am to 5:00 pm. To expedite the schedule, work for task 43 *"Test module integration"* needs to occur on the weekends, around the clock. To create this exception, you'll create a Task calendar by applying the "24 Hours" Base calendar to this task.

1. Double-click the task name of task 43 *"Test module integration"* to open the *Task Information* dialogue box.

2. Select the **Advanced** tab. Then, select "24 Hours" from the **Calendar** pick-list.

3. Check the **"Scheduling ignores resource calendars"** checkbox. This will cause Project to ignore any Resource calendars and use the Task calendar when scheduling.

4. Before you click **OK**, notice that this task is scheduled to start on Thursday, 4/30/20 and finish on the following Wednesday, 5/7/20.

5. Click **OK** to close the *Task Information* dialogue box. Notice that the finish date for task 43 has been updated to Saturday, 5/2/20.

6. To check your results so far, visit www.mspbasics.com. Select "Practice Exercise Solutions" from the menu. Select "Chapter 9" and reference "Checkpoint Images #4 & #5".

Next, you'll switch to the **Task Usage View** to see the how Project scheduled the work on this task.

1. Select the **View** tab.

2. In the **Task Views** group, select the **Task Usage** command.

3. Scroll to task 43 *"Test module integration"*. On the left, you can see that this task has 40 hours of work.

Use the **Scroll to Task** command to bring the work values for task 43 into view.

1. Select the task name.

2. Select the **Task** tab.

3. In the **Editing** group, select the **Scroll to Task** command. On the right, you can see that Project scheduled 14 hours of work on Thursday, 4/30/20, 24 hours of work on Friday, 5/1/20 and the remaining 2 hours of work on Saturday, 5/2/20.

4. Return to the Gantt Chart view by select the **Gantt Chart** icon in the top left corner of the ribbon.

5. **SAVE THIS PROJECT FILE**. You will use this file to complete the Chapter 10 practice exercise.

You've now worked with Project, Resource and Tasks calendars and observed how they function in a schedule.

Now You Can

- Explain the Microsoft Project Work Week

- Explain Base Calendars

- Explain the Project Calendar

- Create a Resource Calendar

- Create a Task Calendar

- Explain Calendar Precedence

- Use Elapsed Duration

Chapter 10 Documenting Your Schedule

IN THIS CHAPTER:

- Reasons to Document the Schedule

- Entering Document Properties

- Adding Notes to Tasks and Resources

- Adding Hyperlinks to Tasks and Resources

- Adding Files to Tasks and Resources

In the last chapter, we added calendars to the schedule. In this chapter, we'll document the schedule. When you're done, you'll be able to use notes, hyperlinks and files to embed useful information about tasks and resources directly into your schedule.

Why Document Your Schedule?

Here are some reasons to document your schedule:

- To Establish Authorship
- To Document Project Issues
- To Document Agreements
- To Document Resource Commitments
- To Document Risks
- To Explain Delays and Cost Overruns
- To Document Initial Assumptions
- To Establish a Lessons Learned Repository

Project includes many useful features for adding important notes and reference material to your schedule. These features will come in handy during the execution and closing phase of your project. We'll start by editing document properties.

Entering Document Properties

When you create a schedule, you may want to include useful information about the project within the file. Such document properties can be used to establish authorship and can be displayed in headers and footers. This information is entered in the *Advanced Properties* dialogue box (*Figure 64* below).

Figure 64 – Advanced Properties Dialogue Box

To enter document properties:

1. Select the **File** tab to go *Backstage*, then select **Info** from the tabs on the left. **Note**: On the right side of the screen under the **Project Information** header, you'll find project data that Project automatically records, such as the project start and finish dates and the Project calendar.

2. From the **Project Information** pick-list, select **Advanced Properties** to open the *Advanced Properties* dialogue box (*Figure 64* above).

3. Select the **Summary** tab.

4. Enter the project information you want to record. Here is where you establish ownership of the file. You can record information like the author, the company and any keywords or comments you'd like to include. Check the "save a preview of file" checkbox to save a preview image of the file that will appear as a thumbnail. When the file is saved, you'll have the option to add the document properties in the header and footer.

5. Click **OK** to close the *Advance Properties* dialogue box.

Adding Task Notes

Task Notes are an excellent way to document additional information about the tasks in your project. Task notes are created in the *Task Information* dialogue box.

To create a Task Note:

1. Double-click the task to open the *Task Information* dialogue box (*Figure 65* below).

2. Select the **Notes** tab, then type the task note in the notes field.

3. Click **OK** to close the *Task Information* dialogue box.

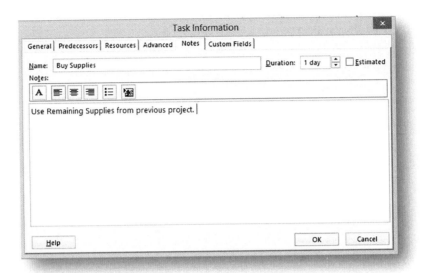

Figure 65 – Adding Task Notes

When you create a task note, Project generates a Notes icon in the Indicators field (*Figure 66* below*).* Hover over the icon to view the task note.

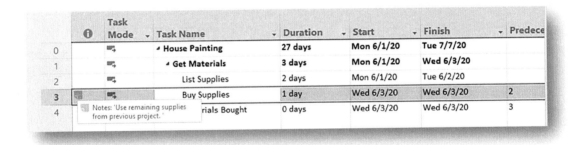

Figure 66 – Task Note Indicator

Adding Hyperlinks to Tasks

Hyperlinks can be added to tasks to access a website or a file directly from a task. For example, a resource assigned to the task may post important information on a *SharePoint* site. By adding a link to the site, you can access it directly from a task within your project file. You can also add a link to a file stored on your computer. For example, you can attach a Job Aid explaining a process related to the task. The advantage of creating a hyperlink to a file (over embedding the file) is that the links always accesses the latest version of the file.

To add a Hyperlink to a website:

1. Right-click the task you want to add the Hyperlink to. From the shortcut menu select **Link** to open the *Insert Hyperlink* dialogue box (*Figure 67* below).

2. In the **Text to display** field, type the text you want to display.

3. In the **Address** field, type the website address.

4. Click **OK** to close the *Insert Hyperlink* dialogue box.

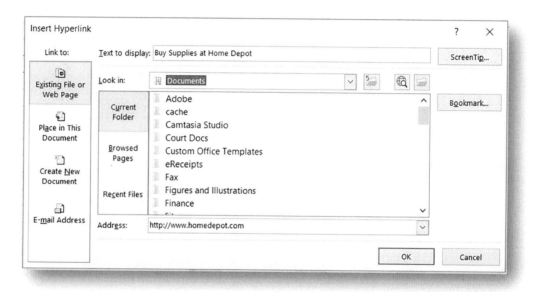

Figure 67 – Adding Hyperlinks to Tasks

To add a Hyperlink to a file:

1. Right-click the task you want to add the file link to. From the shortcut menu select **Link** to open the *Insert Hyperlink* dialogue box.

2. Use the **Look in** field to locate the document.

3. Select the document, then click **OK** to close the *Insert Hyperlink* dialogue box.

After you add a hyperlink to a task, Project will create a hyperlink target in the Indicators field (*Figure 68* below). Hover over the target to view the hyperlink description. Click the hyperlink to access the webpage or file.

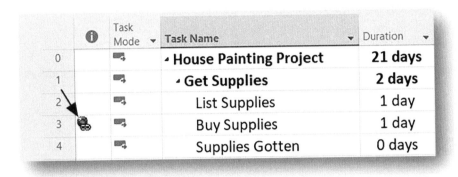

Figure 68 –Hyperlinks Indicator

Adding Resource Notes

In Chapter 8 we discussed adding resource information to your project plan using the *Resource Information* dialogue box. **Resource Notes** are a handy way to add information about a resource to the schedule. For example, you can note when a resource is on vacation.

To create a Resource Note:

1. Go to the **Resource Sheet** by selecting the **View** tab. Then, in the **Resource Views** group, select **Resource Sheet**).

2. Double-click the resource you want to add a note to. The *Resource Information* dialogue box will open (*Figure 69* below).

3. Select the **Notes** tab.

4. Type the note in the notes filed.

5. Click **OK** to close the *Resource Information* dialogue box.

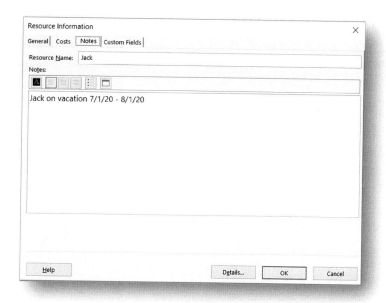

Figure 69 – Adding Resource Notes

After you add a Resource note, Project will create a Notes icon in the Indicators field, next to the resource's name in the Resource Sheet (*Figure 70* below). Hover over the icon to view the note.

Figure 70 – Resource Note Indicator

Adding Hyperlinks to Resources

Like tasks, hyperlinks can be added to resources to access a web or file directly from the Resource Sheet. You may be asking, "why would I need to do this?" Well, many teams use websites for others to request resources from their team or to post expected turn-around times for work requests. In such cases, adding a hyperlink to the resource would keep you from having to leave Project to find the link.

To add a Hyperlink to a website:

1. On the **Resource Sheet**, right-click the name of the resource you want to add the hyperlink to.

2. From the shortcut menu, select **Link** to open the *Insert Hyperlink* dialogue box.

3. In the **Text to display** field, type the text you want to display.

4. In the **Address** field, type the website address.

5. Click **OK** to close the *Insert Hyperlink* dialogue box.

To add a Hyperlink to a file:

1. On the **Resource Sheet**, right-click the name of the resource you want to add the file link to.

2. From the shortcut menu, select **Link** to open the *Insert Hyperlink* dialogue box.

3. Use the **Look in** field to locate the document.

4. Select the document, then click **OK** to close the *Insert Hyperlink* dialogue box.

After you add a hyperlink to a resource, Project will create a hyperlink target in the Indicator's field next to the resource's name (*Figure 71* below).

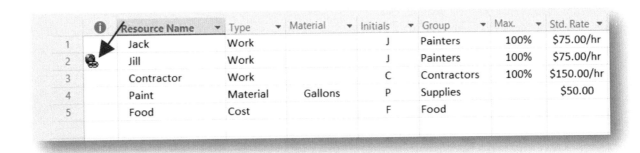

Figure 71 – Adding Hyperlinks to Resources

Adding Files to Task and Resources

So far, we've added files to tasks and resources using hyperlinks. This is handy for accessing the latest version of a file. If your file isn't likely to change often (E.g. vendor contracts), you can add it directly to a task or resource using the Notes field in the *Task Information* dialogue box or the *Resource Information* dialogue box.

151

To add a file to a task:

1. From the Gantt Chart view, double-click the task you want to add the file to. The *Task Information* dialogue box will open.

2. Select the **Notes** tab.

3. In the Notes field, click the **Insert Object** icon (last icon on the right), to open the *Insert Object* dialogue box.

4. Select **Create from File**, then select **Browse** to locate the file.

5. Click **Insert** to add the file. **Note:** Select the **Display As Icon** checkbox if you want the file displayed as an icon that links to the document. Otherwise, the document will be displayed directly in the notes field.

6. Click **OK** to insert the file (depending on the file size, there may be a brief lag as the file loads).

7. Click **OK** again to close the *Task Information* dialogue box.

After you add the file, Project will create a Notes icon in the Indicator's field of the task. Double-click the icon to access the file.

To add a file to a resource:

1. From the Resource Sheet, double-click the resource you want to add the file to. The *Resource Information* dialogue box will open.

2. Select the **Notes** tab.

3. In the Notes field, click the **Insert Object** icon (last icon on the right), to open the *Insert Object* dialogue box.

4. Select **Create from File**, then select **Browse** to locate the file.

5. Click **Insert** to add the file. **Note:** Select the **Display As Icon** checkbox if you want the file displayed as an icon that links to the document. Otherwise, the document will be displayed directly in the notes field.

6. Click **OK** to insert the file (depending on the file size, there may be a brief lag as the file loads).

7. Click **OK** again to close the *Resource Information* dialogue box.

After you add the file, Project will create a Notes icon in the Indicator's field, next to the resource's name. Double-click the icon to access the file.

We've now learned to use notes, hyperlinks and files to embed useful information about tasks and resources directly into the project schedule.

Document the Schedule

Instructions: In this practice exercise, you will document the schedule. You'll work with Task Notes, Resource Notes and Hyperlinks to add task and resource information to the project plan. Visit www.mspbasics.com for "Checkpoint Images" to check your work as you go along.

Follow the steps below to complete this exercise:

Open an Existing Project Plan

Open the "Software Development" project plan that you saved from the Chapter 9 practice exercise. **Note**: The file should contain the completed steps from the Chapter 9 exercise.

Create a Resource Note

In the Chapter 9 practice exercise, you created a Resource calendar for the *Analyst* resource to incorporate vacation days into the schedule. Now, you'll create a Resource Note for the *Analyst* to document the schedule concerning the vacation.

1. Switch to the **Resource Sheet** view by selecting the **View** tab. Then, in the **Resource Views** group, select **Resource Sheet**.

2. Double-click the *Analyst's* name to open the *Resource Information* dialogue box.

3. On the **Notes** tab, in the **Notes** field, type "On Vacation 1/6/20 – 1/10/20".

4. Click **OK** to close the *Resource Information* dialogue box. Notice that Project generated a "note" icon in the Indicators field for the *Analyst* resource. Hover over the icon to read the note.

5. To check your results so far, visit www.mspbasics.com. Select "Practice Exercise Solutions" from the menu. Select "Chapter 10" and reference "Checkpoint Images #1a & #1b".

Create a Task Note

Next, you'll create a Task Note to document additional information about a task. Return to the Gantt Chart view by clicking the **Gantt Chart** icon in the top left corner of the ribbon.

1. Double-click task 14, *"Obtain approvals to proceed (concept, timeline, budget)"* to open the *Task Information* dialogue box.

2. On the **Notes** tab, in the **Notes** field, type "Meet with management to confirm budget approval".

3. Click **OK** to close the *Task Information* dialogue box. Notice that Project generated a "note" icon in the Indicators field for task 14. Hover over the icon to read the note.

4. To check your results so far, visit www.mspbasics.com. Select "Practice Exercise Solutions" from the menu. Select "Chapter 10" and reference "Checkpoint Images #2a & #2b".

Add a Hyperlink to a Task

Last, you'll add a hyperlink to a task. You'll add a link to the hardware vendor's website.

1. Right-click task 70 *"Install/deploy software"*. From the shortcut menu, select **Link** to open the *Insert Hyperlink* dialogue box.

2. In the **Text to display** field, type "Hardware Vendor".

3. In the **Address** field, type http://www.dell.com.

4. Click **OK** close the *Insert Hyperlink* dialogue box.

5. To check your results so far, visit www.mspbasics.com. Select "Practice Exercise Solutions" from the menu. Select "Chapter 10" and reference "Checkpoint Images #3a & #3b".

Notice that Project generated a "link" icon in the Indicator's field. Hover over the link to view for details about the link. The hyperlink is active, so you can access the website directly from the project plan by double-clicking the link. You'll need to first click away from the link.

You've now documented the schedule. You've worked with notes and hyperlinks to add task and resource information to the schedule.

Now You Can

- Add Task Notes
- Add Resource Notes
- Add Hyperlinks to Tasks and Resources
- Add Files to Tasks and Resources

Chapter 11 Compressing Your Schedule

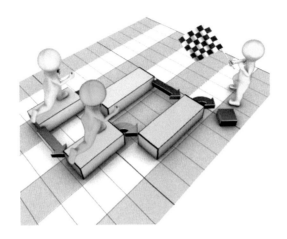

IN THIS CHAPTER:

- Compressing the Schedule
- Viewing the Critical Path
- Understanding Slack
- Using Lead Time Effectively
- Using the Task Path Feature
- Adding Deadlines to Tasks

In the last chapter, we documented the schedule. In this chapter, you'll learn to compress the schedule. When you're done, you'll be able to explain slack and use lead time to compress the schedule. You'll also be able to add Deadlines to tasks, view the Critical Path and use the Task Path feature.

Why Compress Your Schedule?

No justification is needed as to why you'd want to speed up your schedule, but here are some things to consider:

1. **Release Resources Quicker** – The faster you deliver your project; the faster resources can work on other projects.

2. **Exploit Business Opportunities** – Delivering projects faster can enable your business to enter the marketplace sooner.

3. **Speed is Contagious!** – Delivering milestones quicker fosters a results-oriented culture.

4. **Easier Politics** – No one will fault you for being *ahead* of schedule!

5. **Better use of Company Resources** – Compressed schedules allow you to deliver more projects per year.

KEY TERMS – Learning to Talk the Talk

Before we review ways to compress your schedule, you should be familiar with a few terms.

➤ **Critical Path** – the series of tasks in a schedule that have the following characteristics:

1. Each task has no slack.

2. Each task is a driving predecessor to the next task in the series.

3. If any of the tasks is compressed or delayed, the overall schedule will be compressed or delayed accordingly.

4. Their collective sum equals the project duration.

➤ **Slack (or Float)** – The number of days a task can be delayed before it will delay another task(s) or the project schedule. There are two types of Slack – Free Slack and Total Slack.

➤ **Free Slack** – The number of days a task can be delayed before it will delay another task(s).

➤ **Total Slack** – The number of days a task can be delayed before it will delay the project schedule.

➤ **Lead Time** – The number of days a successor task can start before its predecessor finishes.

➤ **Change Highlighting** – The Microsoft Project feature that highlights impacted dates and durations after a change is made to the schedule.

Understanding the Critical Path

The **Critical Path** is the series of tasks that stretch from the start date to the finish date of a schedule and determine its duration. This is the most practical concept in the book, because it tells you which tasks to compress to speed up your schedule. The tasks on the Critical Path are considered "critical" because their scheduling determines the project finish date. Since they have no slack, they cannot be delayed without delaying the schedule. Conversely, a schedule can only be compressed if a task(s) on the Critical Path task is compressed.

To fully understand the Critical Path, you must understand **Slack** (called *Float* in the PMBOK®). As mentioned earlier, there are two kinds of Slack: **Free Slack** and **Total Slack**.

The following examples show how Free Slack and Total Slack impact the schedule:

- ➢ **Example 1** – A task has 10 days of *Total* Slack; which means it can be delayed 10 days without delaying the overall schedule. If it is delayed 10 days, it becomes a Critical Path task because it no longer has slack. If it is delayed 11 days, the overall schedule will be delayed 1 day.

- ➢ **Example 2** – A task has 4 days of *Free* Slack; which means it can be delayed 4 days without delaying the start date of its successor. If it is delayed 5 days, the successor task will be delayed 1 day. Although this will not delay the overall schedule, it will delay the impacted task owner's start date. It would be a good idea to check with the task owner before exceeding the 4 days of Free Slack.

Highlighting the Critical Path

Being aware of your project's Critical Path allows you to manage the project with better intelligence. Microsoft Project automatically calculates the Critical Path and allows you to highlight the Critical Path tasks in your schedule. In *Figure 72* below, the Critical Path tasks are highlighted with red task bars in the Gantt chart graph and red font in the Entry table.

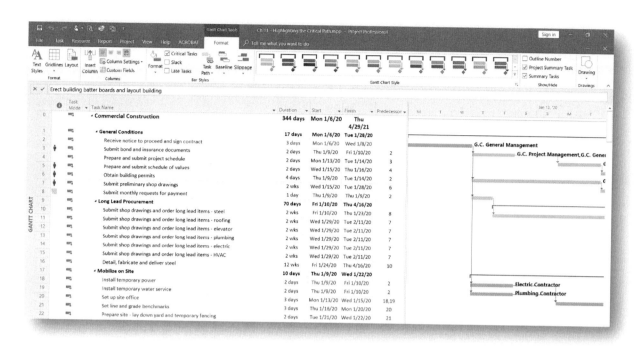

Figure 72 – Highlighting the Critical Path

Highlighting the Critical Path allows you to quickly identify which tasks can be compressed to speed up the schedule. For example, if the schedule in *Figure 72* above needed to be compressed 1 day, you'd know that only the tasks highlighted in red should be considered. Compressing the tasks with blue bars will NOT speed up the schedule.

To highlight the Critical Path task bars in the Gantt chart:

1. On the **Format** tab, in the **Bar Styles** group, select the **Critical Tasks** checkbox.

2. The Critical Path tasks will be formatted with red task bars in the Gantt Chart graph.

To highlight the Critical Path tasks names in the Entry table:

1. On the **Format** tab, in the **Format** group, select **Text Styles** to open the *Text Styles* dialogue box.

2. In the **Item to Change** pick-list, select **Critical Tasks**.

3. In the **Color** field, select the color you want for the font highlighting.

160

How to Compress a Schedule

There are at least three ways to compress a schedule:

1. Reduce the duration of tasks on the Critical Path.

2. Apply Lead time between tasks on the Critical Path.

3. Adjust task relationships between tasks on the Critical Path.

Compressing the Schedule by Reducing Critical Path Task Durations

As explained earlier, a schedule can only be compressed if a task(s) on the Critical Path is compressed. This can be a counter-intuitive notion to some. It's natural to think that a schedule can be compressed by reducing the duration of the longest task in the schedule. For example, the *Commercial Construction* template included in Project has a duration of 344 days and contains a 12-week task (Task 16, "*Detail, fabricate and deliver steel*") that is not on the Critical Path (*Figure 72* above). Even if the duration of this task is reduced from 12 weeks to 1 day, the project duration will still be 344 days!

Compressing the Schedule by Applying Lead Time

As discussed in Chapter 4, **Lead** time is the number of days a successor task can start before its predecessor finishes. To use Lead time to compress the schedule, you must know which tasks are on the Critical Path. Your schedule will only compress if you apply Lead time between tasks on the Critical Path. For example, the Commercial Construction schedule shown in *Figure 73* below has a 344-day duration. Task 21 "*Set line and grade benchmarks*" and Task 22 "*Prepare site - lay down yard and temporary fencing*" are successive Critical Path tasks.

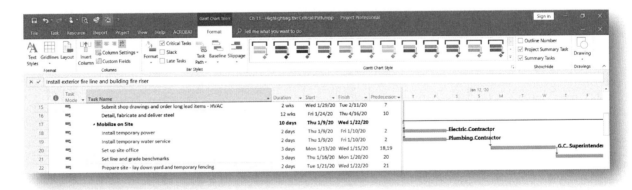

Figure 73 – Using Lead Time

In *Figure 74* below, a 2-day Lead was applied to the successor task (Task 22). This compressed the schedule 2 days and reduced the project duration to 342 days.

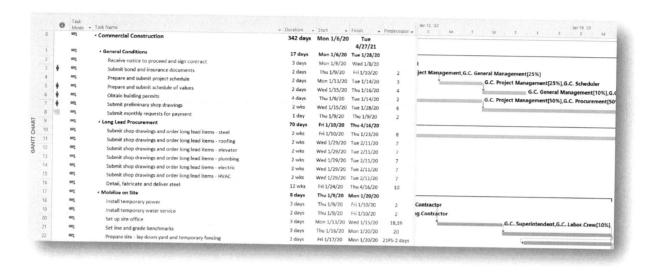

Figure 74 – Using Lead Time

To apply Lead Time:

1. In the Predecessors field of the successor task, enter the predecessor's task ID, then the 2-letter acronym for the task relationship type, then a minus sign, then the Lead time value (E.g. **21FS-2d**).

Compressing the Schedule by Adjusting Task Relationships

Another way to compress the schedule is to adjust task relationships between the tasks on the Critical Path. For example, the Commercial Construction schedule shown in *Figure 75* below has a 342-day duration. Task 20, *"Set up site office"* and Task 21, *"Set line and grade benchmarks"* are Critical Path tasks, with a *Finish-to-Start* task relationship.

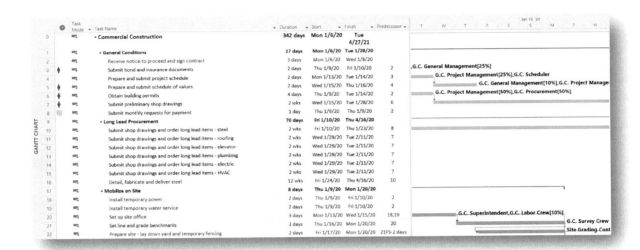

Figure 75 – Compressing the Schedule

Assume that the G.C. Survey Crew negotiated with the G.C. Superintendent and the G.C. Labor Crew to start tasks 20 and 21 on the same day. In *Figure 76* below, tasks 20 & 21 were given a *Start-to-Start* task relationship. This compressed the schedule 3 days and reduced the duration to 339 days.

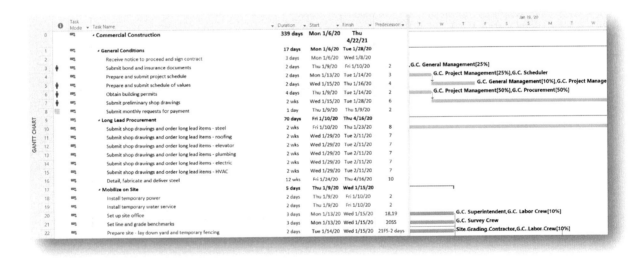

Figure 76 – Compressing the Schedule

Using the Task Path Feature

Although a task may have several predecessors, it can only be delayed by its "driving predecessor(s)". A **Driving Predecessor** has no "wiggle room" and will delay its successor if it is delayed. The **Task Path** feature allows you to identify a task's driving predecessor(s), predecessor(s), driven successor(s), and successor(s) by highlighting their Gantt task bars (*Figure77* below).

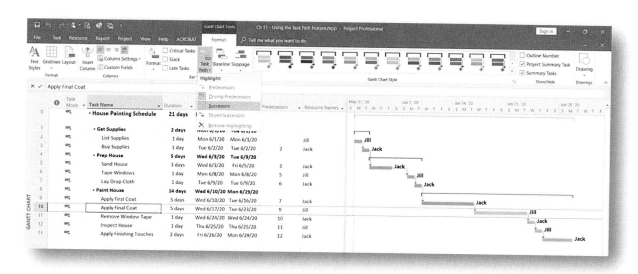

Figure 77 – Task Path Feature

To view the Task Path for a task:

1. Select the task for which you want to view the Task Path.

2. On the **Format** tab, in the **Bar Styles** group select **Task Path**.

3. From the **Highlight** pick-list, select the **Predecessors, Driving Predecessors, Successors** or **Driven Successors** option you want.

Adding Deadlines to Tasks

When managing your schedule, you may need to ensure that a task finishes by a certain date. The **Deadline** feature allows you to flag a task with the latest date you'd like it to finish. When a Deadline is applied to a task, Project will generate a green arrow in the Gantt chart graph as a visual reminder of the date. Project will also generate an alert in the Indicators field if the task exceeds the Deadline (*Figure 78* below).

Figure 78 – Adding Deadlines to Tasks

To add a Deadline to a task:

1. Double-click the task to open the *Task Information* dialogue box.

2. Select the **Advanced** tab.

3. In the **Deadline** field, enter the date or select it from the drop-down calendar (*Figure 79* below*)*.

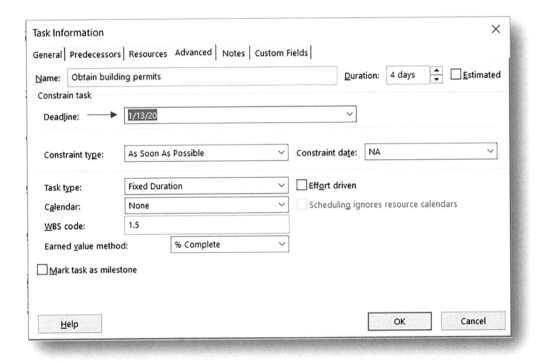

Figure 79 – Adding Deadlines to Tasks

Important Notes about Deadlines

> If you're using Deadlines, be sure to remove them before displaying the Critical Path. While
>
> Deadlines are useful indicators, they introduce negative slack, which alters the Critical Path. To

remove a Deadline, simply delete the date shown in the Deadline field of the *Task Information* Dialogue box. You can always add them back after viewing the Critical Path.

➢ A common mistake that project managers make is to apply *Constraints* to tasks (instead of Deadlines), to ensure a target completion date. In fact, neither a Constraint nor a Deadline will ensure that a task will finish on time. Only good project management practice can keep a schedule from slipping. That said, if you want a visual reminder of the target completion date, applying a Deadline is preferable to applying a Constraint. Constraints impact the schedule and limit scheduling flexibility; whereas deadlines do not. We'll review Constraints in the next chapter.

We've now learned to compress the schedule. We've learned to use Lead time, add Deadlines, view the Critical Path and use the Task Path feature.

CHALLENGE – Practice Exercise

Compress a Schedule

Instructions: In this practice exercise, you'll work with Slack, the Critical Path and Lead time to compress a project schedule. Visit www.mspbasics.com for "checkpoint" images to check your work as you go along.

Follow the steps below to complete this exercise:

Start a Project from a Template

You'll use a project template to complete this exercise. **Note**: The templates are hosted on a companion website. You'll need to be connected to the internet to access them.

1. From the opening view, double-click the "Commercial Construction" project template.

Set the Project Start Date

Your construction site is in Southern California and you've hired "all-season" construction crews. Set the project start date to **5/1/20** as follows:

1. Select the **Project** tab.
2. In the **Properties** group, select the **Project Information** command to open the *Project Information* dialogue box.
3. Enter the project start date in the **Start date** field.
4. Click **OK** to close the *Project Information* dialogue box.

Next, you'll adjust the screen to get a better look at the current view. The **Timeline View** panel is displayed. It provides a summary of the project timeline. It shows all the major phases of the project and their scheduled start and finish dates. It also shows that the project will start on 5/1/20 and finish on 8/25/21.

Hide the timeline view panel as follows:

1. Selecting the **View** tab.

2. In the **Split View** group, uncheck the **Timeline** checkbox.

Next, slide the line that divides the Entry table from the Gantt chart to the right, until you can see the **Add New Column** field in the Entry table.

Highlight the Critical Path

The building you're constructing will obtain the certificate of occupancy on 8/24/21 (task #142). Your client has requested that you compress the schedule by 3 weeks and obtain the certificate of occupancy by 8/3/21. To see which tasks can be compressed to expedite the schedule, you'll highlight the Critical Path in the Gantt chart and Entry table.

To display the Critical Path in the Gantt Chart:

1. Select the **Format** tab.

2. In the **Bar Styles** group, select the **Critical Tasks** checkbox. The Critical Path tasks will be highlighted with red task bars in the Gantt chart graph.

To display the Critical Path tasks in the Entry table:

1. Select the **Format** tab.

2. In the **Format** group, select **Text Styles** to open the *Text Styles* dialogue box.

3. In the **Item to Change** field, select **Critical Tasks** from the pick-list.

4. In the **Color** field, select **red** for the color.

5. Click **OK** to close the *Text Styles* dialogue box. The Critical Path tasks will be highlighted in the Entry table with red font.

6. To check your results so far, visit www.mspbasics.com. Select "Practice Exercise Solutions" from the menu. Select "Chapter 11" and reference "Checkpoint Images #1a & 1b".

Display Total Slack, Free Slack, and Successor Tasks

To get more information about the impact of compressing or delaying tasks, you'll add the Slack and Successor fields. Using the **Add New Column** field, add the **Total Slack**, **Free Slack,** and **Successors** fields to the Entry table as follows:

1. Click on the "Add New Column" heading to display the various fields.

2. Type the name of the field you want.

3. Select the field name to add it to the Entry table.

Scroll to Task 58 *"Strip forms from 2nd floor slab"*. This task has 99 days of Total Slack; meaning, it can be delayed 99 days without delaying the schedule. It finishes on 11/18/20, long before the project finishes. Because of this, it may be tempting to let this task slip. However, this task has zero Free Slack; meaning, it can be delayed zero days before it will delay another *task.*

Notice in the Successors field that this task has several successors – Tasks 69,70, 71 & 72. These tasks are being worked by 4 different trades. It would be a good idea to check with these trade resources and confirm they are still available before delaying Task 58. Notice, the Critical Path tasks have zero Total Slack. They directly impact the project finish date, and can be compressed to meet your client's request date for Task 142.

Applying a Deadline to a Task

Next, you'll apply a Deadline to Task 142 *"Obtain certificate of occupancy"*, as a visual reminder of the **8/3/21** date your client has requested.

1. Double-click Task 142 to open the *Task Information* dialogue box.
2. Select the **Advanced** tab.
3. In the **Deadline** field, type or select **8/3/21**.
4. Click **OK** to close the *Task Information* dialogue box.
5. To check your results so far, visit www.mspbasics.com. Select "Practice Exercise Solutions" from the menu. Select "Chapter 11" and reference "Checkpoint Image #2".

A few things occurred when the Deadline was applied. Project generated a green arrow in the Gantt chart to indicate that the task has a Deadline (see "Checkpoint Image #3). The arrow corresponds with the Deadline date on the timescale. If you can't see the Gantt chart task bar for Task 142, bring it forward using the **Scroll to Task** feature as follows:

1. Select Task 142.

2. Select the **Task** tab.

3. In the **Editing** group, select the **Scroll to Task** command.

Because this task currently finishes on 8/24/21, which exceeds its 8/3/21 Deadline, the task bar extends past the Deadline marker. Project also generated an alert in the Indicators field to notify you of the exceeded Deadline (see "Checkpoint Image #4"). Notice the negative numbers in the "Total Slack" field. When you create a Deadline, Project adds *negative slack* which distorts the Critical Path calculations. Since you'll be using the Critical Path to compress the schedule, you'll remove the Deadline feature for now and add it back later.

To remove the Deadline:

1. Double-click Task 142 to open the *Task Information* dialogue box.

2. Delete the date from the **Deadline** field.

3. Click **OK** to close the *Task Information* dialogue box.

Apply Lead Time

Next, you'll apply **Lead** time to compress the schedule. You'll start by adding Lead time between two Critical Path tasks. Scroll up to Tasks 93 *"Install window wall aluminum and glass"* and 94 *"Install interior stud walls and drywall"*. These tasks have a *Finish-to-Start* relationship. You've spoken to the Window and Drywall contractors and they've agreed that the Drywall contractor can begin Task 94 one week before Task 93 finishes. He can begin to install the interior stud walls and drywall in the areas where the Window contractor has finished. You'll represent this in Project with a 1-week Lead between the tasks.

Apply the Lead time as follows:

1. In the **Predecessors** field of task 94, type **93FS-1w**

2. To check your results so far, visit www.mspbasics.com. Select "Practice Exercise Solutions" from the menu. Select "Chapter 11" and reference "Checkpoint Image #5".

Scroll down to Task 142 to see how the 1-week Lead time compressed the schedule toward your 8/3/21 deadline. The finish date has been compressed to 8/17/21. You'll need to compress the schedule further to make your client's date.

Scroll up to Critical Path Tasks 98 *"Install millwork and wood trim"* and 99 *"Paint walls and woodwork"*. These tasks have a *Finish-to-Start* relationship. They also each have other predecessors, tasks 94 & 95 respectively. You can see by the blue highlighting that these tasks were rescheduled from the 1-week Lead you just applied. You've spoken to the resources assigned to Tasks 98 & 99 and they've agreed that Task 99 can begin one week before Task 98 finishes. You'll represent this in Project with a 1-week Lead between the tasks as follows:

1. In the **Predecessors** field of Task 99, add **98FS-1w**. Be sure not to remove the other predecessor (Task 95). Each predecessor should be separated by a comma.

2. To check your results so far, visit www.mspbasics.com. Select "Practice Exercise Solutions" from the menu. Select "Chapter 11" and reference "Checkpoint Image #6".

Scroll down to Task 142 to see how the 1-week Lead time compressed the schedule toward your 8/3/21 deadline. The finish date has been compressed to 8/10/21. You'll need to compress the schedule another week to make the deadline.

Scroll up to Critical Path Task 105 *"Install building carpet"*. This task currently has a 4-week duration. You've negotiated with the Carpet Contractor to bring in additional resources and complete the task in 3 weeks. Reduce the task's duration as follows:

1. In the **Duration** field of Task 105, enter **3w**.

2. To check your results so far, visit www.mspbasics.com. Select "Practice Exercise Solutions" from the menu. Select "Chapter 11" and reference "Checkpoint Image #7".

Scroll down to Task 142 to see how the duration change compressed your schedule. The task now meets your client's 8/3/21 deadline!

Last, you'll re-add the Deadline to Task 142.

1. Double-click Task 142 to open the *Task Information* dialogue box.

2. Select the **Advanced** tab.

3. In the **Deadline** field, type or select **8/3/21**.

4. Click **OK** to close the *Task Information* dialogue box.

5. To check your results, visit www.mspbasics.com. Select "Practice Exercise Solutions" from the menu. Select "Chapter 11" and reference "Checkpoint Image #8".

6. **SAVE THIS PROJECT FILE**. You will use this file to complete the Chapter 12 practice exercise.

In the Entry table, notice that since Task 142 no longer exceeds its deadline, there is no alert in the Indicators field. In the Gantt chart, notice that the end of the task bar now corresponds with the Deadline marker. If you can't see the Deadline marker in the Gantt chart, slide the zoom slider in the bottom right corner to the right to increase the Timescale. Then, scroll to the Deadline marker.

You've now worked with Slack, the Critical Path and Lead time to compress a schedule.

Now You Can

- Compress a Schedule
- View the Critical Path
- Explain Slack
- Use Lead Time Effectively
- Use the Task Path Feature
- Add Deadlines to Tasks

Chapter 12 Constraining Your Schedule

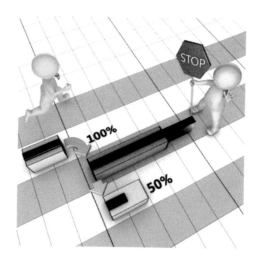

IN THIS CHAPTER:

- Constraint Types

- Scheduling from the Start or Finish Date

- Applying Constraints to Tasks

- When to Use and Not Use Constraints

- Scheduling Conflicts and The Planning Wizard

In the last chapter, we compressed the schedule. We used the Critical Path and applied Lead time to reduce the project duration. In this chapter, you'll learn to constrain the schedule. Constraints are one of the most misused features of Microsoft Project. In this chapter, we'll discuss the proper way to use them. When you're done, you'll be able to explain constraint types, apply constraints, identify when a task has been constrained and use the Planning Wizard to resolve scheduling conflicts.

Although the Microsoft Project scheduling engine is very efficient, the way it schedules may not always fit your business reality. In such cases, you may need to constrain your schedule. Constraints allow you to cater the scheduling behavior of Project to your business realities.

Here are some practical use cases for constraining the schedule:

> ➢ Funding may be delayed, thereby preventing the task from starting as soon as possible.

> ➢ A task may be temporarily unworkable (despite its predecessor being complete).

> ➢ A task may be delayed until a resource has finished working on a higher priority project.

By default, Project begins all tasks as soon as possible. In each of the use cases above, Project's default scheduling behavior must be constrained to support the business realty.

Constraint Types

A **Constraint** is a restriction applied to a task that impacts the start or finish date of a task. There are eight constraint types available in Microsoft Project.

Here's a description of each:

> ➢ **As Soon As Possible** (default) – The task will **start** as soon as possible

> ➢ **As Late As Possible** – The task will **start** as late as possible.

> ➢ **Finish No Earlier Than** – The task will **finish** on the specified date or later.

> ➢ **Finish No Later Than** – The task will **finish** on the specified date or sooner.

> ➢ **Must Finish On** – The task will **finish** on the specified date.

> ➢ **Must Start On** – The task will **start** on the specified date.

> ➢ **Start No Earlier Than** – The task will **start** on the specified date or later.

> ➢ **Start No Later Than** – The task will **start** on the specified date or sooner.

Here's a note of caution. The *Must Finish On* and the *Must Start On* constraint can only guarantee that a task finishes or starts on the specified date, if your schedule supports it. It's tempting to use these constraints to guarantee that a deadline is met. These constraints <u>can</u> guarantee that a task starts or finishes on a specified date within an allowable range, but they cannot guarantee that you meet your project deadline. Use the methods discussed in Chapter 11, "Compressing Your Schedule" to ensure you meet your deadline. If you apply a *Must Finish On* or *Must Start On* constraint and the specified date is not supported by your schedule, Project will issue a warning to alert you of the scheduling conflict.

Scheduling from the Start or Finish Date

Project automatically schedules tasks to start as soon as possible by applying the *As Soon as Possible* constraint to all new tasks. This causes the overall schedule to finish as soon as possible. Stated differently, Project schedules tasks from the project start date. You can also schedule tasks from the project finish date. For example, your project may need to finish by a certain date before the resources get assigned to a different project. In such a case, it would be helpful to know when to start the project so that the resources can remain on your project until it finishes. *Figure 80* below shows the settings for both scheduling options.

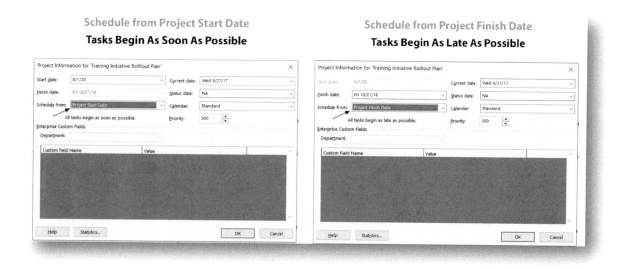

Figure 80 – Schedule from Start or Finish Date

To adjust the settings to schedule from the project finish date:

1. Select the **Information** command on the **Project** tab to open the *Project Information* dialogue box.

2. Select **Project Finish Date** from the **Schedule from** pick-list.

3. Click **OK** to close the *Project Information* dialogue box.

Applying Constraints to Tasks

To apply a Constraint to a task:

1. Double-click the task you want to apply the constraint to. The *Task Information* dialogue box opens (*Figure 81* below).

2. Select the **Advanced** tab.

3. From the **Constraint type** pick-list, select the constraint type you want.

4. Enter the date in the **Constraint date** field.

5. Click **OK** to close the *Task Information* dialogue box.

6. After the constraint is applied, Project will add a Constraint icon in the Indicator's field of the Entry table in Gantt Chart view (*Figure 81* below).

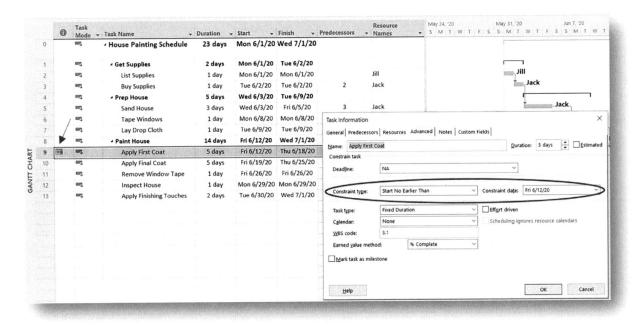

Figure 81 – Applying Constraints

When to Use and Not Use Constraints

> **USE CONSTRAINTS** – When you must override the normal scheduling behavior of Project due to a business driver, such as delayed funding or delayed resource availability.

> **AVOID CONSTRAINTS** – When the business driver, such as the need to make a critical date, is better solved by using the Critical Path, Lead Times and Deadlines (see Chapter 11).

Scheduling Conflicts and the Planning Wizard

Constraints must be used appropriately to avoid **Scheduling Conflicts**. Scheduling conflicts occur when conflicting requirements are imposed on a task. If you set a constraint for a task that causes a scheduling conflict, Project will alert you of the conflict and offer options to resolve the issue using the **Planning Wizard** (*Figure 82 below*).

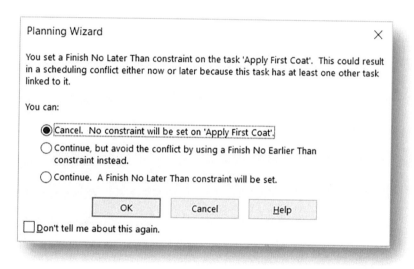

Figure 82 – Planning Wizard

We've now reviewed constraints and Project's default scheduling behavior. We've reviewed proper use cases for applying constraints, learned to identify when a task has been constrained and how the Planning Wizard can assist with identifying and resolving scheduling conflicts.

CHALLENGE – Practice Exercise

Constrain a Schedule

Instructions: In this practice exercise, you will constrain a schedule. You'll work with different constraint types to create exceptions to override Project's default scheduling behavior. Visit www.mspbasics.com for "Checkpoint" images to check your work as you go along.

Follow the steps below to complete this exercise:

Open an Existing Project Plan

Open the "Commercial Construction" project plan that you saved from the Chapter 11 practice exercise. **Note**: The file should contain the completed actions from the Chapter 11 exercise.

Apply Constraints to Tasks

Note the current project finish date of 8/4/21. You'll reference it later in the exercise. Scroll to Task 6 *"Obtain building permits"*. This task is scheduled to start on 5/6/20. You've been notified that no building permits will be approved before 6/1/20. Therefore, this task cannot begin on the scheduled start date. To account for this delay, you'll apply a *Start-No-Earlier-Than* constraint to the task as follows:

1. Double-click Task 6 *"Obtain building permits"* to open the *Task Information* dialogue box.
2. Select the **Advanced** tab.
3. In the **Constraint type** field, select **Start No Earlier Than**.
4. In the **Constraint date** field, enter or select **6/1/20**.
5. Click **OK** to close the *Task Information* dialogue box.

6. To check your results so far, visit www.mspbasics.com. Select "Practice Exercise Solutions" from the menu. Select "Chapter 12" and reference "Checkpoint Image #1".

Notice that Project generated a "calendar" icon in the Indicators field. This indicates that the task has a constraint applied. Hover over the icon for details about the constraint. Also, notice that Project rescheduled this task to start on 6/1/20 (see "Checkpoint Image #2).

Scroll to Task 15 *"Submit shop drawings and order long lead items – HVAC"*. This task is now scheduled to start on 6/19/20 and finish on 7/2/20. The HVAC Contractor assigned to the task has correctly observed that his shop drawings will not be used until October 26th, when his successor (Task 54) begins. As a favor, he has asked you to delay his task as late as possible, so he can devote resources to more critical projects. Since this task isn't on the Critical Path and has 16.2 weeks of Total and Free slack, you agree to accommodate his request. But, to allow room for potential delays, you'll need him to start the task on 9/1/20. To incorporate this condition into the schedule, you'll apply a *Must Start On* constraint to this task as follows:

1. Double-click Task 15 *"Submit shop drawings and order long lead items – HVAC"* to open the *Task Information* dialogue box.

2. Select the **Advanced** tab.

3. In the **Constraint type** field, select **Must Start On**.

4. In the **Constraint date** field, enter or select **9/1/20**.

5. Click **OK** to close the *Task Information* dialogue box.

6. To check your results so far, visit www.mspbasics.com. Select "Practice Exercise Solutions" from the menu. Select "Chapter 12" and reference "Checkpoint Image #3".

7. Project opens the **Planning Wizard** to notify you that you applied a *Must Start On* constraint to the task and that this could result in a scheduling conflict because the task is linked to other tasks. Select option 3, *"Continue. A Must Start On constraint will be set"*.

8. Click **OK** to close the Planning Wizard.

Notice that Project generated the "calendar" icon in the Indicators field and rescheduled the task to start on 9/1/20 (see "Checkpoint Image #4). Notice that this task is now on the Critical Path (indicated by the red highlighting). This is because delaying the start date removed the Total Slack.

Scroll to Task 104 *"Hang Wallpaper"*. This task is currently scheduled to start on 6/7/21 and finish on 6/18/21. The Painting Contractor has called in a favor and has asked you to delay his task as late as possible because he has a competing project with a more urgent completion target. You've checked your schedule and observed that his task isn't on the Critical Path and has 2 weeks of Total Slack. So, you decide to grant his request. To incorporate this delay into the schedule, you'll apply an *As Late As Possible* constraint to this task as follows:

1. Double-click Task 104 *"Hang Wallpaper"* to open the *Task Information* dialogue box.

2. Select the **Advanced** tab.

3. In the **Constraint type** field, select **As Late As Possible**.

4. Because the task will start as late as possible, do not type a date in the **Constraint date** field. Project will calculate this date.

5. Click **OK** to close the *Task Information* dialogue box.

6. To check your results so far, visit www.mspbasics.com. Select "Practice Exercise Solutions" from the menu. Select "Chapter 12" and reference "Checkpoint Image #5".

Project rescheduled this task to begin on 6/21/21, which is the latest date the task can start without delaying the schedule. This task is now on the Critical Path and its Total and Free slack are now zero (see "Checkpoint Image #6). Like the default *As Soon As Possible* constraint type, Project doesn't generate a constraint indicator for the *As Late As Possible* constraint type.

Scroll to the top of the plan to view the project finish date. Notice that the finish date is still 8/4/21. The constraints didn't affect the project duration. This is because no constraints were applied to the Critical Path tasks. All constraints were applied to tasks with available slack.

You've now worked with constraints to create exceptions to override Project's default scheduling behavior.

Now You Can

- Explain Constraint Types

- Schedule from the Start or Finish Date

- Apply Constraints to Tasks

- Explain When to Use and Not Use Constraints

- Resolve Scheduling Conflicts using the Planning Wizard

Chapter 13 Leveling Your Resources

IN THIS CHAPTER:

- Understanding Max. Units
- Automatic Resource Leveling
- Using the Leveling Gantt View
- Leveling Resources Manually
- Using the Resource Usage View
- Using the Team Planner View
- Splitting Tasks

In the last chapter we learned to constrain the schedule. We reviewed the eight constraint types and use cases for applying them. In this chapter, we'll review resource leveling. We'll learn what those *red men* are and how to get rid of them! In simple terms, resource leveling is about offloading over-committed resources. When you're done with this chapter, you'll be able to explain resource over-allocation and level resources using automatic and manual leveling methods. You'll also be able to use the Resource Usage and Team Planner views to inspect and level over-committed resources.

Resource Leveling

Resource Leveling is the re-distribution of resource assignments or resource assignment units to resolve (or level) the condition of over-committed (or over-allocated) resources. It pertains only to Detailed scheduling because resources are only assigned per their specific availability in a Detailed schedule (Chapter 6). Resource allocation can impact the overall schedule and cost, therefore effective resource leveling is good practice. Conversely, in a Simple schedule resources are not assigned to tasks per their specific availability, as the tasks durations are fixed. Therefore, if resources are over-allocated in a Simple schedule, leveling them will not impact the schedule.

Here are some reasons to level resources:

➢ **Schedules should reflect resource commitments** – Resources should be leveled whenever resource assignments exceed the commitments made by your team.

➢ **To avoid cost over-runs** – Resources should be leveled to avoid cost over-runs. E.g. unapproved overtime cost.

➢ **To avoid unrealistic scheduling expectations** – Because resource leveling can delay the schedule, it should be done before schedules are presented to stakeholders.

Max. Units

As discussed in Chapter 8, **Max. Units** represents a resource's maximum capacity to work on any given day. It's expressed as a percentage of an 8-hour day on the Resource Sheet in the Max. Units field. By default, Project assigns 100% Max. Units to all new resources; which means the resource is available to work on assigned tasks the entire 8-hour work day.

When a resource is scheduled to work beyond their Max. Units value, the resource becomes **over-allocated**. For example, a resource with 50% Max. Units can work on tasks for 4 hours per day without becoming over-allocated. If their collective task assignments on any given day total 5 hours or more, they will become over-allocated. When this occurs, Project will alert you of the over-allocation with a *red man* icon in the Indicators field of the Entry table in the Gantt Chart view (*Figure 83* below). In other views, such as the Resource Usage view and the Team Planner view, over-allocated resources are highlighted with red font.

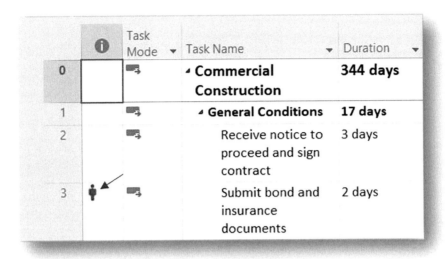

Figure 83 – Over-Allocated Resources

Analyzing Over-Allocations – Using the Resource Usage View

Before you level over-allocated resources, you must identify the task assignments that caused the over-allocation. You can get this information in the **Resource Usage** view. This view shows resources and their task assignment details. The over-allocations and the assignments causing them, are highlighted in red font. You can adjust the view to show the data at different time intervals, such as daily or weekly.

Figure 84 below shows the Resource Usage view. The *G.C. Project Management* resource is over-allocated on June 4th, June 5th, June 10th and June 11th. He's scheduled to work 12 hours on these dates, which exceeds his 100% Max. Units capacity of 8 hours per day. For example, on June 10th, he's scheduled to work 8 hours on the "Prepare and submit schedule of values" task and 4 hours on the "Submit preliminary shop drawings" task. As you can see the Resource Usage view is very useful for determining where over-allocations occur.

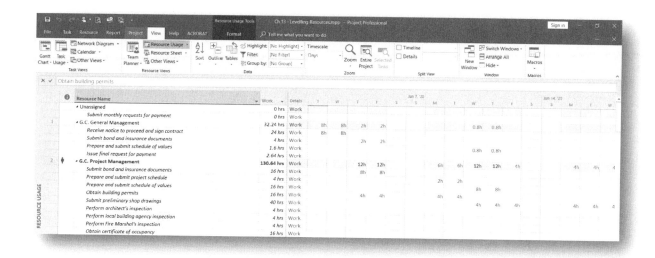

Figure 84 – Resource Usage View

To access the Resource Usage view:

1. Select the **View** tab.

2. In the **Resource Views** group, select **Resource Usage**.

Resource Leveling Methods

Resource leveling can be done **Automatically** or **Manually**. Automatic resource leveling is done by *Project*. Using this feature, Project will automatically resolve over-allocated resources by making adjustments that least delay the schedule. Manual resource leveling is done by *you*. As you'll soon discover, you can do everything Project can do to level resources – such as delaying start dates, splitting tasks and adjusting resource assignment units.

Note: Automatic and Manual resource <u>leveling</u> should not be confused with the Automatic and Manual <u>scheduling modes</u>. The Automatic and Manual scheduling modes are used to control how tasks are scheduled. Automatic and Manual resource leveling are options for leveling resources.

Automatic Resource Leveling

When using Automatic resource leveling, Project will level over-allocated resources per the settings you specify in the *Resource Leveling* dialogue box. The options you select control the adjustments Project can make to your schedule during Automatic leveling.

To access the Resource Leveling dialogue box:

1. Select the **Resource** tab.

2. In the **Level** group, select **Leveling Options**.

Using *Figure 85* below, let's review the leveling options.

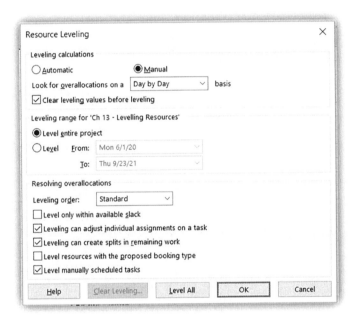

Figure 85– Automatic Resource Leveling Options

Leveling calculations – There are two options for this setting – Automatic and Manual. If you select the Automatic option, Project will level resources as soon as they become over-allocated. If you select the Manual option, Project will level resources <u>only</u> when you tell it to, by invoking the resource leveling feature. General practice is to use the Manual option, as it allows you to control when resource adjustments are made.

Look for overallocations on a …basis – This option lets you choose how granularly Project will look for over-allocations. The choices are Minute by Minute, Hour by Hour, Day by Day, Week by Week and Month by Month. General practice is to use Day by Day.

Clear leveling values before leveling – This option will clear values from a previous leveling attempt.

Leveling range – This option allows you to choose whether Project will level resources across the entire project or only within a specified date range.

Leveling order – This option lets you choose the order in which Project will delay tasks to level resources. There are 3 choices:

> ➤ **ID only** – Project will delay tasks with higher Task ID values first.

> ➤ **Standard** – Project considers the following conditions (in respective order) to determine which tasks to delay: Predecessor relationships, Slack, Dates, Priorities and Constraints.

> ➤ **Priority, Standard** – Project considers the same conditions as the Standard option, except it looks for task priority first. **Note:** You can set task priority by double-clicking a task to open the *Task Information* dialogue box, selecting the **General** tab and then setting the priority in **Priority** field. The higher you set the task priority number, the less likely the task will be adjusted during resource leveling.

Level only within available slack – Project assesses the slack value of tasks and delays them within the available slack. Unchecking this option allows Project to extend the project finish date to resolve over-allocations. Checking this option will prevent Project from extending the finish date but may result in some resources remaining over-allocated.

Leveling can adjust individual assignments on a task – Project adjusts individual assignments on task until the over-allocation condition clears up. For example, a resource that is assigned at 50% Units may be reduced to 25% Units – if that will resolve the over-allocation condition.

Leveling can create splits in remaining work – Project will split the remaining work on a task (delaying the task) to resolve an over-allocation.

Level resources with the proposed booking type – Project will consider the *Booking* Type (proposed or committed) when leveling resources. If selected, Project will make changes to committed resources before making changes to proposed resources. If left unchecked, Project will only impact committed resources. This option relates to **Project Server** only.

Level manually scheduled tasks – Project will include manually scheduled tasks when leveling.

How to Automatically Level Resources

Once you've set your leveling preferences, complete the following steps to Automatically level resources:

1. Select the **Resource** tab.

2. In the **Level** group, select **Level All** to level the entire project <u>OR</u> select **Level Resource** to level a specific resource.

Viewing the Effects of Automatic Leveling – Leveling Gantt View

When using Automatic leveling, you can view the adjustments Project made to resolve over-allocations in the **Leveling Gantt** view. This view shows the before and after effects of Automatic resource leveling. *Figure 86* below shows the Leveling Gantt view.

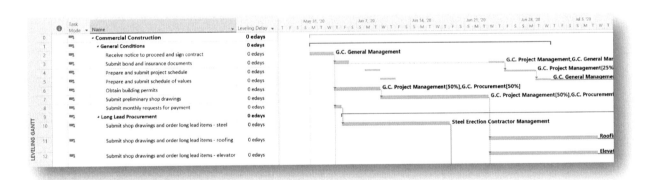

Figure 86 – Leveling Gantt View

The table on the left shows the tasks, their start and finish dates and the amount of leveling delay caused by Automatic resource leveling. In the Gantt chart area, there are two sets of task bars. The task bars depict how Project resolved the over-allocations and show the delay caused by the leveling. The gold task bars on the top represent the tasks <u>before</u> they were leveled. The blue task bars on the bottom represent the tasks <u>after</u> they were leveled. For example, in *Figure 86*, Project split the remaining work on Task 3 to resolve the over-allocation. As you can see, this action delayed the task quite a bit.

To access the Leveling Gantt view:

1. Select the **View** tab.
2. In the **Resource Views** group, select **Other Views**, then select **More Views**.
3. In the *More Views* dialogue box, select **Leveling Gantt**, then select **Apply**.

Leveling Resources Manually

Using the Automatic leveling option allows Project to automatically level resources by making adjustments that least delay the schedule. Though efficient, this option may produce resource schedules that are not manageable in your project environment. For this reason, you may want to consider leveling resources manually. It gives you more control and allows you to make resource adjustments that reflect your business reality. Bear in mind that whether you do it manually or automatically, resource leveling will usually delay your schedule. This is because after the resources are leveled, they will only be working to their Max. Units capacity.

Leveling Resources by Increasing Max. Units

There are several ways to manually level resources. One way is to increase a resource's Max. Units value. For example, in *Figure 87* below, the *G.C. Project Management* resource is over-allocated on June 4th, June 5th, June 10th and June 11th. The resource is scheduled to work 12 hours on these dates, which exceeds their 100% Max. Units capacity of 8 hours per day.

		Resource Name	Work	Details	T	W	T	F	S	Jun 7, '20 S	M	T	W	T	F
		Unassigned	0 hrs	Work											
		Submit monthly requests for payment	*0 hrs*	Work											
1		G.C. General Management	32.24 hrs	Work	8h	8h	2h	2h					0.8h	0.8h	
		Receive notice to proceed and sign contract	*24 hrs*	Work	8h	8h									
		Submit bond and insurance documents	*4 hrs*	Work			2h	2h							
		Prepare and submit schedule of values	*1.6 hrs*	Work									0.8h	0.8h	
		Issue final request for payment	*2.64 hrs*	Work											
2		**G.C. Project Management**	**130.64 hrs**	Work			12h	12h			6h	6h	12h	12h	4h
		Submit bond and insurance documents	*16 hrs*	Work			8h	8h							
		Prepare and submit project schedule	*4 hrs*	Work							2h	2h			

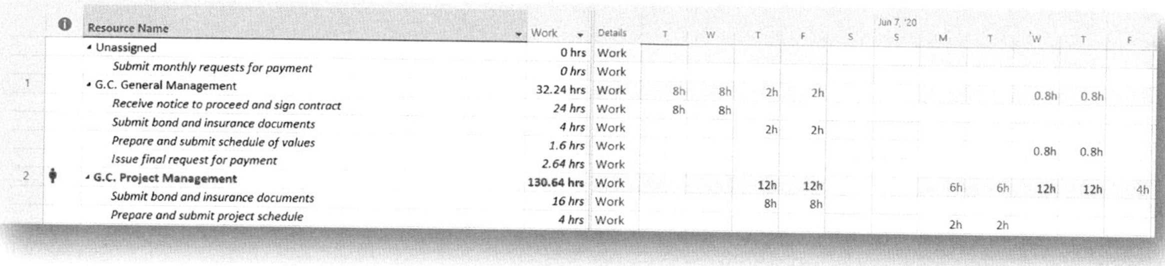

Figure 87 – Over-Allocated Resources

Increasing this resource's Max. Units to 150% (12 hours per day) would resolve the over-allocations. Bear in mind, working 12 hours per day may not be practical. Also, increasing Max. Units can also increase cost, so it may not always be the best solution.

To adjust a resources Max. Units:

1. Select the **View** tab.

2. In the **Resource Views** group, select **Resource Sheet** to access the Resource Sheet view.

3. Adjust the resource's Max. Units in the **Max. Units** field.

Leveling Resources by Redistributing Task Work

Another way to manually level resources is to redistribute task work. For example, in *Figure 87* above, to resolve the over-allocation on June 4th & June 5th, the work hours for the "Submit bond and insurance documents" task could be manually reduced from 8 hours to 4 hours. The remaining 4 hours could be redistributed to another day(s), when the resource can work on the task within their Max. Units capacity. The same adjustment can be made for the "Prepare and submit schedule of values" task on June 10th and June 11th.

Leveling Resources by Splitting a Task

Resources can also be manually leveled by **Splitting a Task**. Splitting a task interrupts the work and resumes it on a later date. For example, in *Figure 88* below, to resolve the over-allocation on June 5th, you could interrupt the work on the "Obtain building permits" task so that no work occurs on June 5th and resume the work on a later date.

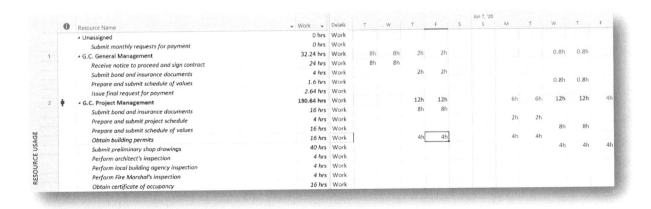

Figure 88 – Resolving Over-Allocations

In *Figure 89* below, Task 6 "Obtain building permits" has been split from 6/5/20 – 6/8/20.

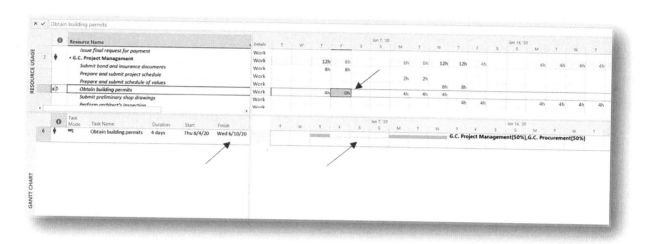

Figure 89 – Splitting a Task

When a task is split, Project indicates the split with a dotted line on the task bar in the Gantt chart (shown in the bottom pane of the split view). In the Resource Usage view (top pane), you can see the "0h" entry on June 5th, indicating that no work occurs. There is no 0h entry on Saturday and Sunday because these are non-working days. The task finish date has been delayed to 6/10/20.

To split a task:

1. In the Entry Table of the Gantt Chart view, select the task you want to split. **Note**: You may need to use the Scroll to Task feature to bring the task bar forward in the Gantt chart. On the **Task** tab, in the **Editing** group, select **Scroll to Task**. You may also need to use the zoom slider in the Quick Access shortcuts (lower right corner) to expand the task bar and make it easier to split.

2. On the **Task** tab, in the **Schedule** group, click the **Split Task** command (the mouse cursor will change to the split task arrow).

3. Hover (don't click) the mouse pointer over the task bar until the date you want the task work to stop appears.

4. Then, click, hold, and drag to the right until the date you want the task work to resume appears, then release.

Leveling Resources Using Constraints

Another way to manually level resources is to use a constraint to delay a task. For example, in *Figure 90* below, the *G.C. Project Management* resource is over-allocated on Wednesday, June 10th and Thursday, 6/11/20. He's scheduled to work 12 hours on both days. To resolve the over-allocation on Thursday, 6/11/20, the "Submit preliminary shop drawings" task can be delayed to Friday, 6/12/20 by applying a *Start No Earlier Than* 6/12/20 constraint.

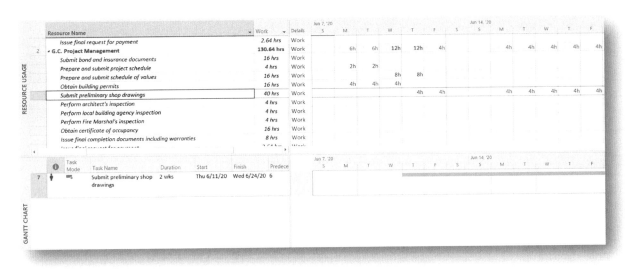

Figure 90 – Leveling Resources with Constraints

To apply a constraint:

1. Double-click the task to open the *Task Information* dialogue box (*Figure 91* below).
2. Select the **Advanced** tab.
3. In the **Constraint type** field, select the constraint type you want from the pick-list.
4. Enter or select the date in the **Constraint date** field.
5. Click **OK** to close the *Task Information* dialogue box.

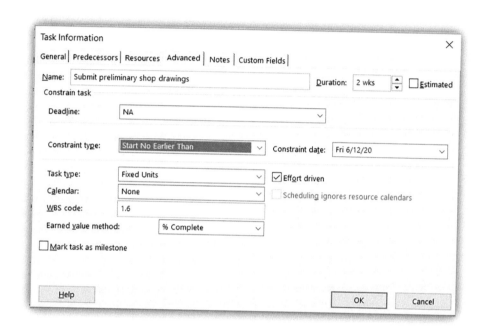

Figure 91 – Applying Constraints

Leveling Resources by Reassigning Work

Another way to manually level resources is to reassign work to another resource. This is done in the *Assign Resources* dialogue box by replacing the over-allocated resource.

To reassign work:

1. Select the task for which you want to reassign the work.

2. Select the **Resource** tab.

3. In the **Assignments** group, select **Assign Resources** to open the *Assign Resources* dialogue box (*Figure 92* below).

4. Select the current resource, then click **Replace** to open the *Replace Resource* dialogue box.

5. Select the new resource, then click **OK**.

6. Select **Close** to close the *Assign Resources* dialogue box.

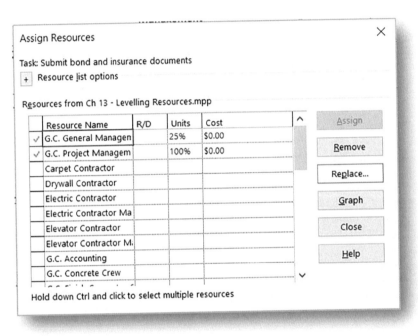

Figure 92 – Replacing Resources

Leveling Resources using the Team Planner View

Over-allocations can also be resolved using the **Team Planner View** (*Figure 93* below). This view is only available in the Microsoft Project Professional version. Like the Resource Usage view, the Team Planner view shows resources and their task assignments. What this view offers that the Resource Usage View doesn't, is a drag and drop feature that allows you make assignment adjustments directly in the view.

The resources are listed on the left. The resources highlighted in red font are over-allocated. The blue task bars on the right, are the tasks they're assigned to. The red outlining reflects the task assignments causing the over-allocation(s). In this view, over-allocations can be resolved by simply dragging and dropping tasks to reschedule or reassign them. While it's tempting to use this method of leveling for its simplicity, bear in mind that any adjustments made in this view can impact the schedule in ways that may not be readily apparent.

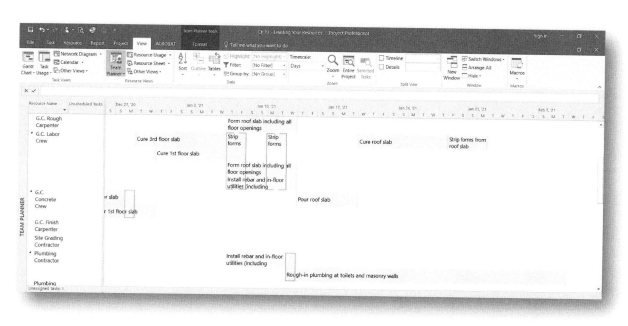

Figure 93 – *Team Planner* View

We've now reviewed resource over-allocation and ways to automatically and manually level resources. We've also seen how the Resource Usage and Team Planner views can help with inspecting and leveling over-committed resources. In summary, resource leveling will generally delay tasks or schedules. Automatic leveling resolves over-allocations with the least amount of schedule delay. Manual leveling requires more work but allows you to balance scheduling efficiency with business realities.

CHALLENGE – Practice Exercise

Level Resources and Resolve Over-Allocations

Instructions: In this practice exercise, you will level over-allocated resources. You'll resolve over-allocations using Manual and Automatic resource leveling. Visit www.mspbasics.com for "Checkpoint" images to check your work as you go along.

Follow the steps below to complete this exercise:

Start a Project from a Template

You'll use a project template to complete this exercise. **Note:** The templates are hosted on a companion website. You'll need to be connected to the internet to access them.

1. From the opening view, double-click the "Marketing Campaign Plan" project template.

First, you'll adjust the screen to get a better look at the current view. The Timeline View panel is displayed. You won't be using it, so you'll hide it to see more of the view.

Hide the Timeline panel as follows:

1. Select the **View** tab.

2. In the **Split View** group, uncheck the **Timeline** checkbox.

Next, slide the line that divides the Entry table from the Gantt chart to the right, until you can see the **Add New Column** field in the Entry table.

Set the Project Start Date and the Current Date

Set the project start date to **6/1/20** as follows:

1. Select the **Project** tab.

2. In the **Properties** group, select the **Project Information** command to open the *Project Information* dialogue box.

3. Enter the project start date in the **Start date** field. DO NOT CLICK OK. Remain in the *Project Information* dialogue box.

4. In the **Current date** field, type or enter **6/1/20**.

5. Click **OK** to close the *Project Information* dialogue box.

6. Take note of the project finish date of **3/12/21**. You'll reference it later in the exercise.

7. To check your results so far, visit www.mspbasics.com. Select "Practice Exercise Solutions" from the menu. Select "Chapter 13" and reference "Checkpoint Image #1".

Identify Over-Allocated Resources

If you scroll down the project plan, you'll notice several tasks with over-allocated resources assigned to them (indicated by the red men icon in the **Indicators** field). To identify which resources are over-allocated and get additional information about their assignments, you'll switch to the **Resource Usage View** as follows:

1. On the **View** tab, in the **Resource Views** group, select **Resource Usage**.

In this view, resources, their task assignments, and cumulative work hours are listed on the left. Their work hours are displayed on the right in the same row. Over-allocations are highlighted in red font. For example, scroll down until you see the Marketing Research resource on the left. Using the scroll bar at the bottom, scroll to the right until you can see the over-allocations for the Marketing Research resource on October 14th,15th & 16th.The work hours will be highlighted in red. This resource is scheduled to work 16 hours on these days, which exceeds their Max. Units of 8 hours per day. Next, you'll manually resolve the over-allocations using various leveling methods.

Manually Level Resources by Increasing Max. Units

As you learned earlier in the chapter, resources become over-allocated when their Max. Units value is exceeded. Next, you'll resolve some of the over-allocations by increasing resources Max. Units.

Switch to the **Resource Sheet View** as follows:

1. Select the **View** tab.

2. In the **Resource Views** group, select **Resource Sheet**.

The following resources are over-allocated:

- Marketing Lead

- Marketing Research

- Marketing Staff

- Marketing Rep

- Internal PR

- PR Company

With the exception of the Marketing Lead, these are *Generic* resource groups and not individual resources. Therefore, the over-allocations can be resolved by increasing Max. Units to reflect the number of resources available in each group. You've spoken with your stakeholders, and each group has allocated up to 5 resources to the project. Each resource in the group is available at 100% Max. Units. Therefore, the collective Max. Units for each resource group is 500%.

Increase the Max. Units for each resource group listed above (excluding the Marketing Lead) to **500%** as follows:

1. In the **Max.** field for each resource, enter **500**.

2. To check your results so far, visit www.mspbasics.com. Select "Practice Exercise Solutions" from the menu. Select "Chapter 13" and reference "Checkpoint Image #2".

The over-allocations for the Marketing Research, Marketing Staff, Marketing Rep, Internal PR and PR Company should be resolved. Next, you'll resolve the over-allocations for the Marketing Lead using other methods.

Manually Level Resources by Applying Constraints

Return to the Gantt Chart view by selecting the **Gantt Chart** icon in the top left corner of the ribbon. The Marketing Lead is over-allocated on tasks 30, 31, 32, 113, 114 & 115. Scroll down until you can see tasks 30, 31 & 32. Use the **Scroll to Task** feature to bring the task bar for task 30 forward as follows:

1. Select task 30.

2. Select the **Task** tab.

3. In the **Editing** group, select **Scroll to Task**.

Notice from the task bars for tasks 30, 31 & 32 that the tasks are scheduled concurrently, rather than in series. This is causing the over-allocation for the Marketing Lead. She's scheduled to work on all three tasks at the same time. Each task has a 5-day duration and is scheduled to start on 9/1/20, when their common predecessor (task 26) finishes. You'll resolve the over-allocations for tasks 31 & 32 by applying *Start No Earlier Than* constraints to delay their start dates as follows:

1. Double-click task 31 to open the *Task Information* dialogue box.

2. Select the **Advanced** tab.

3. In the **Constraint type** field, select **Start No Earlier Than**.

4. In the **Constraint date** field, type or select **9/8/20**.

5. Click **OK** to close the *Task Information* dialogue box.

6. To check your results so far, visit www.mspbasics.com. Select "Practice Exercise Solutions" from the menu. Select "Chapter 13" and reference "Checkpoint Image #3".

The over-allocation for task 31 should be resolved. This task has been rescheduled to start on 9/8/20, which is the next working day after its predecessor (task 30) finishes (see "Checkpoint Image #4).

Apply a *Start No Earlier Than* constraint to task 32 as follows:

1. Double-click task 32 to open the *Task Information* dialogue box.

2. Select the **Advanced** tab.

3. In the **Constraint type** field, select **Start No Earlier Than**.

4. In the **Constraint date** field, type or select **9/15/20**.

5. Click **OK** to close the *Task Information* dialogue box.

6. To check your results so far, visit www.mspbasics.com. Select "Practice Exercise Solutions" from the menu. Select "Chapter 13" and reference "Checkpoint Image #5".

The over-allocation for task 32 should be resolved. It has been rescheduled to start on 9/15/20, which is the next working day after its predecessor (task 31) finishes. This should have also resolved the over-allocation for task 30, because they are no longer scheduled on the same dates. Notice the task bars for tasks 30, 31 & 32 are now positioned in sequence (see "Checkpoint Image #6).

Manually Level Resources by Reassigning Work

Scroll down until you can see tasks 113, 114 & 115. Use the **Scroll to Task** feature to bring the task bar for task 113 forward as follows:

1. Select task 113.

2. Select the **Task** tab.

3. In the **Editing** group, select **Scroll to Task**.

The Marketing Lead is over-allocated on tasks 113, 114 & 115 because their dates overlap. She is scheduled to start tasks 113 and 114 on 3/3/21. She's scheduled to start task 115 on 3/4/21, which overlaps with task 113.

First, you'll resolve the over-allocation for task 114 by reassigning the work to another resource. You've been told that a resource from the Marketing Staff group can replace the Marketing Lead. Replace the resource as follows:

1. Select task 114 *"Review Regional Sales"*.

2. Select the **Resource** tab.

3. In the **Assignments** group, select **Assign Resources** to open the *Assign Resources* dialogue box.

4. Select the **Marketing Lead** resource in the **Name** field, then click **Replace**.

5. In the *Replace Resource* dialogue box, select the **Marketing Staff** resource, then click **OK**.

6. Select **Close** to close the *Assign Resources* dialogue box.

7. To check your results so far, visit www.mspbasics.com. Select "Practice Exercise Solutions" from the menu. Select "Chapter 13" and reference "Checkpoint Image #7".

The Marketing Lead has been replaced with the Marketing Staff resource and the over-allocation for task 114 should be resolved (see "Checkpoint Image #8).

Manually Level Resources by Splitting a Task (Interrupting Task Work)

Next, you will resolve the over-allocations for tasks 113 & 115 by splitting task 113. As discussed earlier in the chapter, splitting a task interrupts the work and resumes it later.

Task 113 *"Evaluate campaign effectiveness"* is a 3-day task. Work is scheduled on 3/3/21, 3/4/21, & 3/5/21. This conflicts with task 115, which is a 1-day task, scheduled on 3/4/21. You'll split task 113 so that no work occurs on 3/4/21 and work resumes on 3/5/21.

Since you'll use the task bar to split task 113, zoom in to get a better view of the task bar as follows:

1. Select the **View** tab.

2. In the **Zoom** group, select **"Days"** from the **Timescale** pick-list.

Split the task as follows:

1. Select task 113.

2. On the **Task** tab, in the **Schedule** group, select the **Split Task** command.

3. Hover (don't click) the mouse pointer over the task bar of task #113 until the **"Scheduled start date"** of **Thursday 3/4/21** appears.

4. Now, click the task bar (don't release) and drag to the right until the **Task Start** of **Friday 3/5/21** appears, then release. The task is now split. The dotted line on the task bar represents the interruption of work (split).

5. To check your results so far, visit www.mspbasics.com. Select "Practice Exercise Solutions" from the menu. Select "Chapter 13" and reference "Checkpoint Image #9".

The over-allocations for tasks 113 & 115 should be resolved. Note the new project finish date of 3/26/21. Our manual resource leveling efforts delayed the schedule 2 weeks.

You've now manually leveled resources by increasing Max. Units, applying constraints, reassigning task work, and splitting a task. Next, you'll level the same resources using **Automatic** resource leveling.

Start a Project from a Template

1. Select the **File** tab, then select **New** to return to the templates in the opening view.

2. Double-click the "Marketing Campaign Plan" template to start a new project.

Set the Project Start Date

1. Set the project start date to **6/1/20**.

2. Take note of the project finish date of **3/12/21**.

Level Resources using Automatic Resource Leveling

1. Notice the over-allocated resources.

2. Select the **Resource** tab.

3. In the **Level** group, select **Level All** to level over-allocated resources for the entire project.

Project has leveled all resources. The updated project finish date should be 5/12/21. Automatically leveling the resources delayed the schedule 2 months.

Note: Automatic resource leveling allows Project to automatically level resources by making adjustments that least delay the schedule. Generally, Automatic leveling results in less delay than Manual leveling. In this case, since we adjusted resource's Max. Units to account for multiple resources in a group (which doesn't occur with Automatic leveling), the Manual method delayed the schedule less.

You've now levelled resources using Manual and Automatic resource leveling.

Now You Can

- Explain Max. Units

- Level Resources Automatically

- Use the Leveling Gantt View

- Level Resources Manually

- Use the Resource Usage View

- Use the Team Planner View

- Split Tasks

Chapter 14 Inspecting Your Schedule

IN THIS CHAPTER:

- Inspection Checklist

- Sorting, Grouping and Filtering Project Data

- Using the Auto Filter

- Creating Custom Groups and Filters

- Using the Task Inspector

In the last chapter, we leveled resources using Manual and Automatic resource leveling. In this chapter, we'll learn to view, organize, and inspect project data before publishing a project schedule. When you're done, you'll be able to sort, group and filter task and resource data, use the Task Inspector and create custom group and filters.

Why Inspect Your Schedule?

Here are eight good reasons to inspect your schedule:

1. To confirm your schedule is accurate
2. To confirm your schedule is aggressive but realistic
3. To confirm dollars are spent wisely
4. To avoid embarrassment
5. To correct mistakes
6. To avoid over-commitment
7. To prepare alternatives
8. Others will!

Things to Inspect

After you've built your schedule, it's a good idea to inspect it, using a robust checklist. Here's a list of 20 things to check before publishing your schedule:

1. Spelling
2. Style (E.g. font, spacing, structure)
3. Project Start Date
4. Project Calendar
5. Resource Calendars
6. Resource Allocation
7. Task Calendars
8. Non-Working Days
9. Work Restriction Periods
10. Project Outline
11. Critical Path
12. Task Relationships
13. Task Type Settings

14. Effort-Driven Settings

15. Constraints

16. Work Estimates

17. Duration Estimates

18. Task Notes

19. Resource Notes

20. Costs

KEY TERMS – Learning to Talk the Talk

When inspecting your schedule, it's helpful to examine your project data in various views, showing different subsets of information. The following features allow you extract and re-sequence task and resource data using the criteria you define:

> **Sorting** – The resequencing of task or resource data per user-defined criteria.

> **Grouping** – The resequencing and grouping of task or resource data into a table that summarizes the group values you specify.

> **Filtering** – The extraction of task or resource data that meets user-defined criteria.

Sorting Project Data

Using the Auto Filter to sort data

There are several ways to sort project data. One way is to use the **Auto Filter** feature. This feature is accessible in most task and resource views and can be used to sort, group or filter data.

To sort the data in any field using the Auto Filter:

1. Click the Auto Filter pick-list next to the field name you want to sort (*Figure 94* below*)*.

2. Select the sorting option you want from the pick-list. For example, you can sort data in ascending or descending order.

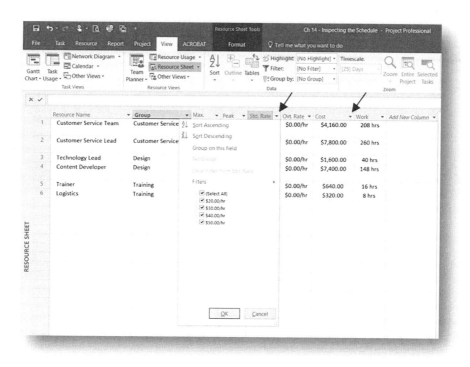

Figure 94 – Using the Auto Filter

Note: If you don't see the Auto Filter pick-lists next to the field names, you'll need to enable them as follows:

1. Select the **View** tab.

2. In the **Data** group, select **Display Auto Filter** from the **Filter** pick-list.

Using the Sort feature to sort data

The **Sort** feature allows you to arrange the data in a view using up to three levels of sorting criteria. For example, you can sort resource data by Group, Cost and Pay Rates. **Note**: To sort resource data by Group, you must enter a group name for each resource in the "Group" field in the Resource Sheet view.

To use the sort feature in a task or resource view:

1. Select the **View** tab.

2. In the **Data** group, select **Sort**, then select **Sort by** to open the *Sort* dialogue box (*Figure 95 below)*.

3. From the **Sort by** and **Then by** pick-lists, select up to three levels of sorting criteria.

4. Select an **Ascending** or **Descending** option for each level.

5. Once you've selected the sorting criteria, click **Sort**.

Figure 95 – Using the Sort Feature

Figure 96 below displays the resource data in the Resource Sheet, sorted by ascending Group, then by descending Cost within those groups.

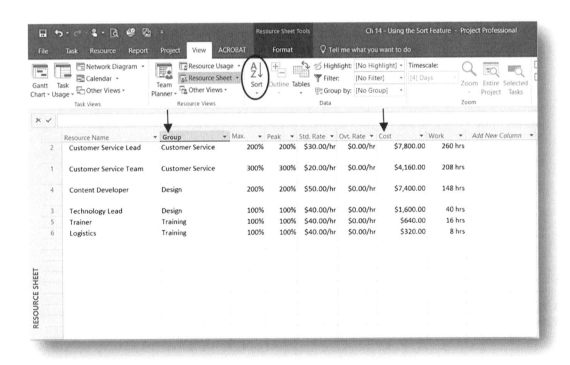

Figure 96 – Using the Sort Feature

Grouping Project Data

Grouping organizes data similarly to sorting. One advantage of Grouping is that Project automatically generates and highlights summary information, including cost values. There are several ways to group data.

Using the Auto Filter to group data

The Auto Filter feature includes the **Group on this Field** option, which is a handy way to group data. This feature allows you to group data by a certain field. In task and resource views containing groupable data, when you use the Auto Filter pick-lists, you'll see *Group on this Field* as an option. For example, in the Resource Sheet view, if you select the Auto Filter pick-list in the **Std. Rate** field, then select *Group on this Field*, the data will be grouped by pay rates (*Figure 97* below). The highlighted areas represent summarized values within the grouping criteria.

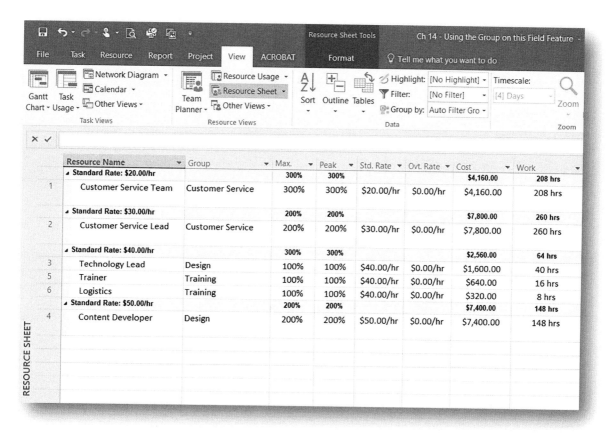

Figure 97 – Group on this Field Feature

Using the Group by feature to group data

Another way to group data is to use the **Group by** feature.

To group data in a task or resource view using the Group by feature:

1. Select the **View** tab.

2. In the **Data** group, from the **Group by** pick-list, select the criteria you want from the **Built-in** options.

Creating Custom Groups

If the grouping criteria you want is not available in the Built-in options, you can create a **Custom Group**. Moreover, if the custom group you want to create is similar to a Built-in group (E.g. "Resource Group"), you can save time by using the **Copy** option to create the custom group.

To create a custom group using the Copy option:

1. Select the **View** tab.

2. In the **Data** group, from the **Group by** pick-list, select **More Groups** to open the *More Groups* dialogue box (*Figure 98* below). **Note**: If you're in a task view, the *task* Built-in groups will be displayed. If you're in a resource view, the *resource* Built-in groups will be displayed.

Figure 98 – Creating a Custom Group

3. Next, select the Built-in group you want to copy, then select **Copy**. The *Group Definition* dialogue box opens (*Figure 99* below).

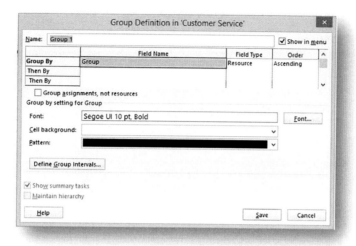

Figure 99 – Group Definition dialogue box

4. In the **Name** field, enter a name for the custom group.

5. Under **Field Name**, the **Group by** criteria will be populated. In the empty cell beneath, in the **Then By** field, enter or select the name of the next grouping criteria you want. In *Figure 100* below, Standard Rate has been selected.

6. In the **Order** field, select **Ascending** or **Descending**.

7. You can change the **Font** type, **Cell background** color and **Pattern** in their respective fields.

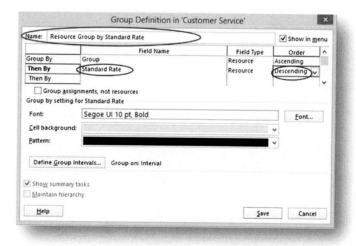

Figure 100 – Group Definition dialogue box

You can also define the grouping intervals as follows:

1. Select **Define Group Intervals** to open the *Define Group Interval* dialogue box.

2. Select **Interval** in the **Group on** field.

3. In the **Group Interval** field, type the interval you want, then click **OK**.

4. Click **Save** to close the *Group Definition* dialogue box. The custom group will appear in the **More Groups** Built-in options.

To apply a custom group to a task or resource view:

1. Select the **View** tab.

2. In the **Data** group, from the **Group by** pick-list, select **More Groups**.

3. Select the custom group from the Built-in options in the Task or Resource groups.

4. Click **Apply** to apply the custom group to the view you're in.

Figure 101 below displays a custom group in which resources are grouped by Group, then by Standard Rate, in intervals of 100.

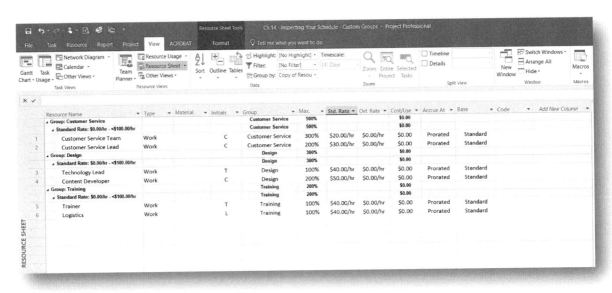

Figure 101 – Custom Groups

Clearing Grouping Results

Before sharing your schedule, you'll want to clear any grouping results you've applied.

To clear Grouping results:

1. Select the **View** tab.

2. In the **Data** group, select **Clear Group** from the Group by pick-list.

Filtering Project Data

Using the Auto Filter to filter data

Filtering allows you to extract task or resource data to view only the criteria that you've specified. There are several ways to filter project information. Project includes many **Pre-Set Filters** that can be applied in most task and resource views (*Figure 102* below*).

To apply a Pre-set filter:

1. Select the **Auto Filter** pick-list in any field.

2. Select **Filters**, then select the Pre-set filter you want.

Figure 102 – Using the Pre-Set Filters

214

Figure 103 below shows tasks in the Gantt Chart view, filtered to display Milestone tasks.

Note: Whenever a filter is applied, the "Filter Applied" notification will appear in the Status Bar (bottom left corner).

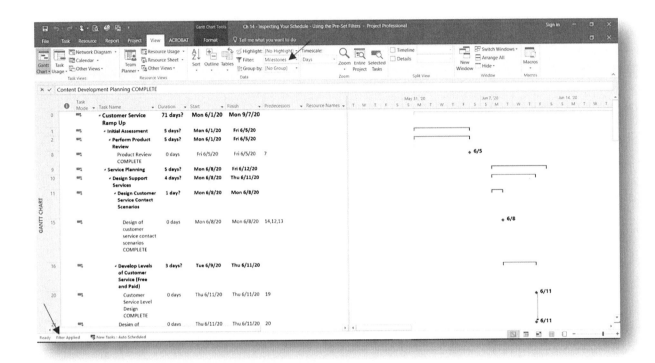

Figure 103 – Using the Pre-Set Filters

Applying a Custom Auto Filter

You can also apply a **Custom Auto Filter** to extract project data. For example, you may want to view only the tasks that are associated with a certain project group (E.g. "Customer Service"). In this case, you could apply a custom Auto Filter to display only the tasks that contain the words "Customer Service".

To apply a Custom Auto Filter:

1. Select the Auto Filter pick-list in any field.

2. Select **Filters**, then select **Custom** to open the *Custom AutoFilter* dialogue box (*Figure 104* below).

Figure 104 – Custom AutoFilter dialogue box

3. In the **Name** field, enter or select the filtering condition you want.

4. In the adjacent field, enter or select the filtering criteria you want.

5. Click **OK** to apply the custom Auto Filter.

Figure 105 below shows the results of the custom Auto Filter specified in *Figure 104*. Project displays only the tasks containing the words "Customer Service".

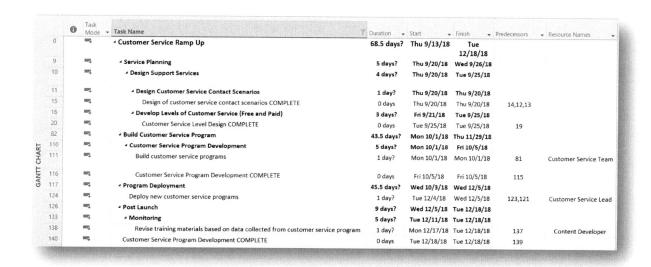

Figure 105 – Applying Custom Auto Filters

Using the Filter feature to filter data

Another way to filter data is to use the **Filter** feature to extract task or resource data using the Built-in filtering criteria.

To filter data in a task or resource view using the Filter feature:

1. Select the **View** tab.

2. In the **Data** group, from the **Filter** pick-list, select the criteria you want from the **Built-in** options.

Creating a Custom Filter

If the filter criteria you want isn't included in the Pre-set or Built-in filters, you can create a **Custom Filter**.

To create a custom filter:

1. Select the **View** tab.

2. In the **Data** group, select **More Filters** from the **Filters** pick-list to open the *More Filters* dialog box. **Note**: If you're in a task view, the pre-set filters for *tasks* appear. If you're in a resource view, the pre-set filters for *resources* appear.

3. Select **New** to open the *Filter Definition* dialog box.

4. In the **Name** field, enter a name for the custom filter.

5. In the first row in the **Field Name** field, enter or select the field you want.

6. In the first row in the **Test** field, select the filtering condition you want.

7. In the first row in the **Value(s)** field, enter or select the value you want to filter by.

8. If you have a second criterion for the filter, complete steps 9 through 12:

9. In the second row, in the **And/Or** field, select **And**.

10. In the second row, in the **Field Name** field, enter or select the field you want.

11. In the second row, in the **Test** field, select the second filtering condition you want.

12. In the second row, in the **Value(s)** field, enter or select the second value you want to filter by.

13. Click **Save** to close the *Filter Definition* dialog box. The new filter will appear among the *More Filters* Task or Resource filters.

To apply a custom filter to a task or resource view:

1. Select the **View** tab.

2. In the **Data** group, from the **Filter** pick-list, select **More Filters**.

3. Select the custom group from the Built-in options in the Task or Resource filters.

4. Click **Apply** to apply the custom filter to the view you're in.

Clearing Filters

Before sharing your schedule, you'll want to clear any filters you've applied.

To clear Filters:

1. Select the **View** tab.

2. In the **Data** group, select **Clear Filter** from the Filter pick-list.

Using the Task Inspector

Next, we'll look at a feature called the **Task Inspector**. The Task Inspector is an efficient way to inspect the tasks in your schedule. This feature allows you to view detailed scheduling information for a specific task, including Scheduling Mode, Start and Finish dates, Predecessor information, Calendars and Constraints (if applied) – *Figure 106* below.

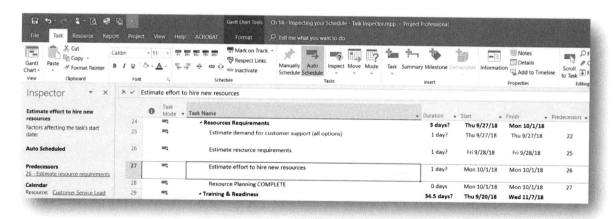

Figure 106 – Using the Task Inspector

To enable the Task Inspector:

1. In a task view, select the task you want to inspect.

2. On the **Task** tab, in the **Tasks** group, select the **Inspect** command. Project will display scheduling information for the selected task in a pane on the left. **Note**: To view the scheduling information, you may need to expand the task Inspector pane, by dragging it to the right.

We've now reviewed ways to view, organize and inspect project data before publishing a project schedule.

Bonus Video

To watch this chapter as a video, which includes software demonstrations of the features covered in this chapter, go to www.mspbasics.com. Select "Practice Exercise Solutions" from the menu and select "Chapter 14".

Now You Can

- Sort Project Data

- Group Project Data

- Filter Project Data

- Create Custom Groups and Filters

- Use the Task Inspector

Part Two Summary

This concludes Part Two – Building the Schedule. You've learned to apply the B.A.S.I.C.S. acronym to consistently build reliable schedules. You've learned to add resources, calendars and documentation to your schedule. You've learned to compress your schedule, constraint it, level resources and perform an in-depth inspection before beginning the execution phase. In Part Three – Executing the Schedule, we'll take the schedule through the execution and closing phases of the project life cycle.

PART THREE: Executing Your Schedule

IN PART THREE, you'll learn to execute your schedule, track project cost, create stunning project status reports, consolidate two different schedules into one master view, create dependencies between schedules, officially close your project and customize the Project 2019 interface. You'll also learn key skills measured by Microsoft Project Exam 74-343.

Chapter 15 Executing Your Schedule

IN THIS CHAPTER:

- Saving a Baseline

- Moving the Project

- Tracking Your Schedule

- Entering Progress Data (Actuals)

- Updating Your Schedule

- Using the Tracking Gantt

- Inactivating Tasks

In the last chapter we inspected the schedule by using the sorting, grouping, and filtering features to inspect resource and task data. In this chapter, we'll executive the schedule. We'll apply the "S" in the B.A.S.I.C.S. acronym, which stands for "Start the Project". When you're done, you'll be able to set a baseline, explain the tracking fields available in Project, move the project start date, view expected outcomes before collecting progress data, enter progress data, inactivate a task and update the schedule.

The Execution Phase – Starting the Project!

So far, you've learned to build a Simple and a Detailed schedule. You've added resources, calendars, and documentation to the schedule. You've compressed and constrained the schedule and you've leveled resources. In PMBOK® jargon, you've completed the **Planning** phase. Now, you're ready to begin the **Execution** phase.

Before we begin executing the schedule, let's look at a list of job qualifications for an ideal candidate for an open position. Try to guess the profession.

- Well Organized
- Assertive
- Firm Decision Maker
- Composed under Pressure
- High in Situational Awareness
- Able to Analyze Risk in real-time
- Highly Flexible
- Excellent Communicator

You may have concluded that the profession is a Project Manager. However, these are the qualities of an Air-Traffic Controller. Project Managers and Air-Traffic Controllers share some of the same characteristics. For example, the distance from Los Angeles to Chicago can be travelled by air in about 2 hours. However, the average commercial flight time is about 4 hours. This is because commercial airlines don't use direct travel routes. Consequently, much of the flight is spent off course. The air-traffic controller's job is to make course corrections along the way and sequence the aircraft for an on-time landing. In like manner, typical projects spend much of their life cycle off schedule. The project manager's job is to make corrections along the way, and deliver the project per the latest agreed upon date. Microsoft Project includes useful features for making real-time scheduling updates while your project is in flight. We'll begin with Baselines.

Baselines

Before task work begins on your project, you'll want to record key information from the Planning phase that you can compare against actual project performance. To do this, you'll need to **Baseline** the project plan. A baseline is essentially a saved copy of the original schedule. It includes the original Start and Finish dates and the original Duration, Work, and Cost estimates. It also includes a time-phased distribution of Work, Duration, Cost, and Resource Allocation.

When you save a baseline, Project takes a snapshot of the original plan and saves it within the plan. You can save up to 11 baselines. The first one is labeled *Baseline* (also called *Baseline 0*). Additional baselines are labeled *Baseline 1* through *Baseline 10*. Although up to 11 baselines are allowed, best practice is to re-baseline only in justifiable cases (like major scope changes).

To set a Baseline:

1. Select the **Project** tab.

2. In the **Schedule** group, select **Set Baseline**, then select **Set Baseline** again to open the *Set Baseline* dialogue box (*Figure 107* below).

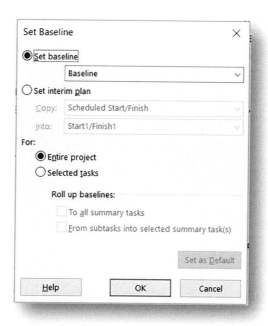

Figure 107 – Set Baseline Dialogue Box

3. With the **Set Baseline** option selected, select the baseline you're saving (0 through 10) from the **Set Baseline** pick-list.

4. In the **For** section, select **Entire project** to baseline the entire project or select **Selected tasks** to baseline selected tasks.

5. Click **OK** to close the *Set Baseline* dialogue box.

Interim Plans

As you update your schedule, you may want to keep a history of weekly performance against the baseline. An **Interim Plan** is useful for this purpose. An Interim Plan (also called an Interim Baseline) is a partial copy of the original schedule. It only includes the current start and finish dates for all tasks. No resource or time-phased values are saved. You can save up to 10 Interim plans. The first one is labeled *Start1/Finish1*. Additional Interim plans are labeled *Start2/Finish2* through *Start10/Finish10*.

To set an Interim Plan:

1. Select the **Project** tab.

2. In the **Schedule** group, select **Set Baseline**, then select **Set Baseline** again to open the *Set Baseline* dialogue box.

3. Select **Set Interim plan**.

4. In the **Copy** field, *Scheduled Start and Finish* is selected by default. This option will copy the start and finish dates from the current plan.

5. In the **Into** field, select the Interim plan you want to save (1 through 10).

6. Click **OK** to close the *Set Baseline* dialogue box.

Interim plan data is saved in the Start and Finish fields. To view Interim plan data, you'll need to use the *Add New Column* field to add the Start and Finish fields to the current view. Add the Start and Finish fields that corresponds to the Interim plan you saved in the **Into** field of the *Set Baseline* dialogue box. For example, if you saved Interim plan "Start1/Finish1", add the "Start 1" and "Finish 1" fields to the view to see the Interim plan data.

Using the Interim Plan to Copy Baselines

You can also use the Interim plan to streamline the process of copying baselines from one slot to another. For example, by selecting *Baseline* from the **Copy** pick-list and *Baseline 1* from the **Into** pick-list, you can copy the data from *Baseline 0* into *Baseline 1*. Although you're using the Interim baseline feature, if you populate the **Copy** and **Into** fields with baselines, the entire baseline will be copied, and not just the start and finish dates. This is a useful feature because although you can save up to 11 baselines, Project always references *Baseline 0* in reports and field values, such as the Earned Value metrics. Therefore, it's a good idea to save your latest baseline as *Baseline 0* and migrate prior versions to the other baseline slots.

Here's how it works:

1. Save your initial baseline as *Baseline* (i.e. *Baseline 0*).

2. Save a copy of the initial baseline as *Baseline 1*.

3. When you re-baseline, save it as *Baseline 0*.

    Note: When you override *Baseline 0*, Project will alert you that you already saved a baseline and ask if you're sure you want to override the data. If you've already saved a copy of the data in *Baseline 1*, click "Yes". Now, when you generate a report, Project will use the latest baseline data, saved in *Baseline 0*.

4. If you should need to re-baseline again, save a copy of the next baseline as *Baseline 2*.

The idea is – every time you re-baseline, over-ride *Baseline 0* for reporting <u>and</u> save a copy as the next sequential baseline for history.

Clearing Baselines and Interim Plans

Project also allows you to **Clear a Baseline or Interim plan**. Suppose an additional phase was added to your project. You would of course want this phase included in the baseline. If no progress data was entered before the phase was added, you could clear the Baseline or Interim plan and set a new one that includes the new phase.

To Clear a Baseline or Interim Plan:

1. Select the **Project** tab.

2. In the **Data** group, select the **Set baseline** command, then select **Clear Baseline** to open the *Clear Baseline* dialogue box.

3. To clear a Baseline, in the **Clear baseline plan** field, select the baseline you want to clear, and click **OK**.

4. To clear an Interim plan, in the **Clear interim plan** field, select the Interim plan you want to clear, and click **OK**.

Viewing Baseline Information

To view the baseline values saved in your plan, you'll need to switch to a table that shows baseline metrics, such as the *Baseline* or *Variance* tables. *Figure* 108 below shows the *Variance* table, which displays the Scheduled Start and Finish values and the Baseline Start and Finish values. This view allows you to compare actual project results against baseline projections.

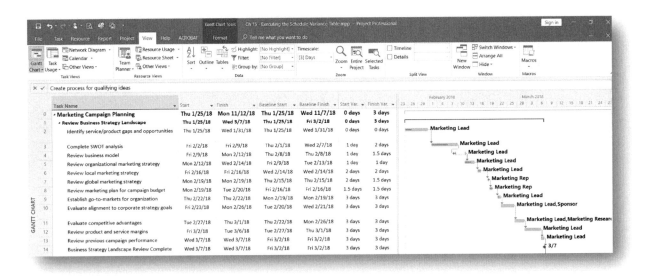

Figure 108 – Variance Table

Moving the Project

There may be times when a project cannot begin on the scheduled start date. Delayed funding and unavailable resources are common reasons. In such cases, consider **Moving the Project**, rather than changing the project start date in the *Project Information* dialogue box. This will move the <u>entire</u> <u>project</u> forward, whereas changing the start date will only move the tasks impacted by a revised project start date.

To move the project:

1. Select the **Project** tab.

2. In the **Schedule** group, select **Move Project** to open the *Move Project* dialogue box (*Figure 109* below).

3. Enter the new start date in the **New project start date** field.

4. Click **OK** to close the *Move Project* dialogue box.

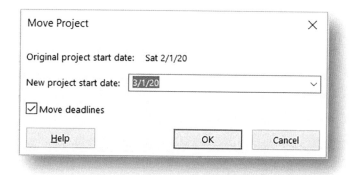

Fig 109 – Move Project dialogue box

Collecting Progress Data (Actuals)

Once you've baselined your schedule, you can begin to collect **Progress Data** (Actuals) to track progress against the plan. Project includes several fields for tracking the schedule through the Execution phase. The type of schedule you've built (Simple or Detailed) should determine the progress data you collect.

➤   For a Simple schedule, collect **Actual Duration** and **Remaining Duration**.

➤   For a Detailed schedule, collect **Actual Work** and **Remaining Work**.

➤   For either schedule type, collect **Actual Start** and **Actual Finish**

When you collect progress data from your team, you'll need to note the date through which the work was performed. This date is called the **Status Date**. Project includes a field for capturing the status date and it references this date when rescheduling uncompleted task work and for Earned Value calculations. If the status date is not set, Project will use the current date.

Tracking Fields

As mentioned earlier, Project includes several fields for tracking the schedule through the Execution phase. Here are some common tracking fields and the definition of each:

> **Duration** – Actual Duration + Remaining Duration

> **Work** – Actual Work + Remaining Work

We've been using the term Duration throughout this book to refer to the number of working days required to complete a task. By definition, Duration is *Actual* Duration + *Remaining* Duration. Since we've been in the Planning phase, whenever we've seen Duration, *Actual* Duration has been zero. For example, if a task in the Planning phase has a 10-day duration, this means that Actual duration is 0 days and Remaining duration is 10 days. The same applies to the term Work. Work is the sum of *Actual* Work and *Remaining* Work.

> **Actual Start** – The actual date the task started

> **Actual Finish** – The actual date the task finished

> **% Complete** – Percentage of Duration Complete

> **% Work Complete** – Percentage of Work Complete

It may be tempting to use the "% Complete" icons (Task tab, Schedule group) to record progress, but unless the progress is 0% or 100%, this practice should be avoided. It's best to track Actual and Remaining Duration or Actual and Remaining Work. For example, optimistic resources may over estimate completion percentages and pessimistic resources may under estimate them. Also, who can accurately assess whether a task is 30% or 40% complete? On a 10-day critical path task, this difference can delay the schedule by 1 day. Entering inaccurate progress data will result in an inaccurate schedule.

Viewing Expected Outcomes

Before you meet with your project team to collect progress data, you should have an idea which tasks should have progressed since the last status check. You won't need to get status from every resource assigned to your project; just from those who should have done work since the last status date. A handy way to get this information is to apply a **Filter for Late Tasks**. Applying the late task filter will display the tasks that should have progressed by the current date. This gives you the option of meeting only with the resources expected to have progress data.

To Filter for Late Tasks:

1. In the Gantt Chart view, select the **Auto-filter** pick-list in the **Task Name** field.

2. Select **Filters**, then select **Late Tasks**. Project will display only the tasks that should have work progress as of the current date.

Entering Progress Data (Actuals)

After you've collected actuals from your team, you'll need to enter the updates into Project. There are several ways to enter actuals. As mentioned earlier, the type of schedule you've built (Simple or Detailed) should determine the progress data you collect. It should also determine the fields and views you use to enter the progress data.

Entering Progress Data in a Simple schedule

To enter actuals for a Simple schedule, simply add the relevant tracking fields to the Entry table in the Gantt Chart view. Using the *Add New Column* field, add the "Actual Start", "Actual Duration" and "Remaining Duration" fields. Enter the actuals directly into these fields and Project will update the duration values in real-time. After you enter a value for Actual Duration, Project will populate the Remaining Duration field per the initial duration estimate. For example, if the initial duration was 10 days, and you enter 7 days in the Actual Duration field, Project will populate the Remaining Duration field with 3 days. If your actuals exceed this value, simply type over this projection with the actual Remaining Duration value. *Figure 110* below shows progress data for tasks 1 through 5 in a Simple schedule. Task 5 has a Baseline Duration value of 10 days. However, the Actual Duration value of 7 days and the Remaining Duration value of 5 days show that the task is delayed, and exceeds the Baseline Duration by 2 days. Because Duration is the sum of Actual Duration and Remaining Duration, Project updated the Duration field to 12 days.

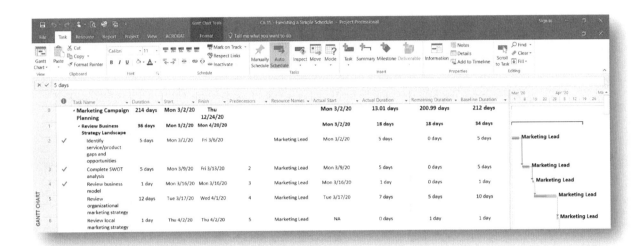

Figure 110 – Entering Progress Data in a Simple Schedule

Here's an important note. When you enter progress data into Project, always use cumulative values for Actual Duration entries. For instance, in the previous example, the Actual Duration value was 7 days. If the resource reports that she completed the remaining 5 days during your next status check, you would enter the cumulative Actual Duration value of 12 days and not the incremental value of 5 days. Project is not designed to keep a record of prior Actual Duration entries.

Entering Progress Data in a Detailed schedule

For a Detailed schedule, you can also enter values directly into the relevant tracking fields. Using the *Add New Column* field, add the "Actual Start", "Actual Work" and "Remaining Work" fields. Enter the actuals directly into these fields and Project will update the Work values in real time. As with the duration fields, after you enter a value for Actual Work, Project will populate the Remaining Work field per the initial work estimate. If your actuals exceed this value, simply type over this projection with the actual Remaining Work value.

Figure 111 below shows progress data for tasks 1 through 5 in a Detailed schedule. Task 5 has a Baseline Work value of 20 hours. However, the Actual Work value of 18 hours and the Remaining Work value of 6 hours show that the task is delayed, and exceeds the Baseline Work value by 4 hours. Because Work is the sum of Actual Work and Remaining Work, Project updated the Work field to 24 hours. Since the resource assigned to this task (Marketing Lead) is assigned at 25% Units (2 hours per day), the additional 4 hours of work will result in a 2-day delay. For this reason, the Duration value exceeds the Baseline Duration value by 2 days.

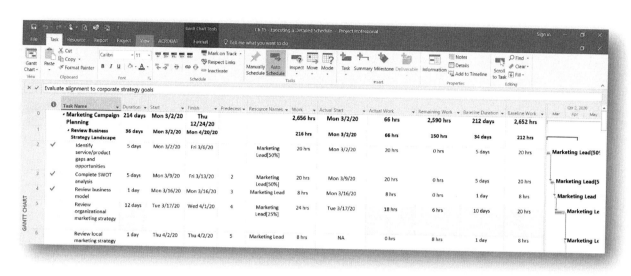

Figure 111 – Entering Progress Data in a Detailed Schedule

As with Simple schedules, when you enter progress data into Project for a Detailed schedule, always use cumulative values for Actual Work entries. For instance, in the previous example, the Actual Work value was 18 hours. If the resource reports that she completed the remaining 6 hours during your next status check, you would enter the cumulative Actual Work value of 24 hours and not the incremental value of 6 hours.

Entering Progress Data at the Task and Assignment Level

When multiple resources are assigned to a single task, you'll need to enter progress data for each resource individually. This can be done by splitting the view and using the "Work" Task Form. Create the combination view as follows:

Split the view and display the "Work" Task Form in the bottom pane:

1. In the Gantt Chart view, select the **View** tab.

2. In the **Split View** group, select the **Details** checkbox to split the view.

3. To display the "Work" Task Form, right-click anywhere in the gray area on the right side of the screen in the bottom pane to display the Task Form pick-list, then select **Work**.

This combination view allows you to enter progress data at the **Task Level** or the **Assignment Level.** A task level entry is an entry that "rolls down" to the assignment level. This means that the value entered at the task level will be distributed among the resources assigned to the task. For example, in *Figure 112* below, 26 hours of Actual Work was entered at the task level for task #10 (top pane).

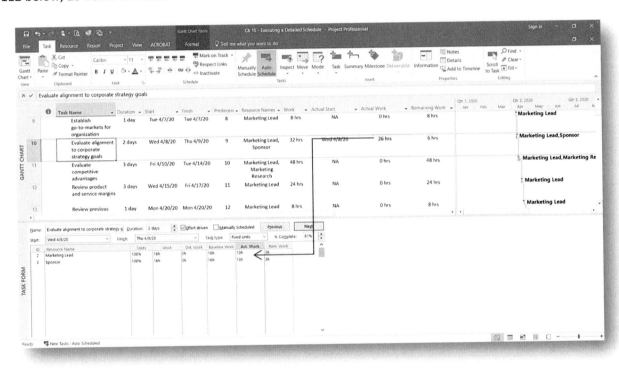

Figure 112 – Entering Progress Data at the Task Level

As you can see in the Task Form (bottom pane), Project divided the 26 hours of Actual Work evenly between the two resources (Marketing Lead and Sponsor) at the assignment level. This even distribution of work was determined by Project and may not reflect the actual progress of either resource.

Conversely, an assignment level entry "rolls up" to the task level. This means that if progress data is entered for each resource assigned to the task, the collective sum will be reflected at the task level. For example, in *Figure* 113 below, the 26 hours of Actual Work for task #10 was entered at the assignment level as 16 hours of Actual Work for the *Marketing Lead* resource and 10 hours of Actual Work for the *Sponsor* resource. The collective sum is reflected at the task level (top pane).

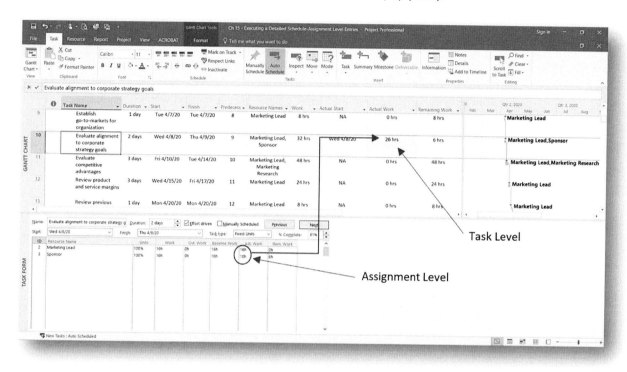

Figure 113 – Entering Progress Data at the Assignment Level

Entering progress data at the task level versus the assignment level yields dramatically different results in terms of duration and cost. Therefore, when multiple resources are assigned to a single task, it is advisable to enter progress data at the assignment level.

The same guideline applies when entering other tracking data, such as Actual Start and Actual Finish dates. If the resources' Actual Start and Actual Finish dates are not the same, you'll want to enter those values at the assignment level as follows:

1. Display the **Resource Usage View** in the top or bottom pane.
2. Then, add the "Actual Start" and "Actual Finish" fields to the view.

3. To enter the actuals, find the task under each resource's name and enter the dates in the respective fields.

Updating the Schedule

Once you've entered your Actuals, your schedule will need to be updated. All uncompleted work that was supposed to occur before the status date will need to be rescheduled. Every time you enter your team's progress data, follow these steps to update the schedule:

1. Select the **Project** tab.

2. In the **Status** group, select **Update Project** to open the *Update Project* dialogue box.

3. Select the **Reschedule uncompleted work to start after** option, then enter the status date in the **Date** field. **Note**: the status date is the date on which you are entering the actuals.

4. In the **For** field, select **Entire Project**, then click **OK** to close the *Update Project* dialogue box. Project will then reschedule any uncompleted tasks if necessary.

Using the Tracking Gantt

After updating your schedule, it would be helpful to see how the updated schedule compares with the baselined schedule. The Tracking Gantt was developed for this purpose. As discussed in Chapter 2, the Tracking Gantt can be used to compare baseline values with actual values. In this view, Project displays two set of Gantt bars. The top, blue task bars represent tasks as they are currently scheduled (Critical Path tasks are highlighted with red task bars). The bottom, gray task bars represent the original, baseline schedule.

To display the Tracking Gantt view:

1. Select the **Task** tab.

2. In the **View** group, from the **Gantt Chart** pick-list, select **Tracking Gantt**.

Inactivating Tasks

As your project progresses, certain tasks may become unnecessary. For example, some tasks may be outsourced. You may not want to delete the task(s), as to keep the task information in your plan. In this case, you can **Inactive a task**. Inactivating a task will keep the task details in the plan, but the task will not affect the timeline. This feature is only available in the Project Professional version of the software.

To Inactivate a Task:

1.   Select the task(s) you want to inactivate.

2.   On the **Task** tab, in the **Schedule** group, select the **Inactivate** command.

3.   Inactive tasks are indicated in grayed out, strikethrough font (*Figure 114* below)

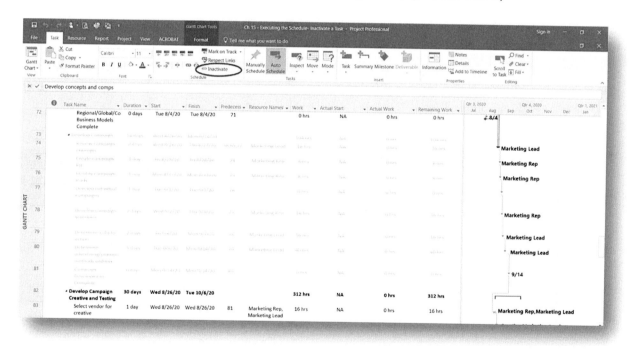

Figure 114 – Inactive Tasks

We've now learned to execute a schedule! We've learned to set a baseline, use the tracking fields available in Project, move the start date, view expected outcomes before collecting progress data, enter progress data, inactivate a task and update the schedule based on newly entered progress data.

Challenge – Practice Exercise

Execute a Simple Schedule

Instructions: In this practice exercise, you'll complete the final step in the B.A.S.I.C.S. scheduling approach – "**S**tart the Project". You will execute the Simple schedule you built in the Chapter 7 practice exercise. Visit www.mspbasics.com for "Checkpoint" images to check your work as you go along.

Follow the steps below to complete this exercise:

Open an Existing Project Plan

1. Open the Simple "House Painting" project plan that you saved from the Chapter 7 practice exercise.

2. To confirm you're starting with the right file, visit to www.mspbasics.com. Select "Practice Exercise Solutions" from the menu. Select "Chapter 15" and reference "Checkpoint Image #1".

Set a Deadline for the Project Finish Date

Set a deadline for the project finish date by applying a deadline to the last task in the schedule (task 16), which is the milestone for the "House Painting" phase.

Set the Deadline as follows:

1. Double-click task 16 to open the *Task Information* dialogue box.

2. Select the **Advanced** tab.

3. In the **Deadline** field, enter 6/26/20.

4. Click **OK** to close the *Task Information* dialogue box.

Set the Current Date

Assume the current date is 6/1/20. Set this date as the "current date" in Project, as follows:

1. Select the **Project** tab.

2. In the **Properties** group, select **Project Information** to open the *Project Information dialogue* box.

3. In the **Current Date** field, enter or select **6/1/20**.

4. Click **OK** to close the *Project Information dialogue* box.

NOTE: You should see a vertical green line in the Gantt chart indicating the current date (the indicator will correspond with 6/1/20 on the timescale). If you don't see the vertical green line, use the Zoom slider in the bottom right corner to zoom in on the timeline.

Baseline the Schedule

Set a Baseline as follows:

1. Select the **Project** tab.

2. In the **Schedule** group, select **Set Baseline**, then select **Set Baseline** again to open the *Set Baseline* dialogue box.

3. Be sure that **Set Baseline** is selected and that "**Baseline**" is populated in the baseline field.

4. Click **OK** to close the *Set Baseline* dialogue box.

Confirm the baseline was set as follows:

1. On the **Project** tab, in the **Schedule** group, select **Set Baseline**, then select **Set Baseline** again to open the *Set Baseline* dialogue box. The baseline field should now read "Baseline (last saved on [current date])".

2. Click **Cancel** to close the *Set Baseline* dialogue box.

Update the Current Date and Set the Status Date

Assume that 1 week has passed and the current date is now Monday, 6/8/20. You met with your team on Friday, 6/5/20 to collect progress data. Set 6/8/20 as the new "Current date" and 6/5/20 as the "Status date" as follows:

1. On the **Project** tab, in the **Properties** group, select **Project Information** to open the *Project Information* dialogue box.

2. In the **Current date** field, enter or select **6/8/20**.

3. In the **Status date** field, enter or select **6/5/20**.

4. Click **OK** to close the *Project Information* dialogue box. You should now see the Status date of 6/5/20 in the **Status** group on the ribbon.

Apply the Late Tasks Filter

You're ready to enter the actuals you received from your team on 6/5/20. To make this task easier, you'll apply a **Late Task** filter to see which tasks should have work done as of the current date (6/8/20). For a review on the Late Tasks filter, see Chapter 15, "Viewing Expected Outcomes".

Filter for Late Tasks as follows:

1. In the **Task Name** field, select the Auto-filter pick-list.

2. Select **Filters**, then select **Late Tasks**. Tasks 1 through 6 should be displayed. These are the tasks that should have work done as of 6/8/20.

3. To confirm you're on the right track, visit www.mspbasics.com. Select "Practice Exercise Solutions" from the menu. Select "Chapter 15" and reference "Checkpoint Image #2".

Add the Tracking Fields

Next, you'll add the tracking fields for a Simple schedule to the Entry table. Using the *Add New Column* field, add the "Actual Start", "Actual Duration" and "Remaining Duration" fields. **Note**: If you don't see the *Add New Column* field, slide the line that divides the Entry table from the Gantt chart to the right, until you can see the *Add New Column* field.

To add each Tracking Field:

1. Click on the *Add New Column* heading. This will display the fields you can add to the table.
2. Type the tracking field name and when it appears, select it.

Enter the Progress Data (Week 1)

The project team has given you the following progress data ("actuals") for the past week.

RESOURCE	TASK	ACTUAL START	ACTUAL DURATION	REMAINING DURATION
Jill	#2 – List Supplies	06/01/20	4 hours	0
Jack	#3 – Buy Supplies	06/03/20	1 day	0
Jack	#6 – Sand House	06/04/20	3 days	1 day

1. Enter the "Actual Start", "Actual Duration" and "Remaining Duration" values shown in the table above into the respective tracking fields.

Since the predecessors to the milestone "Supplies Bought" are complete, mark this milestone 100% complete as follows:

1. Select the **Task** tab.
2. Select task 4 ("Supplies Bought").
3. In the **Schedule** group, select the **100% Complete** icon.

Notice the checkmarks in the Indicator's field of tasks 1 through 4. This indicates that the tasks are 100% complete, with no Remaining Duration. In the Gantt chart, notice the task bars for tasks 2, 3 & 6 now have a dark blue progress bar inside the task bar, indicating the task's completion progress.

Clear the Late Task Filter

Now, you'll clear the Late Task filter to display the entire schedule.

Clear the filter as follows:

1. Select the **View** tab.

2. From the **Filter** pick-list, select **Clear Filter**.

3. To check your results so far, visit www.mspbasics.com. Select "Practice Exercise Solutions" from the menu. Select "Chapter 15" and reference "Checkpoint Image #3".

Schedule Tracking Questions:

1. Is the project on schedule, ahead of schedule or behind schedule?

2. If the project is not on schedule, by how many days is it ahead of or behind schedule?

3. For the answers to the tracking questions, visit www.mspbasics.com. Select "Practice Exercise Solutions" from the menu. Select "Chapter 15" and reference "Checkpoint Image #4".

Update the Current Date and Set the Status Date

Assume another week has passed and the current date is Monday, 6/15/20. You will meet with your team today to collect progress data.

Set 6/15/20 as the new "current date" and 6/15/20 as the "Status Date" as follows:

1. On the **Project** tab, in the **Properties** group, select **Project Information** to open the *Project Information* dialogue box.

2. In the **Current date** field, enter or select **6/15/20**.

3. In the **Status date** field, enter or select **6/15/20**.

4. Click **OK** to close the *Project Information* dialogue box. You should now see the Status Date of 6/15/20 in the **Status** group on the ribbon.

Apply the Late Tasks Filter

You're ready to check with the project team to get another status on the current work. To see which tasks should have work done as of the current date (6/15/20), apply the **Late Tasks** filter, as follows:

1. In the **Task Name** field, select the Auto-filter pick-list.

2. Select **Filters**, then select **Late Tasks**. Tasks 5 through 11 should have work done as of 6/15/20.

3. To confirm you're on the right track, visit www.mspbasics.com. Select "Practice Exercise Solutions" from the menu. Select "Chapter 15" and reference "Checkpoint Image #5".

Enter the Progress Data (Week 2)

The project team has given you the following progress data ("actuals") for the past week.

RESOURCE	TASK	ACTUAL START	ACTUAL DURATION	REMAINING DURATION
Jack	#6 – Sand House	06/04/20	4 days	0
Jill	#7 – Tape Windows	06/10/20	1 day	0
Jack	#8 – Lay Drop Cloth	06/11/20	1 day	0
Contractor, Jack	#11 – Apply First Coat	06/12/20	1 day	1 day

1. Enter the "Actual Start", "Actual Duration" and "Remaining Duration" values shown in the table above into the respective tracking fields.

Tasks 6, 7 & 8 should now checkmarks in the Indicator's field because they are 100% complete, with no Remaining Duration.

Clear the Late Task Filter

Clear the Late Task filter to display the entire schedule, as follows:

1. Select the **View** tab.
2. From the **Filter** pick-list, select **Clear Filter**.
3. To check your results so far, visit www.mspbasics.com. Select "Practice Exercise Solutions" from the menu. Select "Chapter 15" and reference "Checkpoint Image #6".

Schedule Tracking Questions:

1. Is the project on schedule, ahead of schedule or behind schedule?
2. If the project is not on schedule, by how many days is it ahead of or behind schedule?
3. For the answers to the tracking questions, visit www.mspbasics.com. Select "Practice Exercise Solutions" from the menu. Select "Chapter 15" and reference "Checkpoint Image #7".

Congratulations! You've now executed a Simple schedule! You've now practiced the last step in the B.A.S.I.C.S. scheduling approach, "Start the Project".

Now You Can

- Save a Baseline

- Move the Project

- Track Your Schedule

- Enter Progress Data (Actuals)

- Update Your Schedule

- Use the Tracking Gantt

- Inactivate Tasks

Chapter 16 Tracking Project Costs

IN THIS CHAPTER:

- Understanding Variance

- Assigning a Project Budget

- Comparing Budget to Cost

- Viewing Cost Variance

- Viewing Earned Value Metrics

- Viewing Earned Value Reports

In the last chapter, we learned to execute a schedule. We baselined the schedule, entered progress data, updated the schedule and inactivated tasks. In this chapter, we'll track project costs. When you're done, you'll be able to assign a project budget, compare budgeted cost to actual cost, view Cost Variance and view Earned Value metrics.

In Microsoft Project, you can track project costs using **Variance** and **Earned Value** metrics. Variance metrics answer the question, "How are we doing against the plan?" Earned Value metrics answer the question, "Are these results worth the investment?"

Variance

Variance refers to what you've done (Actuals), what you still have to do (Remaining) and what you said you would do (Baseline). In Microsoft Project, Variance is defined and calculated as follows:

- **Variance** = Actual Values + Remaining Values − Baseline Values.

There are two kinds of Variance:

- **Actual Variance** = Variance <u>without</u> Remaining Estimate.

- **Estimated Variance** = Variance with Remaining Estimate.

The primary difference between Actual Variance and Estimated Variance is that there's nothing you can do about Actual Variance. This is because it measures results that have already occurred. Conversely, Estimated Variance includes the remaining work, which can be compressed or delayed to meet schedule and cost requirements.

Earned Value Metrics

Now, let's look at **Earned Value** metrics. Again, it answers the question, "Are these results worth the investment?" Projects are chosen based on certain feasibility metrics. The *planned* values in a project have a lot to do with why one project gets funded over another. Earned Value metrics allow you to determine if the value of the project at, say the 25% mark, is still what it was at the beginning of the project. Let's put the term "value" into context. If you bought a stock at $1.00 per share, and six months later it's worth 50 cents per share, what actions would you consider? If you're risk averse, the loss in value might cause you to sell the stock. You're not happy with the loss, but you're thankful for the chance to protect what remains of your investment. Earned Value metrics provides similar feedback to project sponsors. It allows them to make informed decisions based on the project's financial performance trend to date, and the trend that's likely to continue if no corrective action is taken.

Here are the Earned Value metrics available in Project:

> **EV or BCWP (Earned Value)** – the portion of the budgeted cost that should have been spent to complete each task's actual work, up to the status date

> **CPI (Cost Performance Index)** – the ratio of budgeted to actual cost, up to the status date (EV/AC)

> **SPI (Schedule Performance Index)** – the ratio of performed work to scheduled work, up to the status date (EV/PV)

> **PV or BCWS (Planned Value)** – the value of the work scheduled to be completed, as of the status date

> **AC (ACWP)** – the actual cost incurred to complete each task's actual work, up to the status date

> **SV (Schedule Variance)** – the difference between the budgeted cost of work performed and the budgeted cost of work scheduled, up to the status date (EV – PV)

> **CV (Cost Variance)** – the difference between the budgeted and actual cost of work performed, up to the status date (EV – AC)

> **EAC (Estimate At Completion)** – the expected total cost of a task based on performance, up to the status date (AC + (Baseline Cost X – EV) / CPI)

> **BAC (Budget At Completion)** – the total planned or baselined cost (this value equals the Cost field value when the baseline is saved)

> **VAC (Variance At Completion)** – the difference between the BAC (Budget At Completion) an the EAC (Estimate At Completion) (BAC – EAC)

Assigning a Project Budget

To track project costs, it's helpful to assign a project budget. This can be done by creating and assigning a **Budget Cost Resource**. Once you enter progress data, you can use the Budget Cost resource to compare the original project budget to actual cost.

Budget Cost resources are created in the Resource Sheet view. They are assigned to the Project Summary Task only and cannot be assigned to individual tasks. Before you can assign the Budget Cost resource to the Project Summary Task, you must first identify the resource as a "Budget" resource.

Identify "Budget" resources when you want to track budgeted work, material or costs against actual work, material or costs.

To create a Budget Cost Resource:

1. Select the **View** tab.

2. In the **Resource Views** group, select **Resource Sheet**.

3. In the **Resource Name** field, name the resource "Budget".

4. In the Type field, select **Cost**.

5. Double-click the resource name to open the *Resource Information* dialogue box (*Figure 115* below).

6. Select the **General** tab.

7. Check the **Budget** checkbox to designate the resource as a "Budget" resource.

8. Click **OK** to close the *Resource Information* dialogue box.

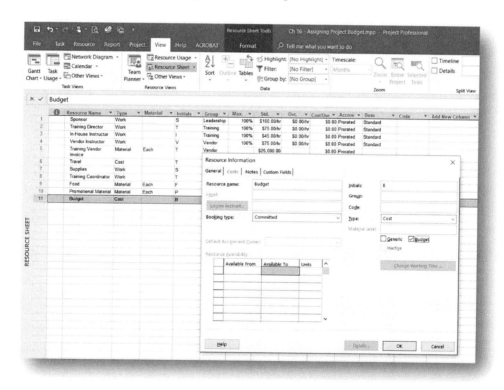

Figure 115 – Creating Budget Cost Resources

Once you've created the Budget Cost resource, you'll need to assign the resource to the Project Summary Task. Here's how.

1. In the Gantt Chart view, select the Project Summary Task.

2. On the **Resources** tab, in the **Assignments** group, select **Assign Resources** to open the *Assign Resources* dialogue box.

3. Select the "Budget" resource, then click **Assign**.

4. Select **Close** to close the *Assign Resources* dialogue box.

After you've assigned the Budget resource to Project Summary Task, follow these steps to assign a project budget:

1. Switch to the **Task Usage** view by selecting the **View** tab. Then, in the **Task Views** group, select **Task Usage** icon.

2. Using the *Add New Column* field, add the "**Budget Cost**" field.

3. In the **Budget Cost** field for the "Budget" resource, enter the value for the project budget.

Figure 116 below shows an assigned project budget of $100,000.00.

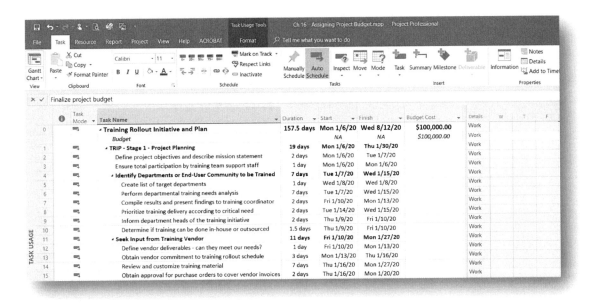

Figure 116 – Assign a Project Budget

Comparing Budget to Cost and Viewing Cost Variance

If resource pay rates have been added to the Resource Sheet, Project will accrue cost in the background as you enter progress data. As your project progresses, you may want to compare the budget to actual cost. A simple way to view cost values is to switch to the Cost table in the Gantt Chart view and add the Budget Cost field, as follows:

1. Select the **View** tab.

2. In the **Data** group, from the **Tables** pick-list, select **Cost**.

3. Using the *Add New Column* field, add the "Budget Cost" field.

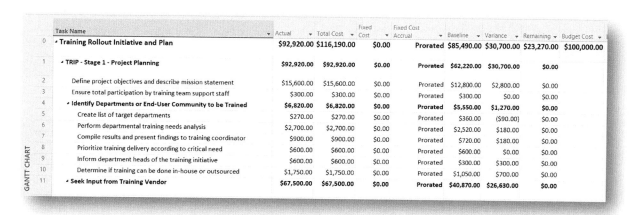

	Task Name	Actual	Total Cost	Fixed Cost	Fixed Cost Accrual	Baseline	Variance	Remaining	Budget Cost
0	⊿ **Training Rollout Initiative and Plan**	**$92,920.00**	**$116,190.00**	**$0.00**	Prorated	**$85,490.00**	**$30,700.00**	**$23,270.00**	**$100,000.00**
1	⊿ **TRIP - Stage 1 - Project Planning**	**$92,920.00**	**$92,920.00**	**$0.00**	Prorated	**$62,220.00**	**$30,700.00**	**$0.00**	
2	Define project objectives and describe mission statement	$15,600.00	$15,600.00	$0.00	Prorated	$12,800.00	$2,800.00	$0.00	
3	Ensure total participation by training team support staff	$300.00	$300.00	$0.00	Prorated	$300.00	$0.00	$0.00	
4	⊿ **Identify Departments or End-User Community to be Trained**	**$6,820.00**	**$6,820.00**	**$0.00**	Prorated	**$5,550.00**	**$1,270.00**	**$0.00**	
5	Create list of target departments	$270.00	$270.00	$0.00	Prorated	$360.00	($90.00)	$0.00	
6	Perform departmental training needs analysis	$2,700.00	$2,700.00	$0.00	Prorated	$2,520.00	$180.00	$0.00	
7	Compile results and present findings to training coordinator	$900.00	$900.00	$0.00	Prorated	$720.00	$180.00	$0.00	
8	Prioritize training delivery according to critical need	$600.00	$600.00	$0.00	Prorated	$600.00	$0.00	$0.00	
9	Inform department heads of the training initiative	$600.00	$600.00	$0.00	Prorated	$300.00	$300.00	$0.00	
10	Determine if training can be done in-house or outsourced	$1,750.00	$1,750.00	$0.00	Prorated	$1,050.00	$700.00	$0.00	
11	⊿ **Seek Input from Training Vendor**	**$67,500.00**	**$67,500.00**	**$0.00**	Prorated	**$40,870.00**	**$26,630.00**	**$0.00**	

Figure 117 – The Cost Table

The Cost table (*Figure 117* above) displays the following cost fields:

- The **Actual Cost** field shows costs incurred for work already performed by resources on their tasks, along with any other recorded costs associated with the task.

- The **Total Cost** field shows the total or projected cost for a task, resource or assignment, based on costs already incurred by work performed by resources assigned to the task, in addition to the costs planned for the remaining work.
    - ❖ Project calculates total cost as Actual Cost + Remaining Cost.

- The **Fixed Cost** field shows any non-resource task expense.

- The **Fixed Cost Accrual** field provides choices for how and when fixed cost are to be charged to the cost of a task. The options are Start, Prorated and End.

- The **Baseline Cost** field shows the planned costs at the time the project is baselined.

- The **Variance** field shows the difference between the Baseline cost and Total cost for a task, resource, or assignment.

    ❖ Project calculate Cost Variance as Cost – Baseline cost.

➤ The **Remaining Cost** field show the remaining scheduled expense that will be incurred in completing the remaining scheduled work. When you first create a task, the Remaining Cost field is the same as the Cost field. Once resources begin to work on the task and report actual work, Project calculates Remaining Cost as Remaining Work X Standard Rate + Remaining Overtime Cost.

Viewing Earned Value Metrics

All variances we've reviewed so far can be characterized as simple variance. As mentioned earlier, Variance answers the question, "How are we doing against the plan?" We can get a more comprehensive view by accessing the Earned Value metrics, which answer the question, "Are these results worth the investment?" To view accurate Earned Value Metrics, you'll need to have baselined your Detailed schedule, added resource pay rates and entered progress data through your status date.

To view Earned Value metrics, you'll need to display an Earned Value table. Project includes three Earned Value tables – "Earned Value" (for tasks and resources), "Earned Value Cost Indicators" and "Earned Value Schedule Indicators".

To display an Earned Value table:

1. Select the **View** tab.

2. In the **Data** group, from the **Tables** pick-list, select **More Tables** to open the *More Tables* dialogue box.

3. Select the Earned Value table you want, then click **Apply**.

Using Reports to View Cost and Earned Value Metrics

Starting with the 2013 version of Project, the reporting features were greatly enhanced. The new reports are customizable and now include dynamic graphs, charts, and tables to view and share project data. There are several Cost and Dashboard reports that can be used to view and track project costs, including Earned Value metrics. Access the reports from the Reports tab (*Figure 118* below).

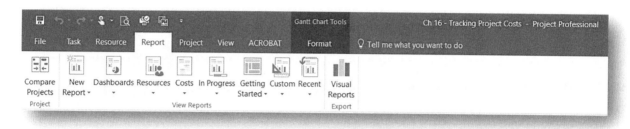

Figure 118 - Reports

To view Earned Value metrics using Reports:

1. Select the **Reports** tab.

2. In the **View Reports** group, select **Costs**, then select **Earned Value Report**. Project displays the Earned Value metrics for your project (*Figure 119* below).

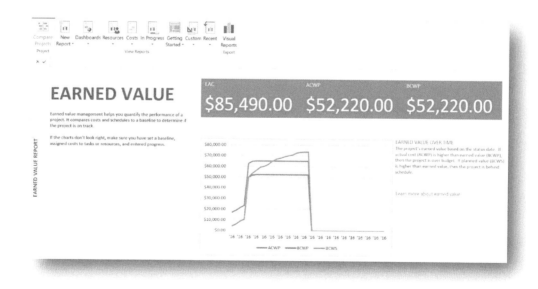

Figure 119 – Earned Value Report

As you've seen, Project offers a variety of tables, views and dynamic reports to track and manage project costs.

We've now learned to track project costs. We've assigned a project budget, compared budgeted cost to actual cost, viewed cost variance and viewed Earned Value metrics.

Execute a Detailed Schedule

Instructions: In this practice exercise, you'll complete the final step in the **B.A.S.I.C.S.** scheduling approach – "**S**tart the Project". You will execute the Detailed schedule you built in the Chapter 8 practice exercise. Visit www.mspbasics.com for "Checkpoint" images to check your work as you go along.

Follow the steps below to complete this exercise:

Open an Existing Project Plan

1. Open the Detailed "House Painting" project plan that you saved from the Chapter 8 practice exercise.

2. To confirm you're starting with the right file, visit www.mspbasics.com. Select "Practice Exercise Solutions" from the menu. Select "Chapter 16" and reference "Checkpoint Image #1".

Set a Deadline for the Project Finish Date

Set a deadline for the project finish date by applying a deadline to the last task in the schedule (task 16), which is the milestone for the "House Painting" phase.

Set the Deadline as follows:

1. Double-click task 16 to open the *Task Information* dialogue box.

2. Select the **Advanced** tab.

3. In the **Deadline** field, enter 6/22/20.

4. Click **OK** to close the *Task Information* dialogue box.

Set the Current Date

Assume the current date is 6/1/20. Set this date as the "current date" in Project, as follows:

1. Select the **Project** tab.

2. In the **Properties** group, select **Project Information** to open the *Project Information dialogue* box.

3. In the **Current Date** field, enter or select **6/1/20**.

4. Click **OK** to close the *Project Information dialogue* box.

NOTE: You should see a vertical green line in the Gantt chart, indicating the current date (the indicator will correspond with 6/1/20 on the timescale). If you don't see the vertical green line, use the Zoom slider in the bottom right corner to zoom in on the timeline.

Baseline the Schedule

Set a Baseline as follows:

1. Select the **Project** tab.

2. In the **Schedule** group, select **Set Baseline**, then select **Set Baseline** again to open the *Set Baseline* dialogue box.

3. Be sure that the **Set Baseline** option is selected, and that "**Baseline**" is populated in the baseline field.

4. Click **OK** to close the *Set Baseline* dialogue box.

Confirm the Baseline was set as follows:

1. On the **Project** tab, in the **Schedule** group, select **Set Baseline**, then select **Set Baseline** again to open the *Set Baseline* dialogue box. The baseline field should now read "Baseline (last saved on [current date])".

2. Click **Cancel** to close the *Set Baseline* dialogue box.

Update the Current Date and Set the Status Date

Assume that 1 week has passed and the current date is Monday, 6/8/20. You met with your team on Friday, 6/5/20 to collect progress data. Set 6/8/20 as the new "Current date" and 6/5/20 as the "Status date" as follows:

1. On the **Project** tab, in the **Properties** group, select **Project Information** to open the *Project Information* dialogue box.

2. In the **Current date** field, enter or select **6/8/20**.

3. In the **Status date** field, enter or select **6/5/20**.

4. Click **OK** to close the *Project Information* dialogue box. You should now see the Status date of 6/5/20 in the **Status** group on the ribbon.

Apply the Late Tasks Filter

You're ready to enter the actuals you received from your team on 6/5/20. To make this task easier, you'll apply a **Late Task** filter to see which tasks should have work done as of the current date (6/8/20). For a review on the Late Tasks filter, see Chapter 15, "Viewing Expected Outcomes".

Filter for Late Tasks as follows:

1. In the **Task Name** field, select the Auto-filter pick-list.

2. Select **Filters**, then select **Late Tasks**. Tasks 1 through 6 should be displayed. These are the tasks that should have work done as of 6/8/20.

3. To confirm you're on the right track, visit www.mspbasics.com. Select "Practice Exercise Solutions" from the menu. Select "Chapter 16" and reference "Checkpoint Image #2".

Add the Tracking Fields

Next, you'll add the tracking fields for a Detailed schedule to the Entry table. Using the *Add New Column* field, add the "Actual Start", "Actual Work" and "Remaining Work" fields. **Note:** If you don't see the *Add New Column* field, slide the line that divides the Entry table from the Gantt chart to the right, until you can see the *Add New Column* field.

To add each Tracking Field:

1. Click on the *Add New Column* heading. This will display the fields you can add to the table.

2. Type the tracking field name and when it appears, select it.

Enter the Progress Data (Week 1)

The project team has given you the following progress data ("actuals") for the past week.

RESOURCE	TASK	ACTUAL START	ACTUAL WORK	REMAINING WORK
Jill	#2 – List Supplies	06/01/20	4 hours	0
Jack	#3 – Buy Supplies	06/03/20	4 hours	0
Jack	#6 – Sand House	06/04/20	8 hours	8 hours

1. Enter the "Actual Start", "Actual Work" and "Remaining Work" values shown in the table above into the respective tracking fields.

Since the predecessors to the milestone "Supplies Bought" are complete, mark this milestone 100% complete as follows:

1. Select the **Task** tab.

2. Select task 4 ("Supplies Bought").

3. In the **Schedule** group, select the **100% Complete** icon.

4. To confirm you're on the right track, visit www.mspbasics.com. Select "Practice Exercise Solutions" from the menu. Select "Chapter 16" and reference "Checkpoint Image #3".

Notice the checkmarks in the Indicator's field of tasks 1 through 4. This indicates that the tasks are 100% complete, with no Remaining Work. In the Gantt chart, notice the task bars for tasks 2, 3 & 6 now have a dark blue progress bar inside the task bar, indicating the task's completion progress.

Clear the Late Task Filter

Now, you'll clear the Late Task filter to display the entire schedule.

Clear the filter as follows:

1. Select the **View** tab.

2. In the **Data** group, from the **Filter** pick-list, select **Clear Filter**.

3. To check your results so far, visit www.mspbasics.com. Select "Practice Exercise Solutions" from the menu. Select "Chapter 16" and reference "Checkpoint Image #4".

Display the Tracking Gantt and Cost Table

Next, you'll Change the view to display the **Tracking Gantt** and the **Cost Table**. This view will enable you to compare the original schedule to the updated schedule and track project cost.

To display the Tracking Gantt:

1. Select the **Task** tab.

2. In the **View** group, from the Gantt Chart pick-list, select **Tracking Gantt**.

To display the Cost table:

1. Select the **View** tab.

2. In the **Data** group, from the **Tables** pick-list, select **Cost**.

3. To check your results so far, visit www.mspbasics.com. Select "Practice Exercise Solutions" from the menu. Select "Chapter 16" and reference "Checkpoint Image #5".

Cost Tracking Questions:

1. Is the project on schedule, ahead of schedule or behind schedule?

2. Is the project over or under the Baseline cost?

3. By what amount is it over or under the Baseline cost?

4. Which task(s) is over or under the Baseline cost?

5. For the answers to the cost tracking questions, visit www.mspbasics.com. Select "Practice Exercise Solutions" from the menu. Select "Chapter 16" and reference "Checkpoint Image #6".

Update the Current Date and Set the Status Date

Assume another week has passed and the current date is Monday, 6/15/20. You met with your team on Friday, 6/12/20 to collect progress data.

Set 6/15/20 as the new "current date" and 6/12/20 as the "Status Date" as follows:

1. Select the **Project** tab.

2. In the **Properties** group, select **Project Information** to open the *Project Information* dialogue box.

3. In the **Current date** field, enter or select **6/15/20**.

4. In the **Status date** field, enter or select **6/12/20**.

5. Click **OK** to close the *Project Information* dialogue box. You should now see the Status Date of 6/12/20 in the **Status** group on the ribbon.

Switch to the Entry Table

1. Select the **View** tab.

2. In the **Data** group, from the **Tables** pick-list, select **Entry**.

3. Slide the line that divides the Gantt chart from the Entry table to the right until you can see the "Actual Start", "Actual Work" add "Remaining Work" fields in the Entry table.

Apply the Late Tasks Filter

You're ready to check with the project team to get another status update. To see which tasks should have work done as of the current date (6/15/20), apply a **Late Tasks** filter.

Apply the Late Tasks filter, as follows:

1. In the **Task Name** field, select the Auto-filter pick-list.

2. Select **Filters**, then select **Late Tasks**. Tasks 6, 7, & 8 should have work done as of 6/15/20.

3. To confirm you're on the right track, visit www.mspbasics.com. Select "Practice Exercise Solutions" from the menu. Select "Chapter 16" and reference "Checkpoint Image #7".

Enter the Progress Data (Week 2)

The project team has given you the following progress data ("actuals") for the past week.

RESOURCE	TASK	ACTUAL START	ACTUAL WORK	REMAINING WORK
Jack	#6 – Sand House	06/04/20	16 hours	0
Jill	#7 – Tape Windows	06/09/20	2 hours	0
Jack	#8 – Lay Drop Cloth	06/10/20	4 hours	0

1. Enter the "Actual Start", "Actual Work" and "Remaining Work" values shown in the table above into the respective tracking fields.

Tasks 6, 7, & 8 should now have checkmarks in the Indicator's field because they are 100% complete, with no Remaining Work.

Clear the Late Task Filter

Clear the Late Task filter to display the entire schedule, as follows:

1. Select the **View** tab.
2. From the **Filter** pick-list, select **Clear Filter**.

Since the predecessors to the milestone "House Prepped" are complete, mark this milestone 100% complete as follows:

1. Select the **Task** tab.
2. Select task 9 ("House Prepped").
3. In the **Schedule** group, select the **100% Complete** icon.
4. To confirm you're on the right track, visit www.mspbasics.com. Select "Practice Exercise Solutions" from the menu. Select "Chapter 16" and reference "Checkpoint Image #8".

Switch to the Cost table:

1. Select the **View** tab.

2. In the **Data** group, from the **Tables** pick-list, select **Cost**.

3. To confirm you're on the right track, visit www.mspbasics.com. Select "Practice Exercise Solutions" from the menu. Select "Chapter 16" and reference "Checkpoint Image #9".

Cost Tracking Questions:

1. Is the project on schedule, ahead of schedule or behind schedule?

2. Is the project over or under the Baseline cost?

3. By what amount is it over or under the Baseline cost?

4. Which task(s) is over or under Baseline cost?

5. For the answers to the cost tracking questions, visit www.mspbasics.com. Select "Practice Exercise Solutions" from the menu. Select "Chapter 16" and reference "Checkpoint Image #10".

6. **SAVE THIS FILE**. You will use it in the Chapter 17 Practice Exercise.

Congratulations! You've now executed a Detailed schedule! You've now practiced the last step in the B.A.S.I.C.S scheduling approach, "Start the Project".

Now You Can

- Explain Variance

- Assign a Project Budget

- Compare Budget to Cost

- View Cost Variance

- View Earned Value Metrics

- View Earned Value Reports

Chapter 17 Creating Project Status Reports

IN THIS CHAPTER:

- Sharing Gantt Chart Reports

- Using the Copy Picture Feature

- Using the Timeline View

- Using the Built-In Reports

In the last chapter, we tracked project costs. We assigned a project budget, compared budgeted cost to actual cost and reviewed Cost Variance and Earned Value metrics. In this chapter, we'll create status reports. When you're done, you'll be able to share Gantt chart reports, customize and share Timeline reports, use the dynamic, built-in reports to share project information and use the Copy Picture feature to capture project data and export it to other applications like PowerPoint.

A key function of the project manager role is to effectively communicate project status. Microsoft Project contains many features to help you create visually stunning status reports.

Sharing Gantt Chart Reports

As mentioned in Chapter 2, the Gantt Chart view is the most common view in Project. It contains an at-a-glance view of your project schedule, including tasks, resources, costs, and a graphical depiction of the timeline. Because of the information contained in this view, many users provide status updates by simply forwarding a copy of the Microsoft Project plan. This is not always the best approach, because some stakeholders may not have the Microsoft Project software. Even if the recipient has the software, the level of detail included in the entire project can be overwhelming. Project offers many alternatives for sharing Gantt Chart reports and other project details.

Using the Copy Picture Feature

The **Copy Picture** feature is a handy way to share a snapshot of your project details. It captures an image of the current view or selected content and copies it to the clipboard. You can render the image for screen (suitable for use in applications like PowerPoint, Word or Outlook), for printing, or you can save the image as a GIF file.

To use the Copy Picture feature:

1. Select the **Task** tab.

2. In the **Clipboard** group, select **Copy Picture** from the **Copy** pick-list to open the *Copy Picture* dialogue box (*Figure 120* below).

Figure 120 – Copy Picture Dialogue Box

3. In the **Render image** section, the **For screen** option captures an image with a resolution that's suited for viewing on a monitor. The **For printer** option captures an image that is suited for printing. The **To GIF image file** option saves the image as a GIF file.

4. In the **Copy** section, select **rows shown on the screen** to copy the current view, or select **copy any specific rows** to copy selected rows.

5. In the **Timescale** section, select **as shown on the screen** to copy the timeline from the current view or choose specific dates using the **From** option.

6. Select **OK** to copy the image to the clipboard and close the *Copy Picture* dialogue box.

After the image is copied to the clipboard, you can share the content by printing, pasting, or exporting the image to other applications.

Using the Timeline View

Another way to communicate project status is to share an image of the **Timeline View**. The Timeline view is a customizable summary of the project timeline. It includes only the tasks and milestones you choose to display. Depending on how your version of Project is configured, the Timeline view will be displayed when you open a new project or a project template. For new projects, the Timeline view will be empty. If the Timeline view panel is not displayed, display it as follows:

1. Select the **View** tab.

2. In the **Split View** group, select the **Timeline** checkbox.

Before you capture an image of the Timeline view, you'll need to add the tasks you want to share.

To add tasks to the Timeline View:

1. Click anywhere in the Timeline panel. When the timeline is selected, the words **"Timeline Tools"** will appear above the Format tab. The Timeline Tools are contextual commands for customizing the timeline.

2. In the **Insert** group, select **Existing Tasks** to open the *Add Tasks to Timeline* dialogue box.

3. Select the tasks you want to add to the timeline.

4. Select **OK** to close the *Add Tasks to Timeline* dialogue box. The selected tasks will appear as timeline bars in the view.

After you add tasks to the timeline, you can customize the view. Use the Timeline Tools to change the font and color of timeline bars, display callout tasks and make other customizations (*Figure 121* below).

Using *Figure 121*, let's review the formatting commands in the Timeline Tools.

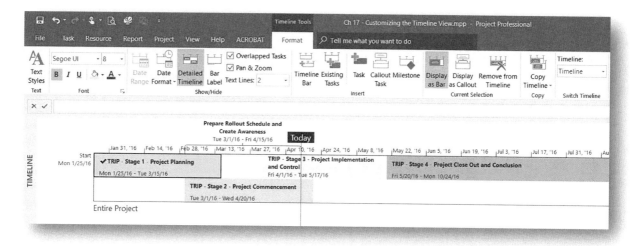

Figure 121 – Customizing the Timeline View

> Use the **Text Styles** command to change the style of the text for an item in the view.

> Use the commands in the **Font** group to format the background or font for an item in the view.

> The **Date Range** commands let you customize the selected timeline bar to show a specific date range.

> The **Date Format** command lets you format how the dates appear in the view. You can also use this command to show or hide dates.

> The **Detailed Timeline** command lets you add details, like task names and dates to the view.

> The **Bar Label** command lets you specify names for the timeline bars.

> The **Overlapped Tasks** command lets you display tasks overlapping on multiple rows to improve the readability of task names.

> The **Pan and Zoom** command displays the pan and zoom control, which allows you to use the Timeline view to navigate the main view.

> The **Text Lines** command lets you specify how many lines are used to display the task name.

➢ The **Timeline Bar** command lets you add additional timelines to the view. This is a new feature added to Project 2019.

➢ Use the **Existing Task** command to add tasks that are currently in the project to the view.

➢ The **Task** command lets you add a new task to the project plan. The new task will be added to the Timeline view and the project plan.

➢ The **Callout Task** command lets you add a new task to project plan. The new task will be added to the Timeline view as a Callout Task and to the project plan.

➢ The **Milestone** command lets you add a new milestone to the project plan. The new milestone will be added to the Timeline view and to the project plan.

➢ In the **Current Select** group, the **Display as Bar** and **Display as Callout** commands let you display a selected task as a Timeline Bar or as a Callout Task.

➢ Use the **Remove from Timeline** option to remove tasks from the Timeline view.

After you customize the Timeline view, you can copy it to the clipboard, using the **Copy Timeline** feature. Like the Copy Picture feature, you can paste the image to applications like PowerPoint or Outlook. You can also export it as a PDF or XPS file.

To Copy the Timeline View:

1. Click anywhere in the timeline panel to access the **Timeline Tools**.

2. In the **Copy** group, select **Copy Timeline**.

3. From the Copy Timeline pick-list, select the option you want. You can copy the image for email, presentation or full size. When you select an option, an image of the Timeline view will be copied to the Clipboard.

4. Paste the image into an application, such as PowerPoint.

To Export the Timeline view to a PDF or XPS file:

1. Click the Timeline panel to select it.

2. Select the **File** tab. Then, select **Export**.

3. Select **Create PDF/XPS Document**. Then, select the **Create PDF/XPS** icon.

4. Choose the location where you'd like to save the file and name the file in the **File name** field.

5. In the **Save as type** field, select **PDF Files** or **XPS Files** from the pick-list.

6. Select **OK** to open the *Document Export Options* dialogue box.

7. In the **Publish** range section, select **All** to export all dates or select **From** to select a date range.

8. In the **Include Non-Printing information** section, you can choose to add document properties and show markup.

9. In the **PDF options** section, you can format the file to the PDA/A format. This format will prohibit features ill-suited to long-term archiving and encryption.

10. Click **OK** to save the file and close the *Document Export Options* dialogue box.

You can also display the timeline as its own view (instead of as a panel in the current view). This is a good option for sharing complex or multiple timelines.

To display the Timeline as its own view:

1. Select the **View** tab.

2. In the **Resource Views** group, from the **Other Views** pick-list, select **More Views**.

3. Select **Timeline** from the list. Then, click **Apply**.

Using Built-in Reports to Share Project Status

The built-in reports are a dynamic and effective way to communicate project status. Microsoft Project includes several Task, Resource, and Cost reports. The reports are customizable and include charts, graphs and tables that can be used to share project data. For example, the *Project Overview* report (*Figure 122* below) provides a summary of overall project status. This report combines graphs and tables to shows a status of each phase of the project.

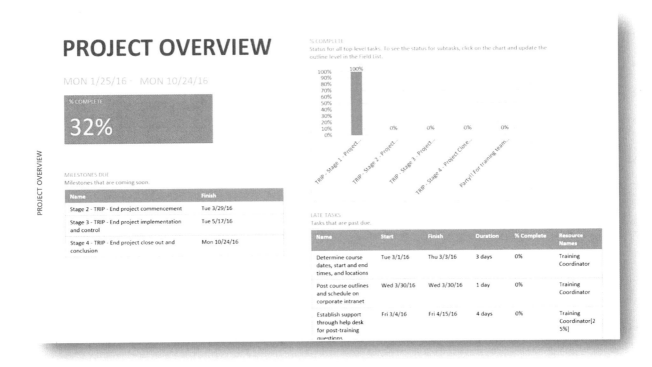

Figure 122 – Project Overview Report

The Report tab includes four report groups – Dashboards, Resources, Cost and In Progress.

Here's a description of each.

Dashboards

As the title suggests, these reports provide a high-level status of the project and should be used primarily with Detailed schedules. The Project Overview report can be used with Simple and Detailed schedules. The reports included in this group are: Burn-Down (popular with Agile projects), Cost Overview, Project Overview, Upcoming Tasks and Work Overview.

Resources

These reports provide resource allocation metrics and should be used exclusively with Detailed schedules, where resources are assigned with specificity. The reports included in this group are: Over-allocated Resources and Resource Overview.

<u>Costs</u>

These reports provide insightful cost metrics and should be used exclusively with Detailed schedules, where work values and pay rates are included, which generate project cost. The reports included in this group are: Cash Flow, Cost Over-runs, Earned Value Report, Resource Cost Overview and Task Cost Overview.

<u>In Progress</u>

These reports allow you to analyze how your project is going and can be used for Simple and Detailed schedules. The reports included in this group are: Critical Tasks, Late Tasks, Milestone Report and Slipping Tasks.

If you prefer Excel or Visio reports, you'll find ten pre-built, customizable PivotTable and PivotDiagram reports using the **Visual Reports** command.

To access the built-in Reports:

1. Select the **Reports** tab.

2. In the **View Reports** group, select the report you want.

Once you've selected the report you want, you can customize it to include the project details you want to share. Project includes many user-friendly customization features in the Report Tools, on the Format tab. You can change the design, the theme and customize the elements in the report, such as graphs, charts and tables. For a video demonstration of these features and many other customizations, visit https://msproject.vhx.tv and check out Chapter 20, "Customizing Microsoft Project 2019".

To Customize a Report:

1. Select an item in the report to display the contextual commands in the **Report Tools**, **Chart Tools**, and **Table Tools**.

2. Use the **Field List** pane to customize, filter and sort elements in the charts and tables.

Using the Copy Report Feature

Like the Copy Picture and Copy Timeline features, the **Copy Report** feature captures an image of a report and saves it to the clipboard. You can paste the image into applications, such as Word or PowerPoint.

To Copy a Report:

1. Click anywhere in the report to access the **Report Tools.**

2. Select the **Design** tab.

3. In the **Report** group, select **Copy Report**. Project copies an image of the report to the clipboard.

4. Paste the report to the application you want.

You can also export reports to a file, as follows:

1. Select the **File** tab. Then, select **Export**.

2. Select **Create PDF/XPS Document**. Then, select the **Create PDF/XPS** icon.

3. Choose the location where you'd like to save the file. Then, name the file in the **File name** field.

4. In the **Save as type** field, select **PDF Files** or **XPS Files** from the pick-list.

5. Select **OK** to open the *Document Export Options* dialogue box.

6. Select the options you want for the file (for a description of each, see the "To Export the Timeline View to a PDF or XPS File" section above).

7. Click **OK** to save the file and close the *Document Export Options* dialogue box.

We've now learned to create status reports. We created Gantt chart reports, customized the Timeline view, used the built-in reports and used the Copy features to copy and export project information into other applications.

Challenge – Practice Exercise

Create a Status Report

Instructions: In this practice exercise, you'll create status reports. You'll use the Copy features and the built-in reports to share project information. **Note**: You'll need access to Microsoft PowerPoint for this exercise. Visit www.mspbasics.com for "Checkpoint" images to check your work as you go along.

Follow the steps below to complete this exercise:

Open an Existing Project Plan

1. Open the Detailed "House Painting" project plan that you saved from the Chapter 16 practice exercise.

2. To confirm you're starting with the right file, visit www.mspbasics.com. Select "Practice Exercise Solutions" from the menu. Select "Chapter 17" and reference "Checkpoint Image #1".

Adjust the view

You'll start by making some changes to the Gantt Chart view for a cleaner presentation of the status report.

Switch to the Gantt Chart view:

1. Select the **View** tab.

2. In the **Task Views** group, select **Gantt Chart** from the Gantt Chart pick-list.

Display the Entry table:

1. On the **View** tab, from the **Tables** pick-list, select **Entry**.

Next, you'll hide the fields in the Entry table that you don't want included in your reports. Hide the "Resource Names" and "Work" fields, as follows:

1. Right-click the field name.

2. Select **Hide Column** from the pick-list.

Slide the line that divides the Gantt chart from the Entry table to the left, until it aligns with the right edge of the "Cost" field.

Next, zoom in to view the entire project in the Gantt chart, using the Entire Project feature:

1. Select the **View** tab.

2. In the **Zoom** group, select **Entire Project**.

To see how your file should look at this point, go to www.mspbasics.com. Select "Practice Exercise Solutions" from the menu. Select "Chapter 17" and reference "Checkpoint Image #2".

Use the Copy Picture feature to Create a Status Report

Now, you've cleaned up the Gantt Chart view and you're ready to a create status report. You'll use the **Copy Picture** feature to capture an image of the Gantt Chart view for a PowerPoint presentation.

To capture an image of the Gantt Chart view, using the Copy Picture feature:

1. Select the **Task** tab.

2. In the **Clipboard** group, from the **Copy** pick-list, select **Copy Picture** to open the *Copy Picture* dialogue box.

3. In the **Render Image** section, select **For Screen**. This will copy an image of the current view to the clipboard that is optimized for use in applications like PowerPoint.

4. Click **OK** to close the *Copy Picture* dialogue box. The image has now been captured to the clipboard.

5. Open a blank presentation in PowerPoint. Select the "Title and Content" layout style for the slide by selecting the **Home** tab. In the **Slides** group, select "Title and Content" from the **Layout** pick-list.

6. Click inside the content box. Using your keyboard, paste the image into the slide by pressing Ctrl-V (Windows) or Cmd-V (Mac).

7. Title the slide "House Painting Project Status". If you have PowerPoint 2019, you can use the "Design Ideas" feature to enhance the slide for a more dynamic report.

8. To see if you're on track, visit www.mspbasics.com. Select "Practice Exercise Solutions" from the menu. Select "Chapter 17" and reference "Checkpoint Image #3".

Customize the Timeline View to share project status

The shareholders have asked for a high-level status of your "House Painting" project. They're particularly interested in the start date of the "Apply First Coat" task, which begins phase 3 of the project. You'll customize the **Timeline View** to create a status report.

To display the Timeline View pane:

1. Select the **View** tab.

2. In the **Split View** group, select the **Timeline** checkbox.

The panel is currently empty and contains only the project start and finish dates. You'll customize the Timeline View by adding tasks and dates to the panel. Add the "Get Supplies", "Prep House", "Paint House" and "Apply First Coat" tasks as follows:

1. Select the **Format** tab.

2. Click anywhere in the Timeline panel to display the **Timeline Tools** on the **Format** tab.

3. In the **Insert** group, select **Existing Tasks** to open the *Add Tasks to Timeline* dialog box.

4. Select the "Get Supplies", "Prep House", "Paint House" and "Apply First Coat" tasks.

5. Click **OK** to close the *Add Tasks to Timeline* dialog box.

The tasks and their start and finish dates should now be added as timeline bars to the Timeline panel. Notice the "Get Supplies" and the "Prep House" timeline bars are shaded in dark blue and have a check mark. This is because these phases are complete. Next, customize the view and give each timeline bar a unique color, as follows:

1. Select the "Get Supplies" timeline bar.

2. In the **Font** group, from the **Background Color** pick-list, select **Gold**.

3. Select the "Prep House" timeline bar.

4. In the **Font** group, from the **Background Color** pick-list, select **Green.**

5. Keep the current background color for the "Paint House" and "Apply First Coat" timeline bars.

Since the stakeholders are interested in the start date of the "Apply First Coat" task, you'll display this task as a **Callout Task**, so that it stands out.

1. Right-click the "Apply First Coat" timeline bar.

2. Select **Display as Callout** from the list.

You've now customized the Timeline view and you're ready to create your status report. To see if you're on track, visit www.mspbasics.com. Select "Practice Exercise Solutions" from the menu. Select "Chapter 17" and reference "Checkpoint Image #4".

Now, you'll use the **Copy Timeline** feature to capture an image of the Timeline view.

1. Select the Timeline panel to display the **Timeline Tools**.

2. In the **Copy** group, from the **Copy Timeline** pick-list, select **For Presentation**. The Timeline View is now copied to the clipboard. You can now paste the image into a PowerPoint or another application to share your timeline. **Note**: When pasting the timeline image, select "Picture" for the paste option.

3. To see if you're on track, visit www.mspbasics.com. Select "Practice Exercise Solutions" from the menu. Select "Chapter 17" and reference "Checkpoint Image #5" to view an image of a Timeline View report in PowerPoint.

Use Reports to Share Project Status

You'll now generate a **Project Overview Report** to share with your stakeholders.

1. On the **View** tab, in the **Split View** group, uncheck the Timeline checkbox.
2. Select the **Report** tab.
3. In the **View Reports** group, from the **Dashboards** pick-list, select **Project Overview**. The *Report Tools* are now displayed on the **Design** contextual tab.
4. In the **Report** group, select **Copy Report** to copy the report to the clipboard. You can now paste the report to PowerPoint or another application. **Note**: When pasting the report image, select "Picture" for the paste option.

5. To see if you're on the right track, visit www.mspbasics.com. Select "Practice Exercise Solutions" from the menu. Select "Chapter 17" and reference "Checkpoint Images #6 & #7" to view images of the Project Overview report in Project and in PowerPoint.

You've now created status reports to share project information. You used the Copy features and the built-in reports to create dynamic status reports!

Now You Can

- Share Gantt Chart Reports

- Use the Copy Picture Feature

- Use the Timeline View

- Use the Built-in Reports

Chapter 18 Consolidating and Linking Schedules

IN THIS CHAPTER:

- Reasons to Consolidate Schedules

- Creating a Master Project

- Using Resource Pools

- Linking Schedules

- Creating External Links

In the last chapter, we generated status reports to communicate project information. We learned to use the Copy and Export features to share Gantt chart reports, Timeline views and the built-in reports. In this chapter, we'll consolidate and link schedules. When you're done, you'll be able to consolidate project plans into a Master Project, create a resource pool and create dependencies between projects.

Consolidating Project Plans

Project managers often manage several projects at the same time, and in many cases, the project schedules are interdependent. To help manage multiple projects, Microsoft Project allows you to combine projects into a **Consolidated Project Plan** – also known as a **Master Project**. Consolidated projects are Microsoft Project files that contain other **Inserted Projects** also called **Subprojects**. The inserted project plans aren't saved in the consolidated project plan. They're linked to it. When you save a master project, changes you've made to its subprojects are saved in the source files as well. Also, if a subproject is updated outside of the master project, the new information will appear in the master project the next time it's opened. You can insert an unlimited number of subprojects into a consolidated project plan.

Why Consolidate Project Plans?

Consolidated project plans enable you to:

> **Get a Program/Portfolio Level View** – see all the projects in a program or portfolio and how they interact with one another in a single view.

> **Manage Resources Across Multiple Projects** – identify resource availability and over-allocations across the entire program or portfolio.

> **Gain Program/Portfolio Level Insights** – query program-level or portfolio-level information for cost, schedule and performance metrics.

> **Manage Phased Deployments** – manage each phase in a project as its own project, while keeping a view of the overall program or portfolio.

> **View the Critical Path of a Program/Portfolio** – gain insights for expediting a program or portfolio by viewing the Critical Path.

Creating a Consolidated Project Plan

To create a Consolidated Project Plan:

1. Open a **Blank Project**.

2. On the **Project** tab, in the **Insert** group, select **Insert Subproject**.

3. Locate and select the files you want to insert. Hold down the Ctrl key to select multiple files.

4. Click **Insert**. Project creates a master project containing the plans you've inserted.

Figure 123 below shows the "New Program" master project, which contains the "New Product Launch", "Marketing Campaign" and "Customer Service Ramp Up" subprojects.

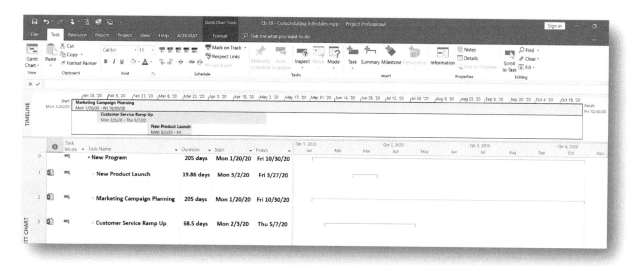

Figure 123 – Creating a Master Project

In a master project, the subprojects are represented as summary tasks in the Task Name field and project plan icons in the Indicators field. Expand a subproject to view its entire schedule. In the Gantt chart, a summary task bar is shown for each subproject. When the Project Summary Task is displayed, it will display the duration of the master project. The start date of the master project will be the start date of the earliest subproject. The finish date of the master project will be the finish date of the latest subproject. For example, in *Figure 123* above, the start date of the master project coincides with the 1/20/20 start date of the earliest subproject, which is the "Marketing Campaign" plan. The finish date coincides with the 10/30/20 finish date of the latest subproject, which is also the "Marketing

Campaign" plan. The 205-day master project duration is automatically calculated from the durations, dependencies and outline level of its subprojects.

Once you've created a master project, you can use the filtering, sorting and grouping features to yield informative project and program-level metrics.

Managing Resources in a Master Project – Creating Resource Pools

When projects are consolidated into a master project, you can view the resources for each subproject in the Resource Sheet view. However, the resources remain separate. You can only assign a resource to the tasks in the subproject it came from. To combine resources and make them available across all subprojects, you'll need to create a shared **Resource Pool**. A Resource Pool is a Microsoft Project file that includes resource information for resources that are shared across projects. The file contains task assignment information, and cumulative costs for all resources linked to the resource pool. For Material resources, the file contains cumulative consumption values for all project plans. This is a useful feature if you assign the same resources to several projects, or the resources on your projects are shared with other projects.

You can use a resource pool to schedule work for multiple projects in one view, identify conflicts between assignments on different projects, and see resource allocation on each project. For example, we know that Project uses the red man indicator to alert you of overallocated resources. This feature works fine at the project level. But what if the resource is over-allocated across the program/portfolio? For example, a resource may show 50% allocated on your project, but they may also be assigned at 50% on three other projects. Resource Pools address this issue by allowing you the see how resources are assigned across an entire program/portfolio.

To share resources across plans in a master project, each plan must be linked to the resource pool. Project plans that are linked to the resource pool are called **Sharer Plans**. Information updated in the resource pool or any of the sharer plans is available to all the linked sharer plans.

To create a Resource Pool:

1. Open a **Blank Project**.

2. Go to the **Resource Sheet** view to create the resources that will be shared across plans in the master project.

3. In the Resource Sheet table, enter the resource information. Include any information you want included in the Resource Pool file (E.g. pay rates if you'll be tracking costs). **Note**: If you elect to copy and paste the resource information from other project plans, be sure that are no duplicate resources.

4. **Save** the Resource Pool file. Name it appropriately (E.g. "New Program Resource Pool").

After you create the resource pool file, you'll need to connect the sharer plans to it. Connecting the sharer plans to the resource pool enables you to see resource allocations across the entire program/portfolio. This is a useful feature, as resources that do not appear over-allocated at the project level may appear over-allocated at the program level.

To connect Sharer Plans to the Resource Pool:

1. Open the resource pool file.

2. Open the project file (sharer plan) you want to connect to the shared resource pool.

3. In the sharer plan file, select the **Resource** tab.

4. In the **Assignments** group, select **Resource Pool**. Then, select **Share Resources** from the pick-list to open the *Share Resources* dialogue box (*Figure* 124 below).

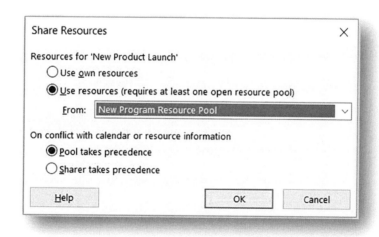

Figure 124 – Share Resources Dialogue Box

5. Select the **Use resources** option. **Note**: This option requires that at least one resource pool file to be open. If you have several Project files open, and the resource pool file you want isn't populated in the **From** field, you'll need to select it from pick-list.

6. In the **On conflict with calendar or resource information** section, select **Pool takes precedence**. This option tells Project to override any conflicting information from the sharer projects with the resource pool file information. The **Sharer takes precedence** option does the opposite.

7. Click **OK** to close the *Share Resources* dialogue box.

8. Repeat steps 2 through 7 for each sharer plan you want to connect to the resource pool.

9. When all the sharer plans have been connected to the resource pool, save and close the sharer plan and resource pool files.

When you open a master project file after the subprojects have been connected to a resource pool, Project will open the *Open Resource Pool Information* dialogue box (*Figure 125* below) to prompt you that the file shares resources from a resource pool. Select the **Open resource pool to see assignments across all sharer files** option to open the resource pool file. Then, click **OK**.

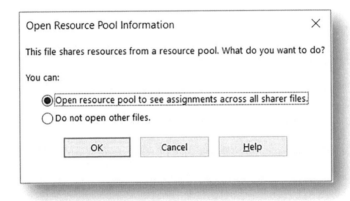

Figure 125 – Open Resource Pool Information Dialogue Box

After you initially save a master project file, Project will prompt you each time after to save changes to all or some of the subproject files (*Figure 126* below).

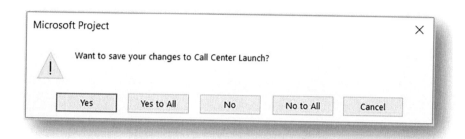

Figure 126 – Saving Master Project Plans

Selecting "Yes to All" tells Project to save changes to all sub-projects in the master project. This is what you'll generally choose. Or, if you haven't made any changes, you can select "No to All". Selecting the "Yes" or "No" option prompts you to save changes for each subproject individually.

Linking Schedules – Creating Inter-Project Dependencies

It's not uncommon for the predecessor of a task to exist in an entirely different project schedule. To address this issue, Project allows you to link two interdependent schedules by creating external predecessors called **External Links**. Linking schedules enables you to manage inter-project dependencies. For example, a server built on one project may be needed on another project or, a resource may need to finish a task on one project because they can work on a different project. Rather than meeting with the project managers of each inter-dependent project, a dependency can be created between the projects. As a result, changes made to the predecessor task in Project A will be automatically reflected in the successor task in Project B. External tasks can be created between projects in a consolidated plan or between independent (non-consolidated) project plans.

To Link Tasks between Projects in a Consolidated Plan:

1. In the master project plan, select the predecessor task you want to link. Then, holding the Ctrl key, select the successor task.

2. Select the **Task** tab.

3. In the **Schedule** group, select the **Link the selected tasks** command. Project creates a *Finish-to-Start* task relationship with an external link between the tasks in the plans.

When an external link has been created, Project will insert the external predecessor task into the plan. The task will be grayed out to indicate the external link. The file path to the predecessor's file will be displayed in the Predecessors field of the successor task. Project also inserts the external successor task in the other project plan. The task names be displayed in grayed-out font, indicating the external links. In *Figure 127* below, the "Launch Product" milestone is an external predecessor to the "Initial Assessment" summary task in the Call Center Launch project.

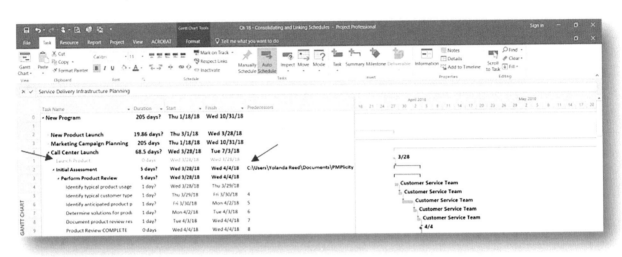

Figure 127 – Creating External Links

Note: To create an external link with a task relationship type other than *Finish-to-Start*, after the file path name, insert the two-letter acronym for the desired task relationship type after the task ID of predecessor, in the Predecessors field of the successor task (E.g. SS or FF).

To Link Tasks between Projects in a Non-Consolidated Plan:

1. In the plan that contains the successor task, double-click the successor task to open the *Task Information* dialogue box.

2. Select the **Predecessors** tab.

3. In the **ID** field, select the cell beneath the existing predecessor's task ID.

4. Type the file name (include the entire file path) of the plan that contains the external predecessor task, then a backslash, then the Task ID of the predecessor (*Figure 128* below).

5. Press the **Tab** key.

6. Select **OK** to close the *Task information* dialogue box.

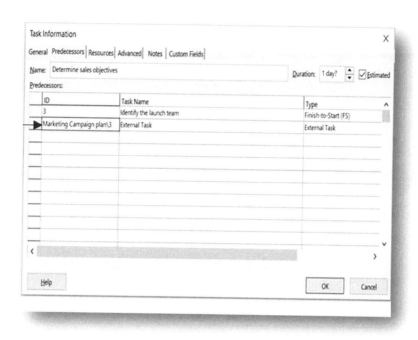

Figure 128 – Creating Inter-Project Dependencies

Project will insert the external predecessor task into the project plan. The task will be displayed in grayed out font to indicate the external link. Project will also create the external successor task in the other plan. It will be displayed in grayed-out font, indicating the external link.

We've now learned to consolidate and link schedules. We've consolidated project plans into a Master Project, created a Resource Pool and created dependencies between projects using External Links.

Bonus Video

To watch this chapter as a video, which includes software demonstrations of the features covered in this chapter, go to www.mspbasics.com. Select "Practice Exercise Solutions" from the menu and select "Chapter 18".

Now You Can

- Create a Master Project

- Create a Resource Pool

- Link Schedules using External Links

Chapter 19 Closing Your Project

IN THIS CHAPTER:

- Reasons to Close Your Project

- How to Close Your Project

- Comparing Planned Estimates to Final Results

- Using the Compare Projects Feature

- Creating a Project Template

In the last chapter, we consolidated and linked schedules. We inserted sub-projects into a Master Project, created a Resource Pool and created dependencies between projects. In this chapter, you'll learn to properly close a project. When you're done, you'll be able to use the software to close out a project, compare final results to planned results and create a template for future projects.

Why Close Your Project?

Now that you've executed your project, it's a good idea to officially close it. Here are some advantages of doing so:

➤ **Accurate Company Records** – Quantifying final project results (e.g. final project cost or final delivery date) establishes accurate company records.

➤ **Future Project Negotiations** – Citing historical data from officially closed-out projects can provide a basis for future project negotiations.

➤ **Answer Future Questions** – Ready access to project details can help explain delays and cost overruns after project closure.

➤ **Establish a Lessons Learned Repository** – Documenting lessons learned with task and resource notes through project closure provides a planning reference for future projects.

➤ **Comply with PMI® Best Practice** – Properly closing a project is a PMI® best practice.

How to Close Your Project

At the end of your project, complete the following steps to officially close your project:

➤ Add task and resource notes (Ch. 10) to document lessons learned for future projects.

➤ Add hyperlinks to tasks and resources (Ch. 10) for quick access to websites and shared files.

➤ For a Detailed schedule, set the **Remaining Work** value to zero for all tasks (Ch. 15).

➤ For a Simple schedule, set the **Remaining Duration** value to zero for all tasks (Ch. 15).

➤ Mark all Milestones 100% Complete – Recall from Chapter 15 that milestones don't automatically get marked complete when their predecessors complete.

Note: You can use the "100% Complete" command on the **Task** tab in the **Schedule** group to quickly mark milestones 100% complete.

➤ Record Actual Start and Actual Finish Dates (Ch. 15).

➤ Record Actual Costs (Ch. 15).

When your project is officially closed out, every task should be marked 100% complete; each task should have a check mark ✓ in the Indicators field. *Figure 129* below shows a properly closed out project.

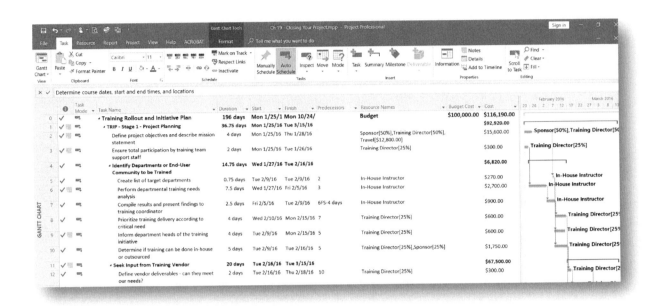

Figure 129 –Closed Out Project

Compare Final Results to Planned Estimates – Using the Compare Projects Feature

Once you've closed your project, you may want to compare your final project results to the planned estimates. You can do this using the **Compare Projects** feature (*Figure 130* below). This feature allows you to compare two versions of a project. When you use this feature, Project will create a "Comparison" report that shows the differences between the two projects.

Figure 130 – Compare Projects

Note: To use the Compare Projects feature to compare your planned estimates to your actual results, you'll need to save a copy of your original plan (after baseline and before entering progress data). You'll then need to rename and save a working copy of the file for entering progress data.

To use the Compare Projects feature:

1. Open the current version of the project plan you want to compare.

2. Select the **Report** tab.

3. In the **Project** group, select the **Compare Projects** command to open the *Compare Project Versions* dialogue box (*Figure 131* below).

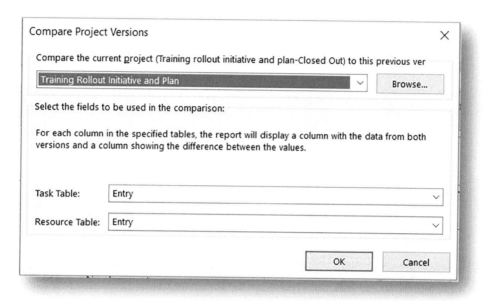

Figure 131 – Compare Project Versions dialogue box

4. In the **Compare the current project to this previous version** field, select **Browse** to locate the previous version of the project file.

5. In the **Task Table** and **Resource Table** fields, select the table that contains the fields you want to display in the comparison report. For each field in the selected table, the report will display a column with the values from both versions and a column showing the differences between the values.

6. Click **OK** to generate the **Comparison Report**.

Figure 132 below shows a Comparison report, that compares two versions of a *Training Rollout and Initiative* project plan.

Figure 132 – Comparison Report

In the top left corner, you'll find a legend that describes the various components of the report. In the bottom panel, the two versions of the plan are displayed side by side. In the top panel, for each field of the specified table, Project displays a column with the data from the current version, a column with the data from the previous version and a column showing the differences between the two. The Gantt Chart displays two sets of task bars. The green task bars represent the current version. The purple task bars represent the previous version.

When the report is generated, the ribbon includes the **Compare Projects** tab, which contains commands for the report. In the **View** group, to compare tasks, select the **Task Comparison** option to show the task view in all three panes. To compare resources, select the **Resource Comparison** option to show the resource view in all three panes. In the **Show** group, use the **Items** and **Columns** commands to select which items and columns are shown in the report. Use the **Go to Item** command to select an item to display in all three views.

Creating a Project Template

It's not uncommon for the projects in an organization to contain similar project details. In this case, rather than creating a new plan for each project, Microsoft Project allows you to create a **Project Template** from an existing project file. Creating a project template from an officially closed out project is ideal for capturing the latest updates to the estimates and task outline.

To Create a Project Template:

1. Open the file you want to create the template from.

2. On the **File** tab, select **Save As.**

3. Select **Browse** to select the location where you want to save the template.

4. In the **File name** field, enter a name for the template.

5. In the **Save as type** field, select **Project Template** from the pick-list. Then, click **Save** to open the *Save As Template* dialogue box (*Figure 133* below).

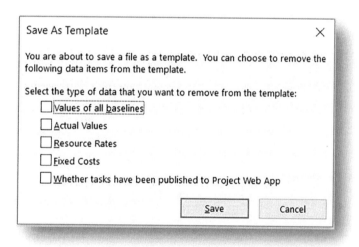

Figure 133 – Save as Template Dialogue Box

6. Select the type of data you want to remove from the template, such as baselines and actual values. Then, select **Save** to save the template as a Microsoft Project mpt. file. To access the template, select the "Project Template" option when locating the file.

You've now learned to use the software to close a project. You can create a Comparison report to compare planned results to final results and create a project template.

Now You Can

- Close Your Project

- Use the Compare Projects Feature to Compare Planned Estimates to Final Results

- Create a Project Template

Chapter 20 Customizing Microsoft Project 2019

IN THIS CHAPTER:

- Customize the Quick Access Toolbar
- Customize the Ribbon
- Create a Status Date Indicator
- Customize the Timeline View
- Customize the Gantt Chart Bars
- Customize the Reports
- Create New Reports
- Create a Custom Field
- Create a Lookup Table
- Create a Graphical Indicator

In the last chapter, we used the software to close a project. We set all tasks to 100% complete, compared final results to planned estimates and created a project template. In this chapter, you'll learn ten useful ways to customize Microsoft Project 2019 to match your style and perhaps meet a specific need.

Throughout this book, we've reviewed many Microsoft Project 2019 features that can make building and managing your schedule easy and efficient. You can also customize many of the features to match your personal preferences and the way *you* work. Customizing Project can also make a difference in how the project information you're sharing is received. In this chapter, we'll demonstrate 10 customizations that can enhance your schedule and help you work more efficiently.

Ten Useful Project 2019 Customizations

1. Customize the Quick Access Toolbar
2. Customize the Ribbon
3. Create a Status Date Indicator
4. Customize the Timeline View
5. Customize the Gantt Chart Bars
6. Customize the Reports
7. Create a New Report
8. Create an Open Text Custom Field
9. Create a Look-up Table
10. Create a Graphical Indicator

Customize the Quick Access Toolbar

The **Quick Access Toolbar** (*Figure 134* below), contains frequently used commands to help you quickly navigate the Project interface. By default, some commonly used commands are already added to the toolbar, such as *Save* and *Undo*.

Figure 134 – Quick Access Toolbar

Projects allows you to customize the Quick Access toolbar to add the commands you use most.

To add commands to the Quick Access toolbar:

1. Select the **File** tab. Then, select **Options** to open the *Project Options* dialogue box.

2. Select **Quick Access toolbar** from the options on the left (*Figure 135* below*)*.

3. On the left, is a list of commands that can be added to the toolbar. Select a group of commands from the **Choose commands from** pick-list. The "Popular Commands" group is selected by default. On the right, you'll find the commands that are currently on the toolbar.

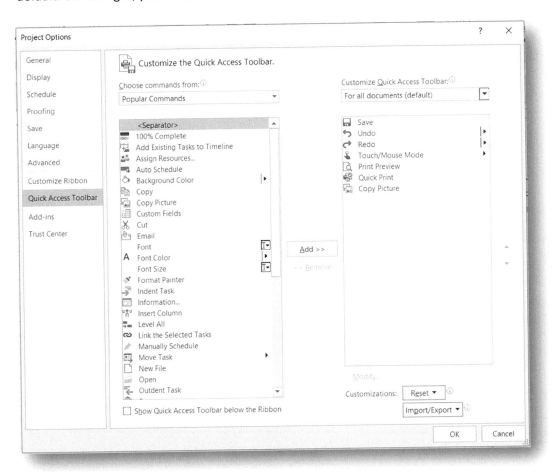

Figure 135 – Customize the Quick Access Toolbar

4. Select a command from the list on the left that you want to add to the toolbar, then click **Add**. The command will appear in the list on the right. Repeat for each command you want to add. To remove a command, select the command from the field on the right. Then, click **Remove**.

5. When you've added all the commands you want, click **OK** to close the *Project Options* dialogue box. The newly added commands will appear on the Quick Access toolbar.

Note: By default, the Quick Access commands you add to the toolbar will appear in all Project documents. To customize the toolbar for the current document only, select that option from the **Customize Quick Access Toolbar** pick-list on the right.

Customize the Ribbon

The **Ribbon** (*Figure 136* below*)* contains all the commands you need to navigate the Project interface. They are organized on tabs, with relevant commands organized into groups. By default, the ribbon includes the *File, Task, Resource, Report, Project, View and Format* tabs. You can customize the ribbon to reorganize, rename, add or remove tabs, groups, and commands. You can also create custom tabs and groups and include the commands you want.

Figure 136 – The Ribbon

To Customize the Ribbon:

1. Select the **File** tab. Then, select **Options** to open the *Project Options* dialogue box.

2. Select **Customize Ribbon** from the options on the left (*Figure 137* below*)*.

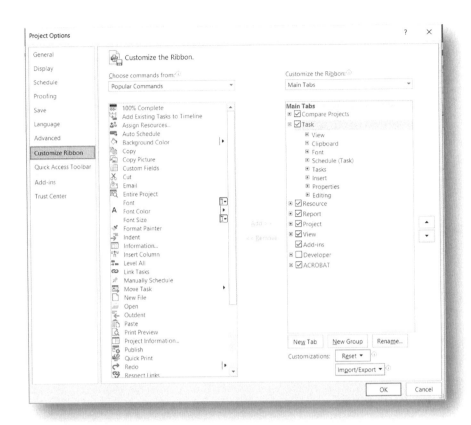

Figure 137 – Customize the Ribbon

3. On the left, is a list of commands that can be added to the ribbon. Select a group of commands from the **Choose commands from** pick-list. The "Popular Commands" group is selected by default.

4. On the right, you'll find the tabs, groups and commands that are currently on the ribbon. Select the group of tabs you want to customize from the **Customize the Ribbon** pick-list on the right. Choose from **All Tabs**, **Main Tabs** (default) or **Tool Tabs**.

5. To remove a tab, simply uncheck the tab's checkbox. The tab, along with its groups and commands will be removed.

6. Use the **Move Up** and **Move Down** arrows on the right to reorder the tabs. When a tab is reordered, its groups and commands will also be reordered.

7. To rename a tab or group, select **Rename** to open the *Rename* dialogue box. Enter the name in the **Display name** field, then click **OK**.

To add commands to a tab on the ribbon, you must first create a **Custom Group** and add the commands to the new group.

To Create a Custom Group:

1. On the right, select the tab you want to add the custom group to. Then, select **New Group**. The new group, "New Group (Custom)" will be added to the tab.

2. To rename the group, select **Rename** to open the *Rename* dialogue box. Enter the name in the **Display name** field. Then, click **OK**.

To Add Commands to the Custom Group:

1. Select the custom group. Then, select a command from the list on the left, and click **Add**. The command will be added to the group. Repeat for each command you want to add. To remove a command, select the command, then click **Remove**.

2. When you've added all the commands you want, click **OK** to close the *Project Options* dialogue box. The new group and the commands will appear on the ribbon, on the tab you designated.

You can also add a **Custom Tab** to the ribbon. This can be helpful if you frequently use commands that are located on various tabs. Creating your own custom tab, will allow you to place the commands you use most on one tab.

To Create a Custom Tab:

1. On the right, select the tab that you'd like the new tab to follow on the ribbon. New tabs are inserted to the right of the selected tab.

2. Select **New Tab**. A new custom tab and group will be added on the right.

3. To rename the tab or group, select it, then, select **Rename** to open the *Rename* dialogue box. Enter the name in the **Display name** field, then click **OK**.

4. To add additional groups to the tab, select the tab, then click **New Groups**.

5. To add commands to a group, select the group. Then, select a command from the list on the left, and click **Add**. Repeat for each command you want to add. To remove a command, select the command, then click **Remove**.

6. You can also change the symbol for a command. Select the command, then select **Rename**. In the *Rename* dialogue box, select the symbol you want, then click **OK**. The new symbol will be displayed with the command on the ribbon.

7. When you've added all the groups and commands you want to the custom tab, click **OK** to close the *Project Options* dialogue box. The new tab, groups and commands will appear on the ribbon.

Export/Import Your Customizations

You can export your customized Quick Access toolbar and ribbon to a file that can be used on other computers. This is a handy feature if you use Project on multiple computers.

To Export Customizations:

1. In the **Quick Access Toolbar** or **Customize Ribbon** window of the *Project Options* dialogue box, select **Import/Export**. Then, select **Export all customizations**.

2. Select the location where you want to save the file, then click **Save**.

3. Click **OK** to close the *Project Options* dialogue box.

To Import Customizations:

1. In the **Quick Access Toolbar** or **Customize Ribbon** window of the *Project Options* dialogue box, select **Import/Export**. Then, select **Import customization file**.

2. Locate the file, then click **Open** to import the customization file.

3. Click **OK** to close the *Project Options* dialogue box.

Note: When you import a customization fie, you lose all prior customizations. If you think you'll want to revert to prior customizations, you should export the current customizations before you import the new file.

Status Date Indicator

While managing your project, you'll often want to know the last date you updated your schedule. In Project, this date is called the **Status Date**. To keep track of your latest status date, it's helpful to create a **Status Date Indicator**. A status date indicator is similar to the *current* date indicator located in the

Gantt chart. Project indicates the current date with a green vertical gridline. A status date indicator is a customized gridline that indicates the project status date.

To Create a Status Date Indicator:

1. Select the **Format** tab.

2. In the **Format** group, select **Gridlines**, then select **Gridlines** again to open the *Gridlines* dialogue box (*Figure 138* below).

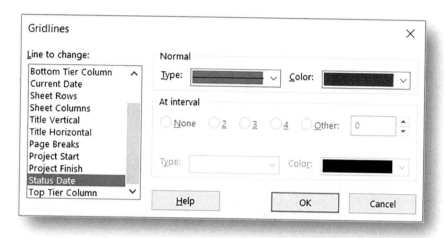

Figure 138 – Gridlines Dialogue Box

3. In the **Line to change** field, select **Status Date.**

4. In the **Normal** section, select a **Type** and **Color** for the gridline from the respective fields.

5. Click **OK** to close the *Gridlines* dialogue box. Project will now display a contrasting vertical gridline to indicate the latest status date in your project plan (*Figure 139* below).

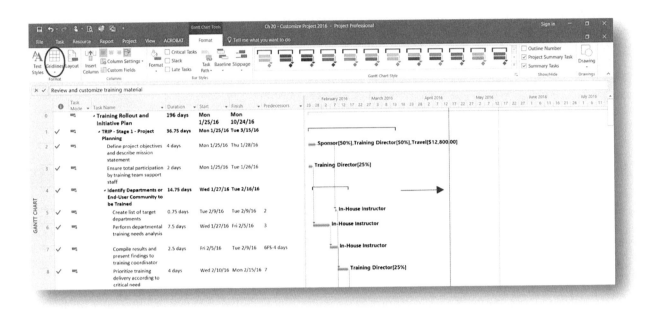

Figure 139 – Status Date Indicator

Customize the Timeline View

The **Timeline View** is a customizable summary of the project timeline (*Figure 140* below). As reviewed in Chapter 17, you can customize the Timeline view to include the tasks and milestones that you want to highlight.

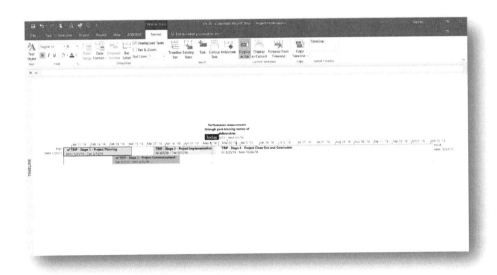

Figure 140 – Customize the Timeline View

To customize the Timeline View:

1. Click anywhere in the Timeline view panel to access the **Timeline Tools**.

2. In the **Insert** group, select **Existing Tasks** to open the *Add Tasks to Timeline* dialogue box.

3. Select the tasks you want to add to the timeline. Then, click **OK**.

4. Use the **Timeline Tools** to change the font and color of timeline bars, display callout tasks and make other customizations. See Chapter 17 for a detailed review of the Timeline Tool commands.

Customize the Gantt Chart Bars

You can customize the Gantt chart by changing the style of the task bars. These small enhancements to the Project interface can make your schedule more engaging for you and for those you're sharing it with.

To Customize the Gantt Chart Bars:

1. Select the **Format** tab.

2. In the **Gantt Chart Style** group, select the bar style you want from the pre-defined styles (*Figure 141* below). You can choose from **Scheduling Styles** or **Presentation Styles**.

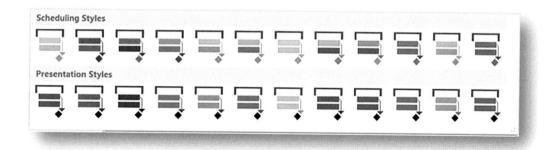

Figure 141 – Customize the Gantt Chart Task Bars

Note: If you choose a style from the "Scheduling Styles", Project will distinguish between Automatic and Manually scheduled tasks. If you select a style from the "Presentation Styles", these distinctions won't appear.

Customize the Reports

Project includes a variety of dynamic reports that can be used to summarize project information and communicate project status. You can customize the reports to change the data, formatting, and other specifics.

To Customize a Report:

1. To format almost any item on a report, such as a chart or table, select the item. Depending on the item selected, the relevant commands will display on the ribbon, on the **Design** and **Format** tabs (*Figure 142* below).

Figure 142 – Customizing the Built-In Reports

2. Use the **Report Tools** to change the theme, colors and font of the report. You can also add shapes, charts, tables and images to the report.

3. Use the **Chart Tools** to change the formatting, data and elements of a chart. Charts can also be quickly customized using the quick access tools that appear next to the selected chart. Use the **Chart Elements** (plus sign) command to quickly change, add or remove chart items such as

labels, gridlines, or legends. Use the **Chart Styles** command (paint brush) to change the chart style and color. Use the **Chart Filters** (funnel) command to edit the data points and names that are visible on the report.

4. Use the **Table Tools** to change the design and layout of a table.

5. Use the **Field List** pane on the right to select the fields shown in a chart or table. You can also use the Field List pane to filter, group and sort information.

   Note: If the field list doesn't display, it will have to be manually toggled on. To do this, on the **Table Tools Design** tab, in the **Show/Hide** group, select **Table Data** to toggle the Field List pane on or off.

Create a New Report

Project includes several built-in task and resource reports to help manage and communicate project information. If you can't find the report you need, you can create a custom **New Report**.

To create a New Report:

1. Select the **Report** tab.

2. In the **View Reports** group, select **New Report**, then, select the option for the type of report you want to create:

   - Select **Blank** to create a report from scratch.

   - Select **Chart** to create a report with a chart. By default, Project generates a chart comparing Work, Actual Work and Remaining Work.

   - Select **Table** to create a report with a table. By default, Project generates a table displaying the Start, Finish, and % Complete fields.

   - Select **Comparison** to compare two charts. Use the Field List pane to add information to each chart to differentiate and compare them.

3. In the *Report Name* dialogue box, enter a name for the report in the **Name** field. Then, click **OK** to generate the report.

4. Use the **Report Tools** to format and add items to the report. Use the **Field List** to add fields and filter the information in a chart or table.

To View a Custom Report:

1. Select the **Report** tab.

2. In the **View** group, select the report from the **Custom** pick-list (*Figure 143* below).

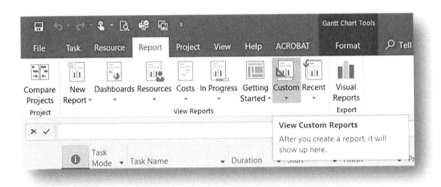

Figure 143 – Viewing Custom Reports

Create a Custom Field

Project includes several tables that allow you to view your project data in various fields. In addition to the fields included in the tables, you may want to include unique information in your project plan. For example, when tracking costs, you may want to include resource cost centers next to the tasks they're assigned to. **Custom Fields** are a good way to add additional information to your project plan. Project supports the following nine custom fields: *Cost, Date, Duration, Finish, Flag, Number, Start, Text* and *Outline Code*. You can create up to 30 custom fields for tasks and resources. Most of the custom fields are available for tasks, resources, and assignments. The *Outline Code* field is available for tasks and resources only.

To Create a Custom Field:

1. Select the **Project** tab. In the **Properties** group, select **Custom Fields** to open the *Custom Fields* dialogue box (*Figure 144* below).

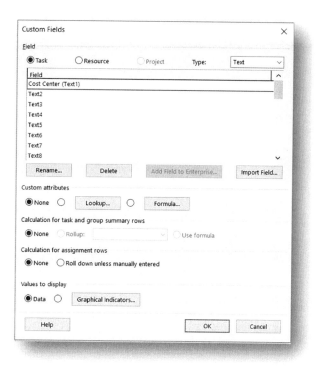

Figure 144 – Custom Fields Dialogue Box

2. Select **Task** to create a task view custom field. Select **Resource** to create a resource view custom field. Select the type of custom field you want to create from the pick-list in the top right corner.

3. Select **Text1** (or the next available custom field), then select **Rename** to name the custom field. The *Rename Field* dialogue box opens.

4. In the **New name for** field, enter a name for the custom field, then select **OK**.

5. Use the **Import field** option to import a custom field from another open project or from a global master template file. Imported custom fields will include any associated value list, formula, or graphical indicators.

6. In the **Custom attributes** section, select **Lookup** to apply a value list for the selected custom field. We'll create a Lookup table later in the chapter. Select **Formula** to apply a formula to calculate the contents of the selected custom field.

7. In the **Calculation for tasks and group summary rows** section, select **Roll-up** to specify that the values of the custom field should be *rolled up* to summary rows. There are several roll-up options to choose from.

8. In the **Calculation for assignment rows** section, select **Roll down unless manually entered** if the contents of the custom field are to be distributed across assignments. With this option, the data will be divided among the assignments, unless it's manually entered into an assignment row.

9. In the **Values to display** section, select **Data** to display actual data in the field contents. Select **Graphical Indicators** to specify the conditions and related indicators to be displayed in the field instead of data. We'll create Graphical Indicators later in the chapter.

10. Once you've selected the options you want, click **OK** to close the *Custom Fields* dialogue box. The new custom field will be included among the existing fields in Project and can be added to any table.

11. To add a custom field to a table, use the **Auto-Filter** pick-list in the **Add New Column** field to locate the custom field.

Figure 145 below shows the "Cost Center" custom field added to the Entry table.

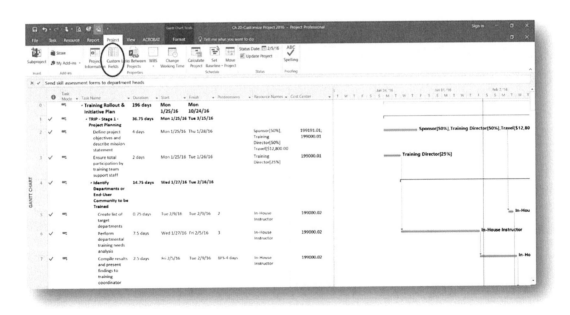

<u>Figure 145 – Using Custom Fields</u>

Note: You'll want to be sure not to use custom fields to enter data that Project also uses to calculate the schedule; namely task durations, predecessors, start and finish dates or resource names. When entering these values, use the default fields already provided in the selected tables, as custom fields have no impact on the schedule.

Rename an Existing Field

You can also rename an existing field, if it already includes the type of data you want to display.

To Rename a Field:

1. Right-click the column header for the field that you want to rename. Then, select **Field Settings** to open the *Field Settings* dialogue box.

2. Enter the new name in the **Title** field. Select the alignment options you want. Then, click **OK**.

Note: If you're a Project Online subscriber, select **Rename** from the column header pick-list. Type the new name, then press **Enter**.

Create a Lookup Table

While managing your project, you may want to monitor certain conditions that affect your project, such as schedule risk. Perhaps, you're unsure if the resources will make their target dates and you'd like them to assign a risk rating to their assigned task. Adding a **Lookup Table** can be useful in this case. Lookup tables can be added to custom fields to apply a value list to the field. For example, if you've created the "Schedule Risk" custom field, you could use a Lookup table to add a risk rating list (E.g. Low, Medium, High) to the field.

To add a Lookup Table to a Custom Field:

1. Select the **Project** tab. In the **Properties** group, select **Custom Fields** to open the *Custom Fields* dialogue box.

2. In the **Field** window, select the custom field you want to add the Lookup table to.

3. In the "Custom attributes" section, select **Lookup** to open the *Edit Lookup Table* dialogue box (*Figure 146* below).

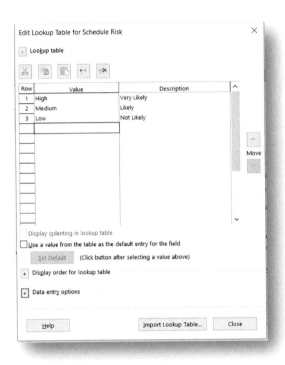

Figure 146 – Edit Lookup Table Dialogue Box

4. In the first row of the **Value** field, enter the first value you want for the table. Then, enter its **Description** in the corresponding field. Add the next value and its description in the next row. Repeat for as many values you would like the value list to include, then select **Close** to close the *Edit Lookup Table* dialogue box.

5. Select **OK** to close the *Custom Fields* dialogue box. The custom field with the new Lookup table is now included among the existing fields in Project.

6. Use the **Auto-Filter** pick-list in the **Add New Column** field to add the custom field with the Lookup table to the current view.

You can now select values for specific tasks from the Lookup table in the custom field (*Figure 147 below*).

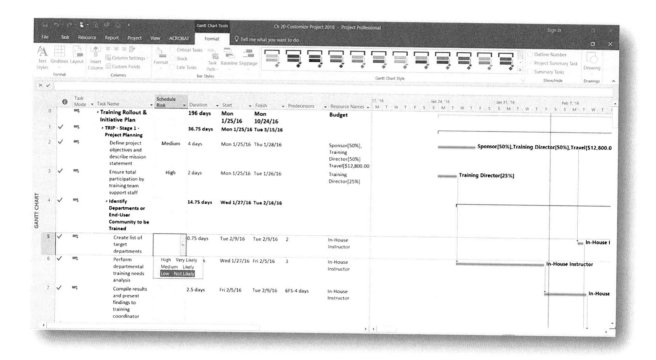

Figure 147 – Using a Lookup Table

Create a Graphical Indicator

To further customize a Lookup table, you can use **Graphical Indicators** to represent the list values. Graphical Indicators are symbols that specify the conditions of the list values and are displayed in the field instead of data. For example, in *Figure* 148 below, the Low, Medium and High schedule risk ratings have been replaced with "flag" graphical indicators. Hovering over the indicator will display the conditions for the corresponding text value.

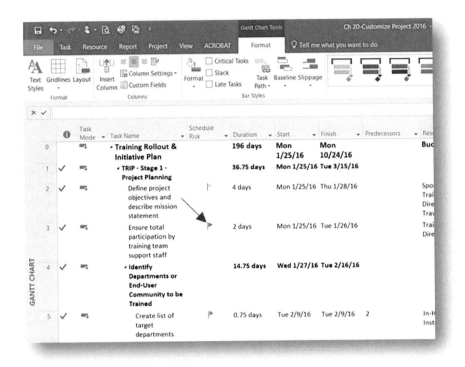

Figure 148 – Graphical Indicators

To Create a Graphical Indicator:

1. Select the **Project** tab. In the **Properties** group, select **Custom Fields** to open the *Custom Fields* dialogue box.

2. In the **Field** window, select the custom field you want to add the Graphical Indicators to.

3. In the "Values to display" section, select **Graphical Indicators** to open the *Graphical Indicators* dialogue box (*Figure 149* below).

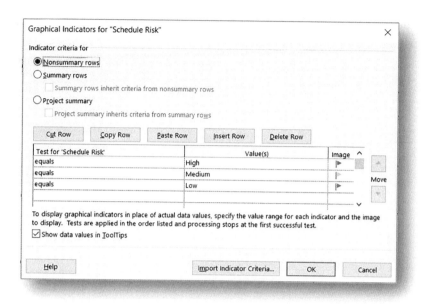

Figure 149 – Graphical Indicators Dialogue Box

4. In the **Test for** field, select **equals** from the pick-list.

5. In the corresponding **Value(s)** field, select the value you want from the pick-list.

6. In the corresponding **Image** field, select the graphical indicator that you want to indicate the value.

7. Repeat steps 4, 5 & 6 for each list value in the Lookup Table, then select **OK**.

You've now learned 10 useful customizations you can do to make the Project fit your personal preferences, enhance your schedule and help you work more efficiently.

Now You Can

- Customize the Quick Access Commands

- Customize the Ribbon

- Create a Status Date Indicator

- Customize the Timeline View

- Customize the Gantt Chart Bars

- Customize the Reports

- Create a New Report

- Create a Custom Field

- Create a Look-up Table

- Create a Graphical Indicator

Chapter 21 Twenty FAQs

IN THIS CHAPTER:

- 20 Frequently Asked Questions about Microsoft Project

In the last chapter, we reviewed 10 useful customizations you can do to Microsoft Project 2019. In this chapter, we'll answer 20 frequently asked questions.

1 - What Does Microsoft Project Do?

Microsoft Project helps you build, manage and track project schedules. With its powerful scheduling engine, Project generates all the scheduling details you need to manage a successful project. You input project data such as the project start date, task outline, task relationships and durations, and Project does the rest! The more information you provide Project, the more information Project provides you.

For example, if you assign resources and include their pay rates, Project will calculate your total project cost. Project does many other things, like create status reports, such as the Earned Value report. It's the premier scheduling solution across many industries and has benefited from years of user feedback and continuous improvement. See Chapter 1 for more information.

2 - What Can Project Do That Excel Can't?

Microsoft Project builds schedules, calculates project cost and creates active status reports. It can perform advanced functions like automatically reschedule resources that are over-extended and calculate the Critical Path, so that you can manage your projects with more intelligence. In short, Microsoft Project helps you build a schedule based on task durations and task dependencies. Excel can't do any of these things. See Chapter 1 for more information.

3 - How Do You Read a Microsoft Project Timeline?

The best way to read a timeline is to zoom in to see the entire timeline. You can do this using the **Entire Project** command (*Figure 150* below). This feature updates the view so that all of the Gantt chart bars are visible on the screen.

1. On the **View** tab, in **Zoom** group, select **Entire Project**.

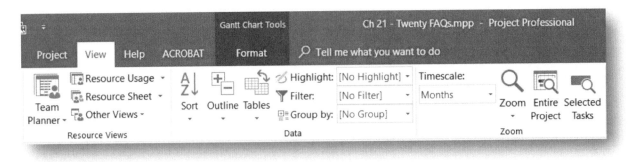

Figure 150 – *Entire Project* Feature

Figure 151 below shows a schedule for a *New Business* plan, built in Microsoft Project.

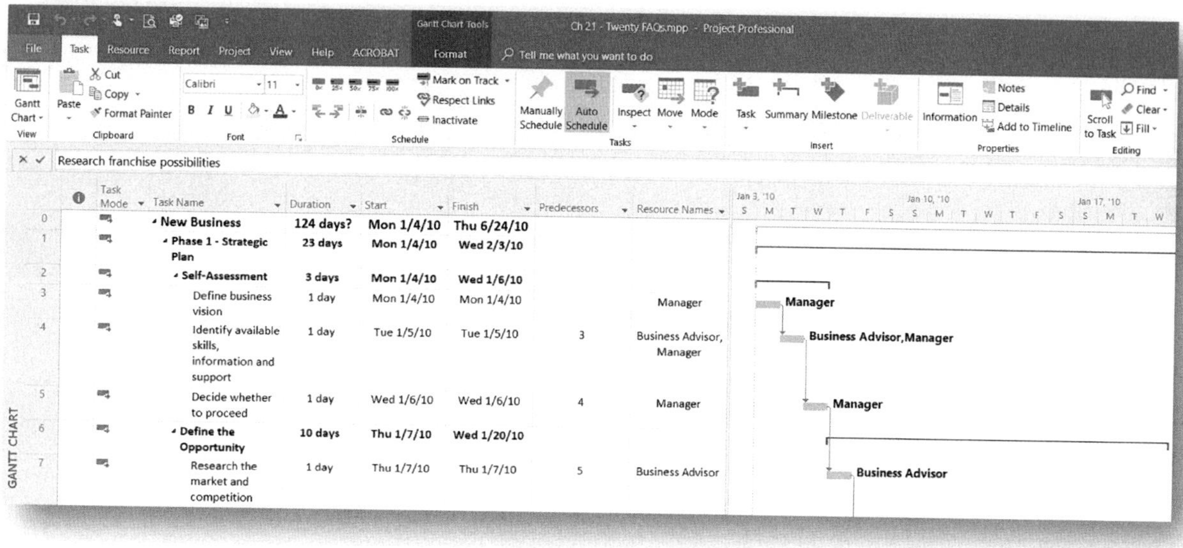

Figure 151

The area on the left is called the **Entry Table**. It's similar to an Excel spreadsheet, and it's where you build your schedule. It includes tasks names, their duration, start and finish dates, predecessors and the resources assigned to them. The graphical chart on the right is called the **Gantt Chart**. It depicts your task durations, start and finish dates and task dependencies. The vertical, green gridline indicates the current date. The gray panel above the Gantt chart is called the **Timescale**. A well-constructed timeline will also include the **Project Summary Task** (task ID zero). It summarizes the entire project and its duration is the duration of the entire project. In *Figure 151*, the Project Summary Task informs us that the project duration is 124 days and is scheduled to finish on 8/11/20. See Chapter 2 for more information.

4 - Can I use Microsoft Project 2019 like I Used the Prior Versions?

Project 2010, 2013, 2016 and 2019 include a feature called user-controlled scheduling. This feature allows users to build a schedule in the Automatic or Manual scheduling mode. By default, the program starts in the Manual scheduling mode. To build a schedule the way you did in versions prior to Project 2010, you'll need to work in the Automatic scheduling mode. See the Chapter 5 for more information.

5 - What is a Milestone?

A **Milestone** are used to signify the completion of a task, phase or significant project event. They have a duration of zero days, so they don't affect the timeline. When naming Milestones, use a noun, past-tense verb nomenclature. For example, "Supplies Gotten" or "House Prepped". Milestones are represented in Project with a diamond icon in the Gantt chart (*Figure 152* below). See Chapter 4 for more information.

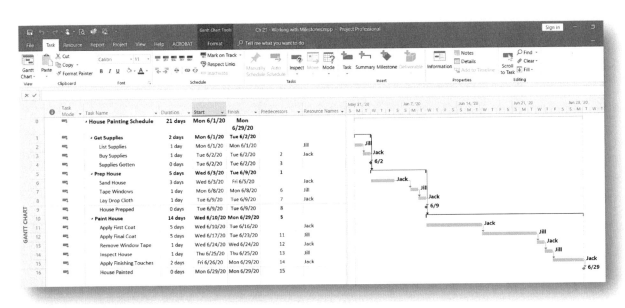

Figure 152 - Milestones

6 - What are Those Red Men?

This is a powerful feature in Microsoft Project. The "Red Man" icon in the Indicator field (*Figure 153* below) alerts you of an over-allocated resource. This means that a resource assigned to the task has exceeded their Maximum Units, which is the maximum number of hours a resource is available to work on any given day. See Chapter 13 for more information.

2			Receive notice to proceed and sign contract	3 days	Mon 6/1/20	Wed 6/3/20		G.C. General Management
3			Submit bond and insurance documents	2 days	Thu 6/4/20	Fri 6/5/20	2	G.C. Project Management 5.C. General
4			Prepare and submit project schedule	2 days	Mon 6/8/20	Tue 6/9/20	3	G.C. Project Management[25%] G.C. Scheduler
5			Prepare and submit schedule of values	2 days	Wed 6/10/20	Thu 6/11/20	4	G.C. General Management[10%] G.C. Project
6			Obtain building permits	4 days	Thu 6/4/20	Tue 6/9/20	2	G.C. Project Management[50%]

Figure 153 – Over-Allocated Resources

7 - How Do I Get Rid of Those Question Marks?

The question marks in the Duration field indicate that the task duration is *estimated*.

To remove the Question Marks:

1. Select the **File** tab. Then, select **Options** to open the *Project Options* dialogue box.

2. Select **Schedule** from the options on the left.

3. In the **Scheduling options for this project** section, uncheck the **"show that scheduled tasks have estimated durations"** checkbox. This will remove the question marks for the currently scheduled tasks (*Figure 154* below).

4. Uncheck the **"New scheduled tasks have estimated durations"** checkbox. This will remove the question marks for new tasks added to the schedule.

5. Click **OK** to close the *Project Options* dialogue box.

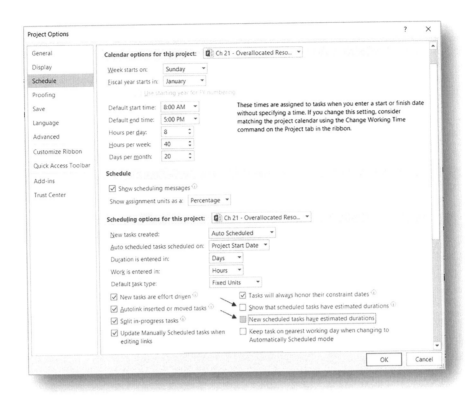

Figure 154 – Project Options Dialogue Box

8 - Should I Enter Start and Finish Dates?

Generally, NO. Project is designed to <u>calculate</u> start and finish dates after you enter task dependences and task durations. Manually entering start dates in the Automatic scheduling mode causes Project to apply a *Start No Earlier Than* scheduling constraint to the task. This limits scheduling flexibility because Project automatically begins each task as soon as possible. If you do want a task constraint in your schedule, you should use the constraint feature. See Chapter 12 for more information.

9 - How Do I Set the Project Start Date?

To Set the Project Start Date:

1. Select the **Project** tab. In the **Properties** group, select **Project Information** to open the *Project Information* dialogue box (*Figure 155* below).

2. Enter the date in the **Start date** field.

3. Click **OK** to close the *Project Information* dialogue box. See Chapter 7 for more information.

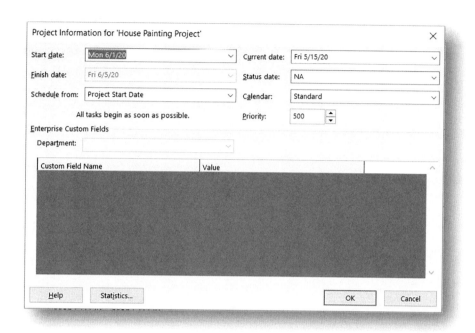

Figure 155 – Set the Project Start Date

10 - Why Do I Get a Constraint Indicator When I Enter a Date?

In the Automatic scheduling mode, entering start or finish dates for tasks creates a *Start No Earlier Than* or *Finish No Earlier Than* constraint respectively. Avoid manually typing in dates unless you want to create either of these constraints. Project is designed to calculate start and finish dates from the task relationships you define in the Predecessors field. See Chapter 12 for more information.

11 - How Do I Get Rid of a Constraint?

To Remove a Constraint:

1. Double-click the task to open the *Task Information* dialogue box (*Figure 156* below).

2. Select the **Advanced** tab.

3. In the **Constraint type** field, select the default *As Soon As Possible* constraint type.

4. Select **OK** to close the *Task Information* dialogue box. See Chapter 12 for more information.

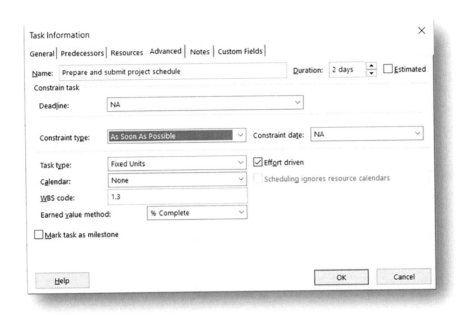

Figure 156 – Task Information Dialogue Box

12 - How Can I Fix My Project Outline?

Use the **Outdent Task** and **Indent Task** commands to outline your schedule. They are located on the **Task** tab, in the **Schedule** group (*Figure 157* below). Promote tasks to create Summary tasks and demote tasks to create subtasks.

Tip: Begin by entering your entire task list first. Structure the project outline after all tasks are entered. This will lead to less re-work. See Chapter 7 for more information.

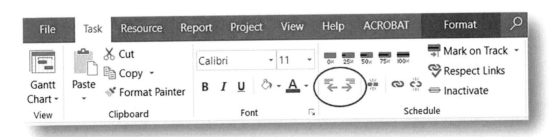

Figure 157 – Structure the Tasks

A handy way to check the outline is to use the **Show Outline** feature. This feature allows you to specify the outline level of the plan you want to view.

To use the Show Outline feature:

1.   On the **View** tab, in the **Data** group, select the outline level you want to view from the **Outline** pick-list.

13 - What is a Baseline and Do I Need One?

A **Baseline** is a detailed copy of your planning estimates. It includes the original start, finish, duration, work and cost estimates. When you save a baseline, Project takes a snapshot of the original plan and saves it within the plan. Setting a Baseline enables you to compare your current performance against your planned performance. It's good to have if you'll be held accountable for the projected performance of the project.

To set a Baseline:

1.   Select the **Project** tab. In the **Schedule** group, select **Set Baseline**, then select **Set Baseline** again to open the *Set Baseline* dialogue box (*Figure 158* below).

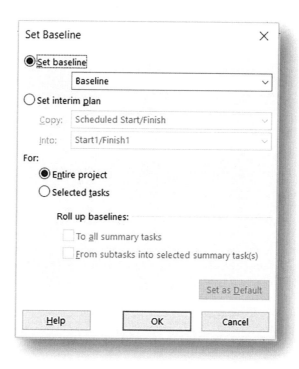

Figure 158 – Set a Baseline

2. With the **Set Baseline** option selected, select the baseline you're saving (0 through 10) from the **Set Baseline** pick-list.

3. In the **For** section, select **Entire project** to baseline the entire project or select **Selected tasks** to baseline selected tasks.

4. Click **OK** to close the *Set Baseline* dialogue box. See Chapter 15 for more information.

14 - How Can I Use the Templates to Get Started Quickly?

The opening view in Project 2019 is filled with starter templates for typical business and personal projects (*Figure 159* below). **Note**: The templates are hosted on a companion website, so you must be connected to the internet to use them.

Follow each step in the B.A.S.I.C.S. scheduling approach to get a quick start on developing your timeline. See Chapter 7 for more information.

Figure 159 – Using the Project Templates

15 - What is the First Thing I Should Do to Build a Schedule?

The first step is to **Break Down the Project**. That's what the "B" represents in the B.A.S.I.C.S. acronym. Gather your team (or yourself!) and create a **Work Breakdown Structure**. Conduct a brainstorming

329

session, use Top-down and Bottom-up planning and be sure to follow the 100% Rule. See Chapter 3 for more information.

16 - What is Task Mode

Task Mode determines how Project will schedule tasks using its scheduling engine. There are two scheduling modes available in Project 2019 – the **Manual** scheduling mode and the **Automatic** scheduling mode. By default, Project schedules new tasks in the Manual scheduling mode. The Task Mode you choose determines how much control you have over the way tasks are scheduled. In the Manual mode, the user defines the start, finish and duration values. In the Automatic mode, tasks are entered without dates. Project automatically calculates start and finish dates based on dependencies, constraints, calendars, and other factors. The ability to toggle between the Manual and Automatic scheduling mode is called **user-controlled scheduling**. The icon in the Task Mode field indicates the task mode you're in. The pushpin icon represents the Manual mode. The task bar icon represents the Automatic mode. See Chapter 5 for more information.

17 - What Does "New Tasks: Manually Scheduled" Mean?

This notification on the Status Bar means that any new task you create will be **Manually** scheduled and not **Automatically** scheduled. In the Manual scheduling mode, users have the option of scheduling tasks manually. The scheduling engine is still engaged, but users are less restricted. For example, text entries are allowed in numeric fields like the Duration field. In this mode, you can enter scheduling details as they become available. Some users may find this mode helpful, as it allows a place for rough estimates when planning details are vague. In the Automatic scheduling mode, the scheduling rules are strictly enforced. If you violate them you will either get a warning or be switched over to the Manual mode, where such violations are allowed. If you'd like to switch to the Automatic mode, select the "Auto Scheduled" option from the Status Bar pick-list. See Chapter 5 for more information.

18 - Where Do I Enter Resource Names?

You could enter resource names directly into the Resource Names field in the Gantt Chart view. This way is fine if all the resources are "Work" resources and all you're interested in is who's assigned to what task. The best place to enter resource names is in the **Resource Sheet View** (*Figure 160* below).

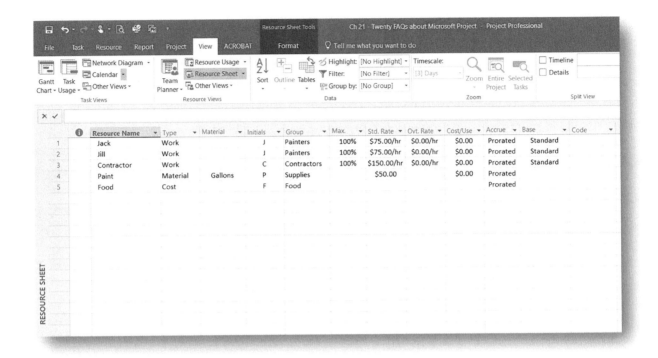

Figure 160 – Creating Resources

To Create Resources in the Resource Sheet View:

1. Select the **View** tab. In the **Resource Views** group, select **Resource Sheet**.

2. Enter resource names, pay rates and other information into the fields of the table.

19 - What Goes in the Predecessors Field?

The **Predecessors** field is where you'll define task relationships. A predecessor is a task that drives another task. In the Predecessors field for a given task, enter the task ID number(s) of its predecessor(s). You can also enter task relationship types, Leads and Lags in this field (*Figure 161* below). See Chapter 4 for more information.

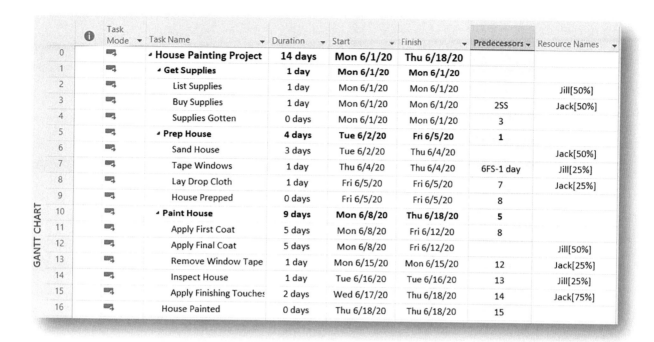

	ⓘ	Task Mode ▼	Task Name ▼	Duration ▼	Start ▼	Finish ▼	Predecessors ▼	Resource Names ▼
0			⊿ House Painting Project	14 days	Mon 6/1/20	Thu 6/18/20		
1			⊿ Get Supplies	1 day	Mon 6/1/20	Mon 6/1/20		
2			List Supplies	1 day	Mon 6/1/20	Mon 6/1/20		Jill[50%]
3			Buy Supplies	1 day	Mon 6/1/20	Mon 6/1/20	2SS	Jack[50%]
4			Supplies Gotten	0 days	Mon 6/1/20	Mon 6/1/20	3	
5			⊿ Prep House	4 days	Tue 6/2/20	Fri 6/5/20	1	
6			Sand House	3 days	Tue 6/2/20	Thu 6/4/20		Jack[50%]
7			Tape Windows	1 day	Thu 6/4/20	Thu 6/4/20	6FS-1 day	Jill[25%]
8			Lay Drop Cloth	1 day	Fri 6/5/20	Fri 6/5/20	7	Jack[25%]
9			House Prepped	0 days	Fri 6/5/20	Fri 6/5/20	8	
10			⊿ Paint House	9 days	Mon 6/8/20	Thu 6/18/20	5	
11			Apply First Coat	5 days	Mon 6/8/20	Fri 6/12/20	8	
12			Apply Final Coat	5 days	Mon 6/8/20	Fri 6/12/20		Jill[50%]
13			Remove Window Tape	1 day	Mon 6/15/20	Mon 6/15/20	12	Jack[25%]
14			Inspect House	1 day	Tue 6/16/20	Tue 6/16/20	13	Jill[25%]
15			Apply Finishing Touches	2 days	Wed 6/17/20	Thu 6/18/20	14	Jack[75%]
16			House Painted	0 days	Thu 6/18/20	Thu 6/18/20	15	

Figure 161 – Using the Predecessors Field

20 - What are the steps for Building a Schedule in Microsoft Project 2019?

To Build a Schedule in Project 2019, use our B.A.S.I.C.S. acronym:

1. First, **B**reakdown the project and organize it into phases.

2. Then, **A**djust the settings to support the type of schedule you plan to build.

3. After that, **S**tructure the tasks into an outline.

4. Then, **I**nitialize the durations.

5. And **C**onnect the tasks.

6. At this point you can **S**tart the project.

And there you have it – answers to 20 frequently asked questions about Microsoft Project 2019!

PART FOUR: Executing Agile Projects

"SOFTWARE IS EATING THE WORLD". This quote, by Marc Andreesson explains what's powering the Agile phenomenon. It's a reference to the disruption caused by software-based companies. For example, Amazon has done much to disrupt traditional retailers, like Sears. In this sense, Amazon is eating Sears. Similarly, Netflix is eating Hollywood, Uber is eating the taxi industry and Expedia is eating travel agencies. By extension, one can ask whether Agile is eating Project Management. Businesses are looking to Agile methodologies the way they once looked to Project Management principles for insights into how to deliver better products, faster than their competitors.

The latest updates to the 6TH edition of the PMBOK (Project Management Body of Knowledge) and Microsoft Project have incorporated the adage "If you can't beat them, join them". The most notable change in both is the integration of Agile workflows. In this section, we'll review the business drivers behind the Agile movement, key Agile concepts, and use cases for Scrum and Kanban workflows.

Chapter 22 Understanding Agile Projects

IN THIS CHAPTER:

- Agile Business Drivers

- Agile Basics

- Kanban Basics

- Scrum Basics

- Selecting the Right Agile Approach

In the last chapter, we reviewed ten useful ways to customize the Microsoft Project interface. In this chapter, we'll provide an overview of the Agile approach. We'll review key aspects of Kanban and Scrum, which are the two Agile approaches you can apply with the newest version of Microsoft Project. When you're done, you'll be able to describe the Agile approach, identify its key business drivers, identify distinctions between Kanban and Scrum and select the right approach for your project.

Agile Business Drivers

The 6th edition of the PMBOK lists six business realities that are driving the need for new, adaptive approaches to product delivery and schedule management.

1. Uncertainty

2. Unpredictability

3. Fast pace of change

4. Global competition

5. Fuzzy, long-term project scope

6. Shifting plans and priorities

Let's expound on these new realities, beginning with uncertainty. The advent of big data has led to more data-driven decisions, which inherently produces more certainty. But who can be certain what data to collect, or what the data means – especially if it's unstructured data? And if one can't glean the proper insights, how can one forecast properly? And on the topic of unpredictability, how much should be invested in emerging technologies, such as A.I.? Who can predict whether new technology is ripe for consumer demand or whether strong demand is further down the road? The answers to these questions are driving the fast pace of change in modern business. If your business isn't disrupting itself with innovation, it could quickly fall behind the competition. Conversely, if your business becomes an early adopter of new technology, what is it that you're adopting, exactly? The concept of a progressively elaborated project scope is more relevant now, than ever. For example, suppose your business decides to incorporate cloud-based solutions to save on long-term expense. At the beginning of the project, it may not be clear which solutions to move to the cloud, or the extent to which those solutions can become fully cloud-based solutions, or what the migration plan should be. This sort of fuzzy, long-term scope is unavoidable if you're an early adopter. Taking it a step further, your plans and priorities may shift many times throughout the project life cycle. These modern business realities have fueled a demand for an approach that is adaptive enough to incorporate changing requirements. The **Agile** approach was designed to accommodate changes and deliver incremental value in time-periods as compressed as two weeks. The promise of this approach has captured the minds and budgets of business leaders world-wide. In the next section, we'll take a closer look at the Agile approach.

Agile Basics

The Agile movement was formalized in 2001, with the publication of the Agile Manifesto for Agile Software Development. This manifesto can be found at http://agilemanifesto.org. It identifies four values, each of which prioritizes principles that lead to seamless, agile software delivery over things that impede it, such as complex processes and tools and rigid plans. These values are distilled into 12 principles, which emphasize key concepts like "welcome changing requirements", "deliver working software frequently" and "work together daily". These principles are realized in several approaches, including Kanban, Scrum, XP and FDD, to name a few. The new Agile features in Microsoft Project are built around the Kanban and Scrum approaches. In the next two sections, we'll review key aspects of these two approaches.

Kanban and Scrum Basics

The Kanban and Scrum approaches are based on building and executing an ever-growing "to-do" list. In a software development project, the to-do list would consist of new software features, requested by the product owner. The to-do list is called a **Backlog**. Each item on the to-do list is called a **User Story**. They're called user stories because they are written by the user, in terms the user can understand. The user that writes the stories is called the **Product Owner**. Since the user story is at the heart of either approach, let's zoom in on this concept by reviewing two examples. The user stories that follow, are from a project to build an e-commerce website for a bookseller who wants to expand the reach of their brick-and-mortar business.

> ### User Story 1
>
> *A website customer can search for books by author, title or ISBN number.*
>
> ### User Story 2
>
> *A website customer can rate and review books.*

The Backlog will consist of as many user stories as required to deliver the final product – a working website that meets client expectations. What distinguishes Kanban from Scrum is how these user stories are pulled from the Backlog and delivered to the client as working software features.

Using Kanban

Using the Kanban method, the team of developers would begin by right-sizing the user stories until each story represents a similar amount work. Then, they will determine the maximum number of stories they can work on at time. This is called the **Work-In-Progress (WIP)** limit. The product owner would then prioritize the user stories in the Backlog. This is when execution begins. Respecting the WIP limit, user stories are pulled from the Backlog and placed on a **Kanban Board**, which is a task board that includes columns, such as: Backlog, Next Up, In Progress and Done.

The user stories are progressed across the Kanban board from the Backlog column to the Next Up, In Progress and Done columns. As you may have deduced, Kanban projects are not driven by a pre-determined schedule. The schedule is generally reversed-engineered from factors like the size of the Backlog and the WIP limit. The reverse-engineered schedule is an expected outcome of the fourth Agile Manifesto value, which reads "responding to change over following a plan". *Figure 162* below, shows a Kanban Board in Microsoft Project. This view is called the *Backlog Board*.

Figure 162 - Backlog Board view

Using Scrum

Using the Scrum method, the team of developers would begin by estimating the amount of work required to deliver each user story. These work estimates are called **Story Points**. The team will then decide how often they can deliver working software to the Product Owner (usually 2 weeks). This 2-week period is called a **Sprint**. Prioritized user stories are then pulled from the Backlog and placed on a **Sprint Board**, which is a task board that includes columns, such as: Sprint 1, Sprint 2, Sprint 3 and so forth. After each Sprint, the client assesses the deliverable and provides feedback. Although there is no schedule at this point, the team will continue to deliver working software every two weeks thereafter. After enough Sprints have gone by, the project manager can determine the team's pace of delivery, which is called **Velocity**. Velocity is the number of Story Points the team can deliver, per Sprint. The schedule can then be reverse-engineered by making projections, using the team's Velocity. *Figure 163* below, shows a Sprint Board in Microsoft Project. This view is called the *Sprint Planning Board*.

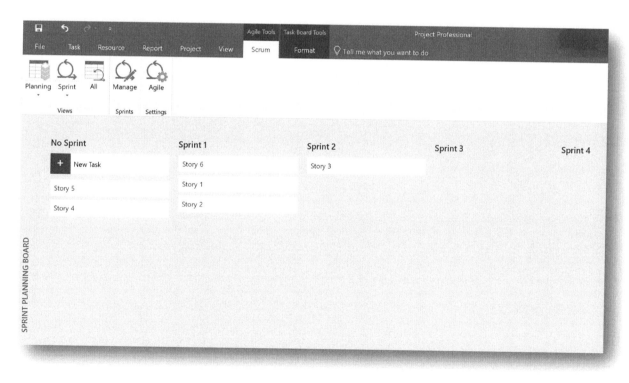

Figure 163 – Sprint Planning Board

To display the activity that occurs within each Sprint, Project includes the **Current Sprint Board** view. *Figure 164* below, shows the detailed progress of Sprint 1. It shows that Story 2 is Done, Story 1 is Next up, and Story 6 is in the Backlog. The striking similarity to the Backlog Board view in *Figure 162* demonstrates that the most noticeable difference between Kanban and Sprint is that one system uses Sprints and the other doesn't.

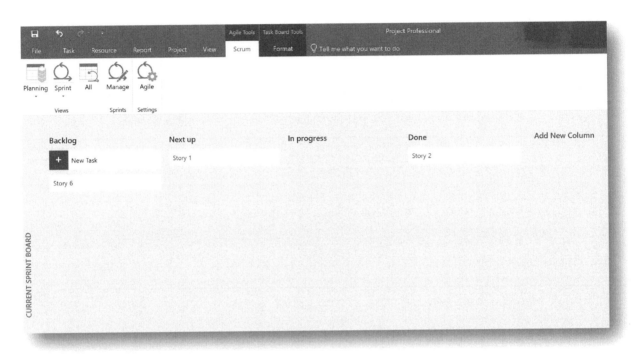

Figure 164 – Current Sprint Board

Selecting the Right Approach

Before selecting a scheduling approach, it's important to determine whether your project warrants an adaptive (Agile) or predictive (Task-based) approach. If your project has never been done before and there is little historical data, then it may be a good candidate for an Agile approach. As mentioned earlier, the Agile approach not only allows for scope changes and shifting requirements, it was designed to accommodate them. Whether you choose Kanban or Scrum should depend upon the volatility of the requirements. If your requirements are more volatile, consider Kanban. If your requirements are less volatile, consider Scrum. If your requirements are stable, consider the traditional task-based scheduling approach described in Parts 1, 2 and 3.

Now You Can

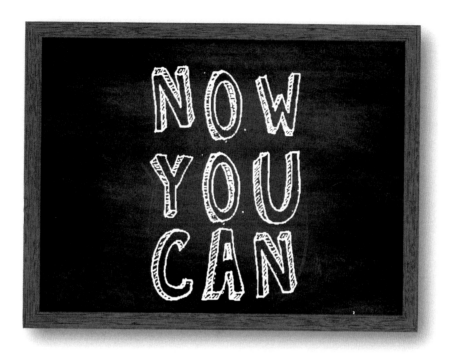

- Explain Agile Business Drivers

- Explain Agile Basics

- Explain Kanban Basics

- Explain Scrum Basics

- Select the Right Agile Approach

Chapter 23 Using the Kanban Features

IN THIS CHAPTER:

- Starting a Kanban Project

- Understanding the Kanban Board

- Using the Kanban Ribbon

- Using the Agile Reports

- Use Case 1 – Sales Kanban Board

- Use Case 2 – IT Support Kanban Board

- Use Case 3 – Digital Marketing Board

In the last chapter, we reviewed the Agile approach and identified business drivers that contribute to the Agile movement. We reviewed key differences between Kanban and Scrum, and guidelines for selecting the right approach for your project. In this chapter, we'll explore the Kanban features available in the Project Online desktop client and apply them using three contextually different use cases. When you're done, you'll be able to start a Kanban project, use the Kanban ribbon, use the Kanban board and use the Agile reports.

Starting a Kanban Project

You can start a Kanban project by selecting the **Kanban Project** template in the opening view of Project Online Desktop client (*Figure 165* below).

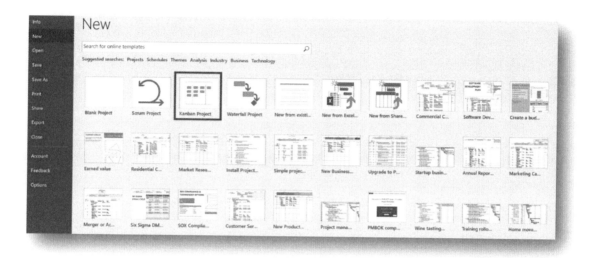

Figure 165 – Opening View

Note: If your interface differs from the images included in this chapter, don't be alarmed. The images included in this chapter are based on Version 1803 (Build 9126.2315 Click to Run). Unlike the desktop version of Project 2019, Project Online receives regular feature updates.

To confirm/update your software build version:

1. Select **Account** from the opening view (*Figure 165* above).

2. Select **About Project** to locate your software build version (*Figure 166* below).

3. In the **Office Updates** section, select **Updates** from the **Update Options** pick-list. Then, select **Update Now**.

Figure 166 – Product Information Page

Understanding the Kanban Board

After selecting the Kanban Project template, you'll be taken to the *Backlog Board* view, shown in *Figure 167* below. The Backlog Board is the Microsoft Project rendition of a Kanban Board.

Figure 167 – Backlog Board view

As mentioned earlier, in this view, tasks (user stories) are added and progressed across the columns. By default, this view includes the Backlog, Next up, In Progress, and Done columns. Each column can be renamed, deleted or moved by right-clicking on its column name (*Figure 168*).

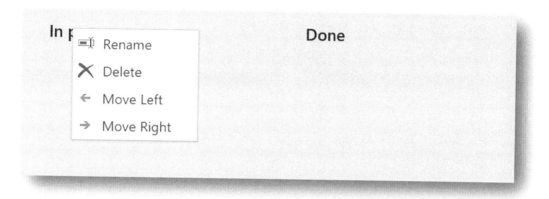

Figure 168 – Editing Columns on the Backlog Board

To add tasks to the board, use the **New Task** command. Simply click the plus sign, enter a task name and select **Add**. By default, new tasks are placed in the Backlog column. To move a task, click and drag the task across the board to the desired column. To add a new column, use the **Add New Column** command to construct the Kanban Board according to your needs. Unlike the Add New Column command available in the Gantt Chart view, in this view, the feature doesn't include a searchable pick-list of pre-set columns.

Using the Kanban Ribbon

When you're in the Backlog Board view, you'll notice that the **Kanban** and **Format** tabs are shaded a darker green. These contextual tabs contain all the tools you'll need for constructing the Kanban Board. The **Agile Tools** are located on the Kanban tab. On this ribbon, you'll find the **Backlog**, **All** and **Agile** commands (*Figure 169* below). If you don't see these commands, select the Kanban tab. The **Task Board Tools** are located on Format tab. This ribbon includes the **Sheet View** and **Customize Cards** commands, which allow you to view and customize Task Boards. In the next section, we'll review each command and discover how they interface with the overall Microsoft Project solution.

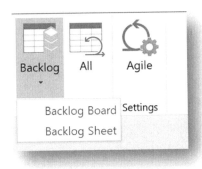

Figure 169 – Backlog Command

Using the Backlog Command

The **Backlog** command contains a pick-list which allows quick access to the **Backlog Board** and the **Backlog Sheet** views. You'll find similar commands among the Scrum features. You can use the Backlog Sheet (*Figure 170* below) to add tasks to the Backlog Board and progress them across the board from Backlog to Done. You can also use it to add more task information than is available in the Backlog Board. The Backlog Sheet is the gateway between the Agile features of Project and the scheduling and reporting features, reviewed in Parts 1 - 3.

Figure 170 – Backlog Sheet View

You can use the Backlog Sheet to add tasks to the Backlog Board by entering them in the Name column. To progress them across the board from Backlog to Done, click on the Board Status column and select the desired status from the pick-list. As mentioned earlier, you can also add more task information than what is shown on the Backlog Board. For example, you can add the work hours to a task. The work hours will not appear on the Backlog Board, as the Kanban Board is only meant to be a simple, customizable view for progressing tasks through the fields on the board. Notwithstanding, if you add work hours, they will appear on the built-in Agile reports. For example, I will use the Backlog sheet to add two tasks to the Kanban Board. I'll call them User Story 1 and User Story 2. I'll also add a work estimate of 20 hours per task and assign them to Jack and Jill. Finally, I'll place User Story 1 in the "In progress" column and User Story 2 in the "Next up" column. *Figure 171* below shows the updated Backlog Sheet.

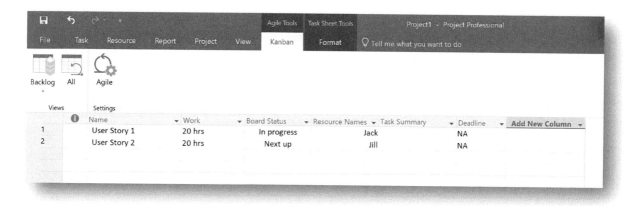

Figure 171 – Backlog Sheet, Populated

Now, let's use the Backlog command to switch back to the Backlog Board. *Figure 172* below shows the

updated Backlog Board.

Figure 172 – Updated Backlog Board

Using the Agile Reports

In *Figure 172* above, notice that work hours are not shown on the Backlog Board. Now, we'll look at the

Board – Work Status Agile report, which shows work hours in various charts and tables. To access this

report, select the **Report** tab. Then, in the **View Reports** group, select **Boards – Work Status** from the

Agile command pick-list. *Figure 173* shows the Board – Work Status report, which reflects the work

status updates that were entered in the Backlog Sheet view.

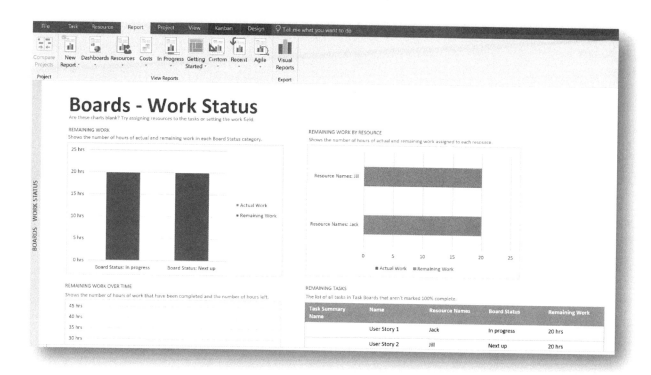

Figure 173 – Boards - Work Status Report

In Chapter 25, we'll review additional Agile reports. For now, take note that to use these reports, you must first use the Backlog Sheet view to add task information such as Work, Actual Work, Remaining Work and Resource Names.

Using the All Command

The **All** command on the Kanban ribbon (*Figure 174* below), let's you view all the tasks that are set to be used in the Agile views. This sheet view includes the **Sprint**, **Name**, **Work** and **Board Status** fields.

Figure 174 – The All Agile Tasks Command

If you select this command with Version 1803 (Build 9126.2315), you'll receive an error message that reads "The view no longer exists…". To some extent, this error message demonstrates the dynamic aspects of the online subscription product. Users must no longer wait three years for updates. However, functionality can vary from release to release. If you're a Project Online subscriber, it's a good idea to check the release log often. You can do so from the **Account** page in the opening view (shown in *Figure 166*). In the **Office Updates** section, select the **View Updates** option from the **Update Options** pick-list. Notwithstanding the error message, if you'd like to see all the tasks that are set to be used in Agile views, here's a work-around.

1. Access any sheet view, such as the Backlog Sheet, Resource Sheet or Sprint Planning Sheet.

2. Use the "Add New Column" field to add the "Agile" column.

3. Any task marked "Yes" will appear in Agile views.

Using the Agile Command

Use the **Agile** command (*Figure 175* below) to select the Agile approach you want to use.

Figure 175 – The Agile Command

Your options are Scrum, Kanban and None (*Figure 176*).

Figure 176 – The Agile Methodology Dialogue Box

Selecting the **None** option will switch the ribbon from the Kanban ribbon to the Gantt Chart ribbon. From there, you can use the Gantt Chart command to switch to the Gantt Chart view and build a traditional task-based schedule, per the methods reviewed in Parts 1 – 3.

Using the Waterfall Project Command

Next, we'll review Case Study examples, to see the Kanban features in use. Before we do, it's worth noting that selecting the **Waterfall Project** option (*Figure 177*), located next to the Kanban Project option in the opening view, will render the same view as the Blank Project command, namely the Gantt Chart view.

Figure 177 – The Waterfall Project Command

The term Waterfall is used in software development projects and represents a sequential software build methodology. In this model, software is designed, then built, then tested, then released. This approach works well with the methodologies discussed in Parts 1 – 3 and is best supported by the Gantt Chart view. Waterfall is considered the antonym of Agile because rather than delivering a *complete* software solution at the end of a *lengthy* build cycle, Agile delivers *partial* software solutions at the end of *compressed* build cycles (E.g. Sprints).

Kanban Use Cases

Use Case 1 – Sales Kanban Board

Sales teams can use Kanban boards to track customers as they move through the sales process (*Figure 178*). In this use case, each of the columns were labeled to represent typical phases in the sales process. On the Backlog Sheet, the task Name field was used for the company name and the Resource Names field was used for the customer contact name. Notice there is no Add New Column field, because six columns were used in this example, which is the maximum.

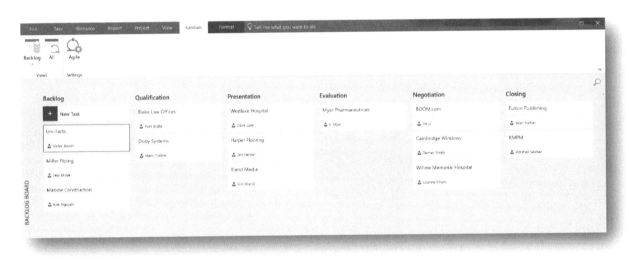

Figure 178 – Sales Kanban Board

Use Case 2 – IT Support Kanban Board

IT Support teams can use Kanban boards to track tickets as they move through the resolution process (*Figure 179*). In this example, each of the columns were labeled to represent typical phases in the ticket resolution process. On the Backlog Sheet, the task Name field was used for the ticket issue description and the Resource Names field was used for the assigned support person.

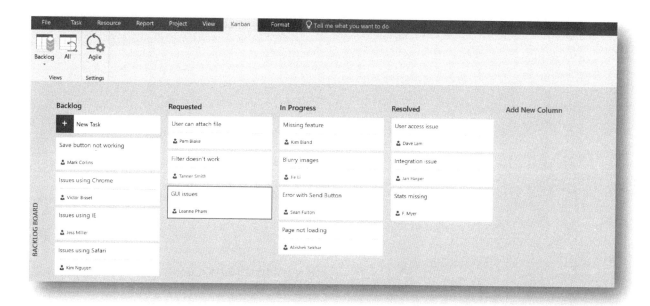

Figure 179 – IT Support Kanban Board

Use Case 3 – Digital Marketing Kanban Board

Digital Marketing professionals can use Kanban boards to track action items (*Figure 180*). In this example, each of the columns were labeled accordingly. On the Backlog Sheet, the task Name field was used for action item descriptions and the Resource Names field was used for the assigned action owners.

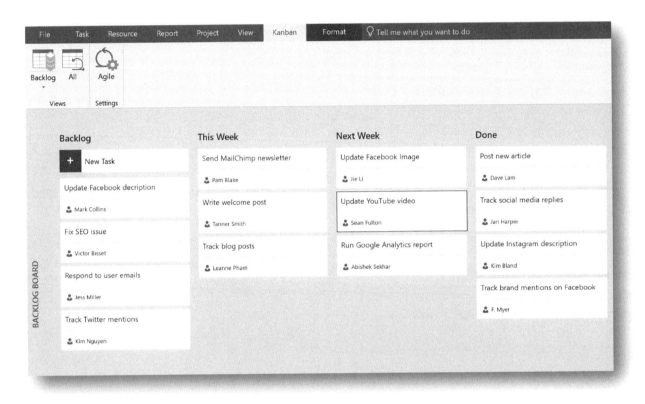

Figure 180 – Digital Marketing Kanban Board

Conclusion

As you can see, there are many ways to apply Kanban boards beyond a software development context. For more examples, visit https://msproject.vhx.tv. When using Kanban, feel free to explore new and interesting use cases. Keep the Agile manifesto values in mind and be flexible and creative in your applications. Value effectiveness over rigidly following the requirements of any Agile approach. In the next two chapters, we'll review the Scrum features and apply them, using a full-fledged software development project.

Now You Can

- Start a Kanban Project

- Use the Kanban Board

- Use the Kanban Ribbon

- Use the Agile Reports

Chapter 24 Using the Scrum Features

IN THIS CHAPTER:

- Starting a Scrum Project
- Understanding the Sprint Boards
- Using the Scrum Ribbon
- Manage Sprints

In the last chapter, we explored the Kanban features available in Project Online. We then applied those features using three contextually different use cases. In this chapter, we'll explore the Scrum features available in the Project Online desktop client. We'll learn to start a Scrum Project, display progress on Boards and manage Sprints using the Scrum Ribbon. When you're done, you'll be able to start a Scrum project, use the Sprint Boards and Manage Sprints using the Scrum Ribbon.

Starting a Scum Project

You can start a Scrum project by selecting the **Scrum Project** template in the opening view of the Project Online desktop client (*Figure 181*).

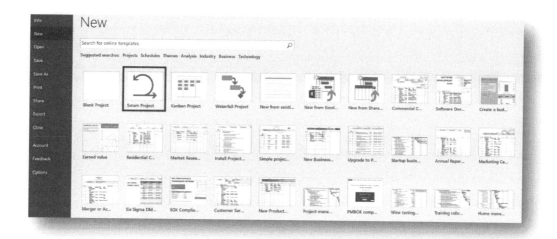

Figure 181 – Sprints Project Command

Understanding the Sprint Planning Board

After selecting the Scrum Project template, you'll be taken to the **Sprint Planning Board** view, shown in *Figure 182*, below. As you can see, this view is essentially a Kanban Board, consisting of Sprints.

Figure 182 – Sprint Planning Board

To add tasks to the board, use the **New Task** command. Simply click the plus sign, enter a task name and select **Add**. By default, new tasks are placed in the **No Sprint** column. To move a task, click and drag the task across the board to the desired Sprint column. By default, this view includes the No Sprint, Sprint 1, Sprint 2 and Sprint 3 columns. Except for the No Sprint column, each column can be renamed by right-clicking on the column header and selecting **Manage Sprints** (*Figure 183*).

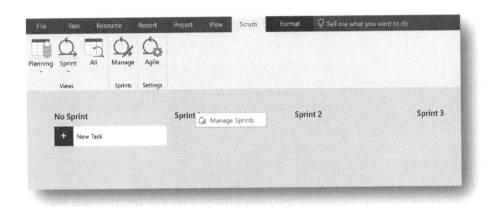

Figure 183 – Manage Sprints

Selecting Manage Sprints will open the *Mange Sprints* dialogue box shown in *Figure 184* below. To change the column names, in the Name field, select the desired Sprint and type over the name.

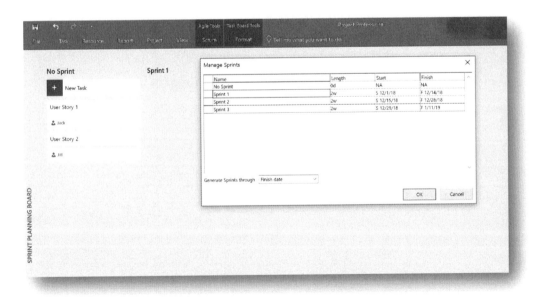

Figure 184 – Renaming Sprints – Manage Sprints Dialogue Box

Using the Scrum Ribbon

When you're in the Sprint Planning Board view, you'll notice that the **Scrum** and **Format** tabs are shaded a darker green. These contextual tabs contain all the tools you'll need to customize and manage Sprints. The **Agile Tools** are located on the Scrum tab. On this ribbon, you'll find the **Planning**, **Sprint**, **All**, **Manage** and **Agile** commands (*Figure 185*). If you don't see these commands, select the Scrum tab. The **Task Board Tools** are located on the Format tab. On this ribbon, you'll find the **Columns** command, which lets you choose which fields are displayed on the Task Board. Your options are Sprint and Board Status.

Figure 185 – The Scrum Ribbon

In the next section, we'll review the commands we haven't covered already in Chapter 23. The **All** and **Agile** commands function the same in the Sprint Planning Board view as they do in the Backlog Board view.

Using the Planning Command

The **Planning** command (*Figure 186* below) lets you see which tasks are scheduled for each Sprint and make any updates. It contains a pick-list which allows quick access to the **Sprint Planning Board** and the **Sprint Planning Sheet** views. This command is similar to the Backlog command on the Kanban ribbon.

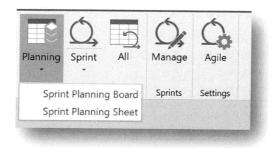

Figure 186 – The Sprint Planning Command

You can use the Sprint Planning Sheet (*Figure 187*) to add tasks to the Sprint Planning Board and place them into the various sprints. You can also add more task information than is available in the Sprint Planning Board view.

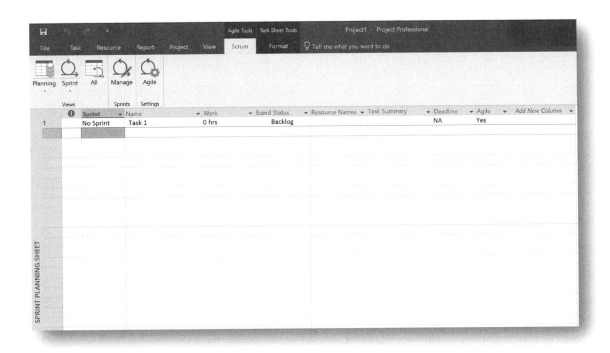

Figure 187 – Sprint Planning Sheet

To add tasks to the Sprint Planning Board from the Sprint Planning Sheet, enter the names in the Name column. To place them in the desired Sprint, select the "No Sprint" cell, then select the desired Sprint from the pick-list. Use the additional fields to add more task information. The Work, Board Status and Resource Names fields function the same in the Sprint Planning Sheet view as they do in the Backlog Sheet view, as described in Chapter 23. The **Task Summary** field is used to display the parent task, if you've defined one. To learn about Summary tasks, see Chapter 4. The **Deadline** field is used to indicate if a task has a deadline applied. If the deadline is exceeded, an alert will be shown in the Indicators column. To learn about deadlines, see Chapter 11. The **Agile** field lets you indicate whether the selected task should be included in Agile views and reports. To make this indication, select the Agile column name, then select Yes or No from the pick-list. As mentioned in Chapter 23, the Agile field can be used as an alternative to the All command, as it displays the same information.

Next, we'll add two user stories to the Sprint Planning Sheet and review the outcome in the Sprint Planning Board. We'll assign 10 hours of work to each task, assign Jack and Jill as resources, place them in Sprints 1 and 2 and use Board Status to place the tasks in the In Progress and Next Up columns. *Figure 188* below shows the populated Sprint Planning sheet.

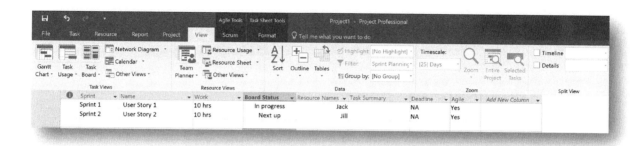

Figure 188 – The Sprint Planning Sheet, Populated

Figure 189 shows the information populated to the Sprint Planning Board. Use the Planning command to access the Sprint Planning Board.

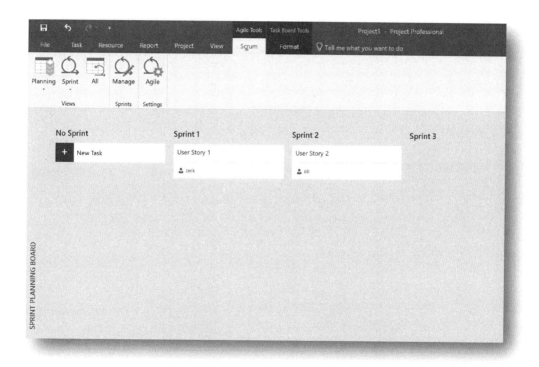

Figure 189 – Updated Sprint Planning Board

Using the Agile Reports

In Figure 189 above, we see the two user stories, and the assigned resources and sprints. We don't see the work hours or the updated Board status. As discussed in Chapter 23, this information can be viewed in the Boards – Work Status report (*Figure 190* below). You can also see the Board status updates in the Current Sprint Board view, which we'll review in the next section.

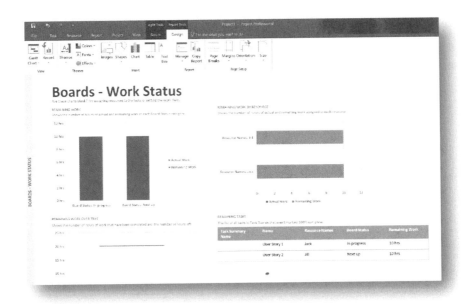

Figure 190 – Boards – Work Status Report

Using the Current Sprint Board Command

The **Current Sprint** command (*Figure 191* below) contains a pick-list which allows quick access to the **Current Sprint Sheet** and the **Current Sprint Board** views. These views allow you to view tasks by Sprints and see how the work is progressing. It functions exactly like the Backlog Command, reviewed in Ch. 23.

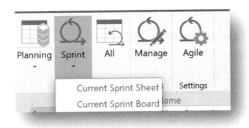

Figure 191 – Current Sprint Command

You can use the Current Sprint Sheet to add tasks to the Current Sprint Board and progress them across the board from Backlog to Done. As with the other Sheet views, you can also add more task information than what is available in the Current Sprint Board view. *Figure 192* below shows the **Current Sprint Sheet**, displaying the information for the example discussed in the previous section. Notice that although we added two user stories, only the data from User Story 1 appears. This is because the <u>current</u> sprint is Sprint 1 and User Story 2 is in Sprint 2. You may be wondering "How does Project know what the current Sprint is?" We'll answer that question when we review the Manage Sprints command.

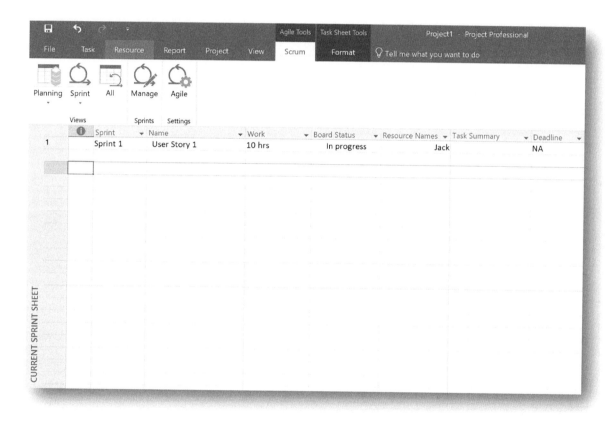

Figure 192 – Current Sprint Sheet

You can use the Current Sprint Sheet to add tasks to the Current Sprint Board by entering them in the Name column. To progress them across the board from Backlog to Done, select the desired status from the pick-list in the Board Status column. As with the previous sheet views, you can add more task information in the Current Sprint Sheet view than in the Current Sprint Board view.

Figure 193 below shows the Current Sprint Board. As expected, it only shows User Story 1 because the current sprint is Sprint 1.

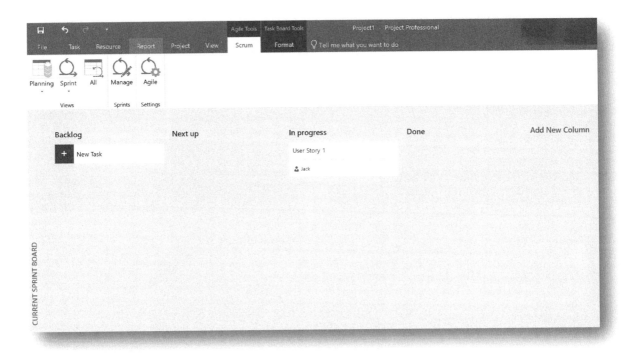

Figure 193 – Current Sprint Board

Using the Manage Sprints Command

The **Manage Sprints** command lets you manage Sprint dates and names. You can use the *Manage Sprints* dialogue box (*Figure 194* below) to generate Sprints, enter unique Sprint names and change Sprint details, such as the duration, start and finish dates. By default, three Sprints are generated with 2-week durations.

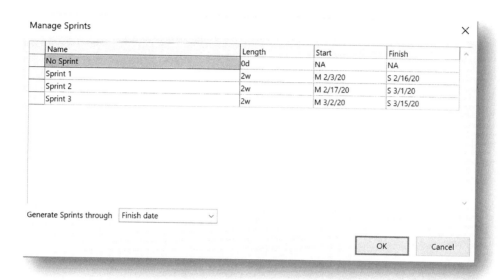

Figure 194 – Manage Sprints Dialogue Box

To quickly generate more Sprints, in the **Generate Sprints through** field, toggle from Finish date to **Custom date**. Then, enter the date in the **Custom date** field. In *Figure 195*, below the Custom date has been set to 5/1/20. Since the project start date is 2/3/20, four additional Sprints were generated. To change Sprint details, such as the length, start or finish date, enter the values directly into the respective fields.

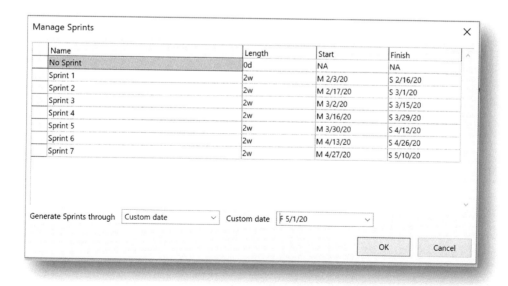

Figure 195 – Manage Sprints Dialogue box – Entering Custom Dates

You can also generate Sprints by scheduling from the project Finish date. To review how to do this, revisit Chapter 12.

Conclusion

As you can see, the new Agile and Scrum features in Project provide a simple, and customizable environment for managing Agile workflows. In the next Chapter, we'll put these features to use on a full-fledged software development project.

Now You Can

- Start a Scrum Project
- Understand the Sprint Boards
- Use the Scrum Ribbon
- Manage Sprints

Chapter 25 An Agile Use Case - Putting it All Together

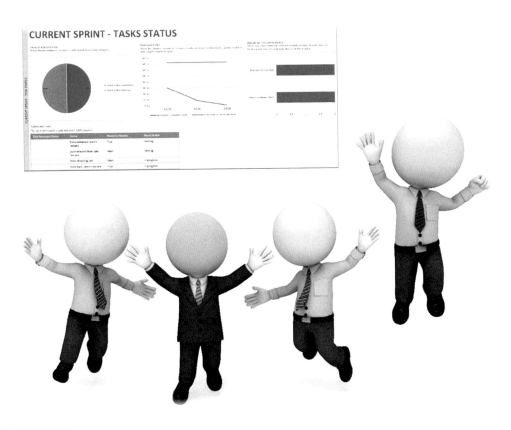

IN THIS CHAPTER:

- An Agile Use Case – Software Development Project

- Entering Progress Data

- Using the 5 Agile Reports: *Boards – Task Status, Boards – Work Status, Current Sprint - Task Status, Current Sprint – Work Status and Sprint Status*

In the last chapter, we explored the Scrum features available in the Project Online desktop client. We learned to start a Scrum Project, display progress on Boards, and Manage Sprints using the Scrum Ribbon. In this chapter, we'll put those features to use on a full-fledged software development project. We'll enter the project information, enter progress data and see how project data is displayed in each of the five Agile reports. Let's get started!

Project Description

Your client sells niche products in a brick-and mortar store and is seeking to grow their business by selling online. Your project is to apply an Agile approach to help the client build a custom e-commerce website. The client has requested the site be implemented within 8 weeks of funding approval and has provided examples of the type of online store they want. You have a small team of two developers and each is only available 20 hours per week. You've met with the client, your project team and relevant stakeholders and have developed a list of abridged user stories. Your team has reviewed each user story, collaborated with the client sponsor and assigned a work estimate to each user story. *Figure 196* below summarizes your project inputs.

User Story	Developer	Work (Hours)
Build basic search feature	Puja	10
Build shopping cart	Mark	10
Build removal from cart feature	Mark	7.5
Build billing interface	Puja	20
Build account set-up feature	Puja	20
Build inventory add-in feature	Mark	10
Build inventory removal feature	Mark	7.5
Build product editing feature	Mark	10
Build enhanced search feature	Puja	10
Build account editing feature	Mark	10
Build recommendation feature	Mark/Puja	40

Figure 196 – Agile Project Inputs

Step 1 – Select a Scheduling Methodology

Software development projects are known to have unstable requirements, so you agree with your client's recommendation to use an Agile, rather than a Waterfall approach. Since your client has an aggressive deadline (8 weeks) and has provided examples of the type of online store they want, you decide to use Scrum, rather than Kanban.

Your reasoning is two-fold:

1. The online store examples will help stabilize requirements, which makes it easier to estimate the work.

2. The use of Sprints will help you to match the client's schedule requirement to your team's availability and organize deliverables into four time-boxed periods, lasting two weeks each.

Step 2 – Start the Scrum Project

From the opening view of Project, select the **Scrum Project** template (*Figure 197*).

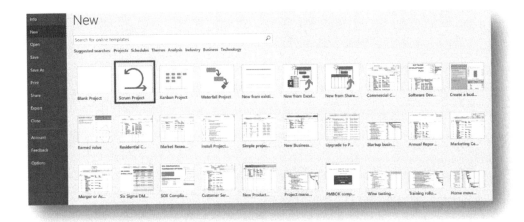

Figure 197 – Starting a Scrum Project

This will open the Sprint Planning Board (*Figure 198*). By default, Project generates 3 Sprints.

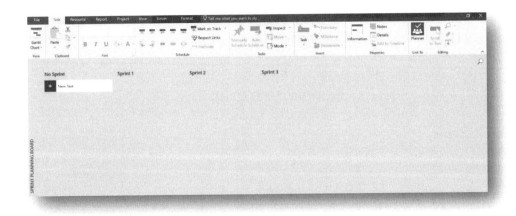

Figure 198 – Sprint Planning Board

Step 3 – Enter Tasks

Use the **New Task** field to enter the 11 user stories. *Figure 199* below shows the finished result.

Note: If you're doing the steps, we entered starting from the bottom of the list, to match the task sequence in *Figure 196*.

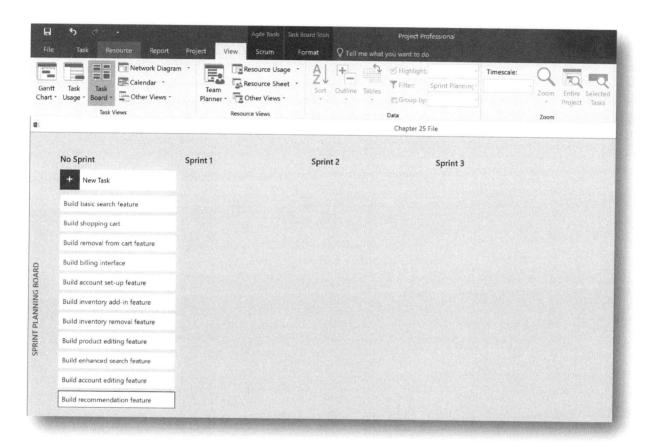

Figure 199 – Sprint Planning Board, Populated

Step 4 – Set the Project Start Date

The client has advised you that funding will be approved on 3/2/20. This will be the project start date.

To set the project start date:

1. Select the **Project** tab to access the Project ribbon.

2. In the **Properties** group, select the **Project Information** command to open the *Project Information* dialogue box.

3. Enter 3/2/20 in the **Start date** field. Since we will be pulling reports, we'll also set the "Current" date to 3/2/20 by entering it in the **Current date** field. Then, click **OK**. For a review on setting the Project start date, see Chapter 7.

Step 5 – Generate a New Sprint

As discussed earlier, we will need four 2-week Sprints to complete the project. Since Project created only three Sprints by default, we'll need to add a fourth one. To do so, select the **Scrum** tab, then select the **Manage Sprints** command to open the *Mange Sprints* dialogue box. If you set the start date correctly in Step 4, your *Manage Sprints* dialogue box should look like *Figure 200*, below.

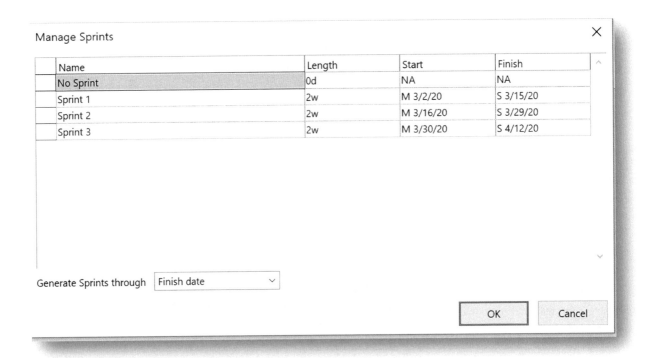

Figure 200 – Manage Sprints Dialogue box

To add the fourth Sprint, in the **Generate Sprints through** field, toggle from Finish date to Custom date. Then, in the **Custom date** field, set the date to 4/26/20. *Figure 201* below shows the updated *Managed Sprints* dialogue box.

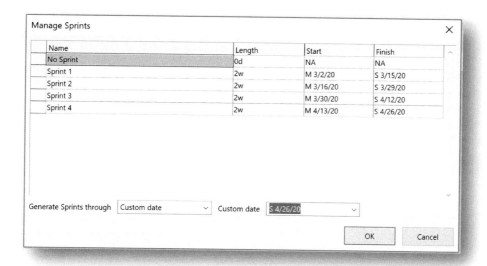

Figure 201 – Manage Sprints Dialogue box, Using Custom Dates

Click **OK** to close the dialogue box and return to the Sprint Planning Board view. *Figure 202* below shows the updated Sprint Planning Board, which includes the fourth Sprint.

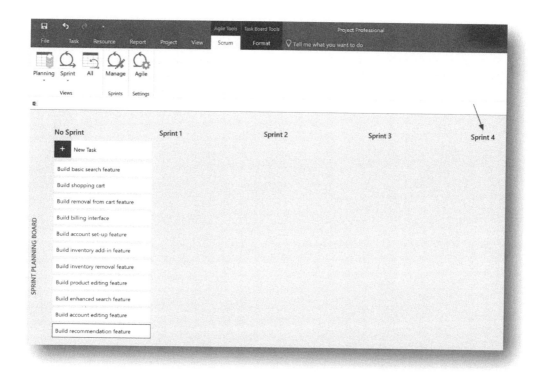

Figure 202 – Sprint Planning Board view – New Sprint Added

Step 6 – Add Resource Names and Work Estimates

Before moving the tasks into Sprints, let's add the resource names and work estimates to each task. This information is entered on the Sprint Planning Sheet. Use the **Planning** command on the Scrum ribbon (*Figure 203)* to switch to the Sprint Planning Sheet.

Figure 203 – Planning Command

Figure 204 below shows the Sprint Planning Sheet with work estimates and resources assigned.

	Sprint	Name	Work	Board Status	Resource Names	Task Summary	Deadline	Agile	Add New Column
11	No Sprint	Build basic search feature	10 hrs	Backlog	Puja		NA	Yes	
10	No Sprint	Build shopping cart	10 hrs	Backlog	Mark		NA	Yes	
9	No Sprint	Build removal from cart feature	7.5 hrs	Backlog	Mark		NA	Yes	
8	No Sprint	Build billing interface	20 hrs	Backlog	Puja		NA	Yes	
7	No Sprint	Build account set-up feature	20 hrs	Backlog	Puja		NA	Yes	
6	No Sprint	Build inventory add-in feature	10 hrs	Backlog	Mark		NA	Yes	
5	No Sprint	Build inventory removal feature	7.5 hrs	Backlog	Mark		NA	Yes	
4	No Sprint	Build product editing feature	10 hrs	Backlog	Mark		NA	Yes	
3	No Sprint	Build enhanced search feature	10 hrs	Backlog	Puja		NA	Yes	
2	No Sprint	Build account editing feature	10 hrs	Backlog	Mark		NA	Yes	
1	No Sprint	Build recommendation feature	40 hrs	Backlog	Mark,Puja		NA	Yes	

Figure 204 –Sprint Planning Sheet

Step 7 – Organize Task by Sprints

Next, we'll organize the tasks into their appropriate Sprints. We could do this in the Sprint Planning Sheet by selecting "No Sprint" for each task, and then selecting the appropriate Sprint. However, it can be done much faster (and funner!) on the Sprint Planning Board, by simply clicking and dragging tasks across the board into their appropriate Sprint. Using the Planning command, let's switch to the Sprint Planning Board and drag each task to its appropriate Sprint. We'll need to respect the 20-hour per week maximum bandwidth for each resource as we select the Sprints. *Figure 205* shows an updated Sprint Planning Board that respects the resource availability limits.

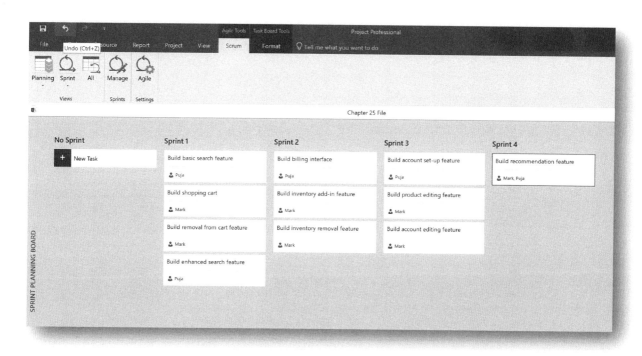

Figure 205 – Updated Sprint Planning Board

Step 8 – Update Board Status for the Current Sprint

We're almost ready to present the plan to the client! Before we do, let's change the Board Status for the tasks in Sprint 1. We'll place 10 hours of work per resource in the **In Progress** column and 10 hours of work per resource in the **Next Up** column. To make these updates, we'll use the **Planning** command to switch back to the Sprint Planning Sheet. If you're following along, notice that the "Sprint" column is now populated, based on the work we did in Step 7. Using the **Board Status** column, toggle the first and second tasks in Sprint 1 to **In Progress** and the third and fourth tasks to **Next Up**. *Figure 206* below shows the updated Sprint Planning Sheet.

Figure 206 – Updated Sprint Planning Sheet

Let's switch to the Current Sprint Board to see the effect of these updates. On the **Scrum** ribbon, select **Current Sprint Board** from the **Sprint** command pick-list. *Figure 207* below shows the Board Status of all the tasks in the current Sprint. If you're following along and don't see any tasks populated in this view, you'll need to set the current date to 3/2/20. Review Step 4 for instructions.

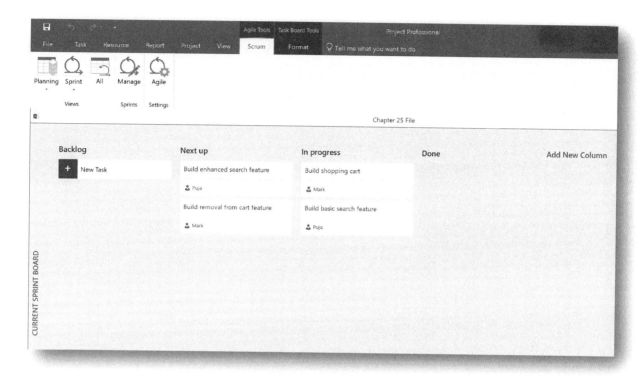

Figure 207 – Current Sprint Board

Step 9 – Enter Progress data and pull Agile Reports

You're now ready to present the plan to the client! We'll use the Agile reports to make an excellent first impression. You've been advised that Mark and Puja have each completed 5 hours of work on the tasks that are In progress. Before we pull the reports, let's enter their progress data in the Current Sprint Planning Sheet. Using the Sprint command, switch to the Current Sprint Sheet. Using the **Add New Column** field, add the **Actual Work** column. Enter Mark and Puja's progress data in the Actual Work column. *Figure 208* shows the updated Current Sprint Sheet.

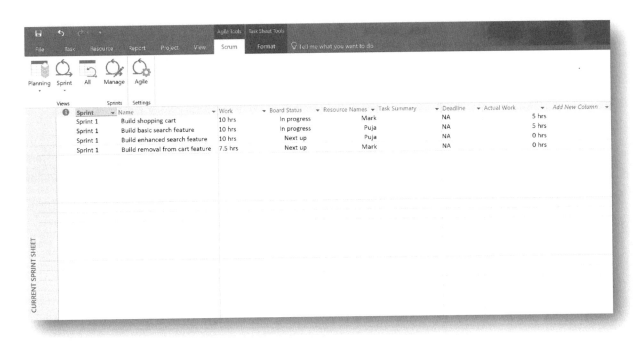

Figure 208 – Current Sprint Sheet with Actual Work

Ready to show off your work? Select the **Report** tab to access the Report ribbon. In the **View Reports** group, select the **Agile** command pick-list. The available Agile reports include the **Boards - Task Status**, **Boards - Work Status**, **Current Sprint - Task Status**, **Current Sprint - Work Status** and **Sprint Status** reports. We'll review each Agile report and send them to the client.

Step 10 –Pull the Agile Report: "Boards – Task Status"

Figure 209 below shows a partial view of the **Boards – Task Status** Agile report. This view includes four graphical elements. Each is described below.

- Tasks by Board Status – A pie chart, showing the percentage of tasks in each Board Status category

- Remaining Tasks – A table, showing all tasks in Task Boards that are not 100% complete

- Remaining Tasks – A burn-down report, showing work on tasks over time

- Remaining Tasks by Resources – A bar chart, showing remaining tasks per resource

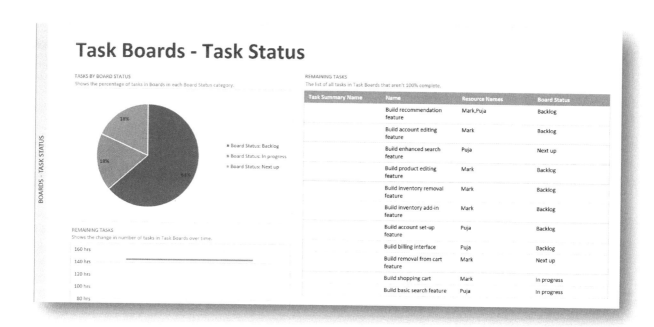

Figure 209 – Boards – Task Status Repot

Step 11 – Pull the Agile Report: "Boards – Work Status"

Figure 210 below shows a partial view of the **Boards – Work Status** Agile report. This view includes four graphical elements. Each is described below.

- Remaining Work – A bar chart, showing Actual and Remaining Work in each Board Status category
- Remaining Work by Resources – A bar chart, showing actual and remaining work per resource
- Remaining Work over Time – A burn-down report, showing remaining work over time
- Remaining Tasks – A table, showing details for tasks that are not 100% complete

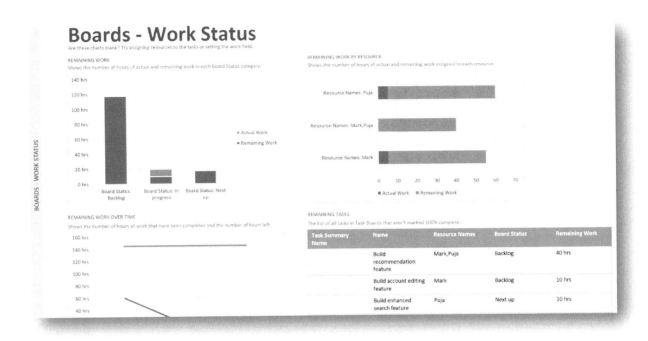

Figure 210 – Boards – Work Status Repot

Step 12 – Pull the Agile Report: "Current Sprint – Task Status"

Figure 211 below shows the **Current Sprint – Task Status** Agile report. This view includes four graphical elements. Each is described below.

- Tasks by Board Status – A pie chart, showing the percentage of tasks in each Board Status category

- Remaining Tasks – A burn-down report, showing remaining work on tasks over time

- Remaining Tasks by Resources – A bar chart, showing remaining tasks per resource

- Remaining Tasks – A table, showing all tasks in Task Boards that are not 100% complete

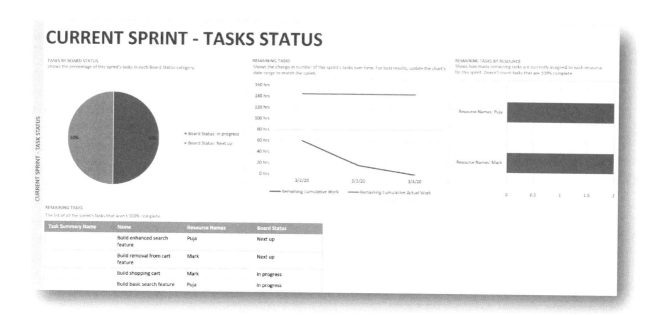

Figure 211 – Current Sprint – Task Status Repot

Step 13 – Pull the Agile Report: "Current Sprint – Work Status"

Figure 212 below shows the **Current Sprint – Work Status** Agile report. This view includes four graphical elements. Each is described below.

- Remaining Work – A bar chart, showing Actual and Remaining Work in each Board Status category

- Remaining Work by Resources – A bar chart, showing actual and remaining work per resource

- Remaining Work over Time – A burn-down report, showing work on tasks over time

- Remaining Tasks – A table, showing the all tasks in Task Boards that are not 100% complete

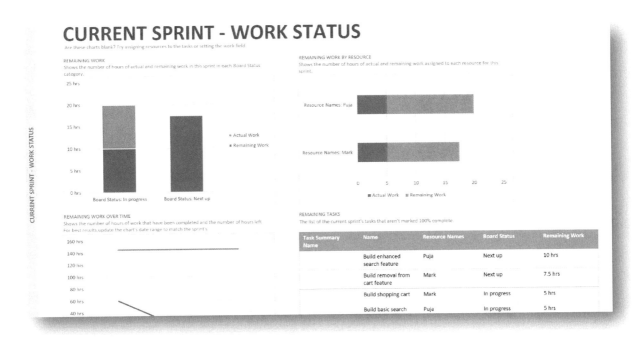

Figure 212 – Current Sprint – Work Status Report

Step 14 – Pull the Agile Report: "Sprint Status"

Figure 213 below shows the **Sprint Status** Agile report. This view includes two graphical elements. Each is described below.

- Tasks per Sprint – A bar chart, showing number of tasks per Sprint
- Work per Sprint – A bar chart, showing Actual and Remaining Work hours per Sprint

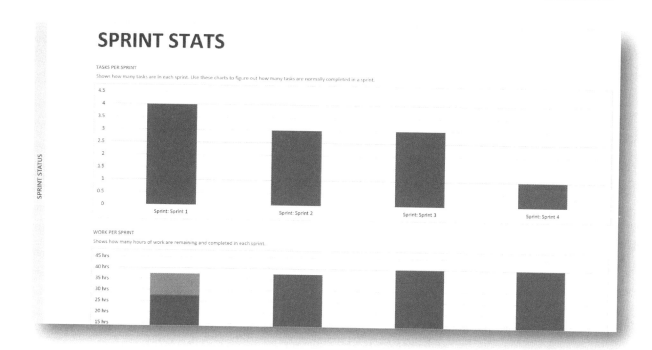

Figure 213 – Sprint Status Report

Conclusion

We've now put the Agile features to use on a full-fledged software development project. We've entered project information, progress data and accessed each Agile report. These reports will make an excellent impression as you work with internal and external clients.

Now You Can

- Execute an Agile Project

- Enter Progress Data

- Use the Boards – Task Status Report

- Use the Boards – Work Status Report

- Use the Current Sprint - Task Status Report

- Use the Current Sprint - Work Status Report

- Use the Sprint Status Report

Video Series

THANK YOU for learning with PMplicity! This book is also available as a streaming video series. It includes a free 30-day trial, software demos and bonus material.

Watch the free trailer at https://msproject.vhx.tv

More Resources

Be sure to bookmark the companion website for this book www.mspbasics.com. You'll find more resources in the ever-expanding "Tips and Tools" section.

For more PMplicity offerings, visit www.pmplicity.com

Glossary

24-Hours Base Calendar – one of three Base calendars in Project used to determine working times for tasks and resources. It has no defined working times and runs continuously.

Actuals – a task's progress data, such as Actual Duration and Remaining Duration.

Actual Duration – the number of working days spent performing a task; mathematically, it is Duration minus Remaining Duration.

Actual Finish – the actual date the task finished.

Actual Start – the actual date the task started.

Actual Variance – Variance that cannot be adjusted, as it does not include remaining cost.

Actual Work – the number of working hours spent performing a task; mathematically, it is Work minus Remaining Work.

Agile – a software development approach, whereby requirements and solutions evolve through the collaborative efforts of a self-organizing, cross functional team consisting of developers, customers, end users, team leaders and project managers.

Assignment – the matching of a resource to a task.

Assignment Units – the percentage of the day resources will work on specific tasks. Assignment Units values are entered in the *Units* field of the *Assign Resources* dialogue box.

AutoFilter – a Microsoft Project feature that allows you to quickly sort, group, or filter task or resource data in a table.

Automatic Scheduling Mode – the scheduling mode in which Project automatically calculates the start, finish and duration values for a task, based on dependencies, constraints, calendars and other factors.

Automatic Resource Leveling – a feature that allows Project to resolve conflicts or over-allocated resources by delaying or splitting tasks, based on the settings in the *Leveling Options* dialogue box.

Backstage View – the view accessed from the File tab, where you manage files and adjust project settings.

Backlog – a list of all the tasks required to deliver a project. It replaces traditional requirements documentation and consists of user-defined requirements, called user stories.

Base Calendar – the calendar that defines the working and non-working times for the project, tasks and resources. Project includes three base calendars – Standard, Night Shift and 24 hours.

Baseline – a saved copy of the original schedule. It includes the original start and finish dates and the original duration, work, and cost estimates. It also includes a time-phased distribution of work, duration, cost, and resource allocation.

Bottom-Up Planning – a method of planning a project, that begins with identifying the tasks in a project, and then organizing them into the major categories or phases of the project.

Budget Cost Resource – a Cost resource that is used as a placeholder for the Project Budget. It is assigned to the Project Summary Task only and cannot be assigned to individual tasks.

Burndown Chart – a graphical representation of the remaining work on a project, where work is shown on the vertical axis and time is shown on the horizontal axis. For example, if a project requires 400 hours of work, this chart will show the pace at which the work "burns down" to completion across a plot line that descends (or burns down) from left to right.

Change Highlighting – a Microsoft Project feature that highlights the values in the schedule that changed due to a schedule edit.

Constraint – a restriction applied to a task that impacts the start or finish date of a task. There are eight constraint types available in Microsoft Project (see Chapter 12 for more details).

Cost Resource – a resource type that acts as a placeholder to capture non-recurring cost items that don't accrue via an hourly rate and cannot be classified as consumable. There are two types of Cost resources – Budget and Expense.

Critical Path – the series of task durations (spanning from the start of the project to the finish of the project) whose collective sum equals the project duration.

Deadline – a Microsoft Project feature that allows you to flag a task with the latest date you'd like it to finish.

Detailed Scheduling (also known as an effort-driven scheduling) – a method of schedule building in which task durations are determined by estimating task work (Work) and resource availability (Units).

Driving Predecessors – predecessor tasks that directly impact or "drive" the start of a successor task.

Duration – the number of working days estimated to complete a task; mathematically, it is the sum of Actual Duration and Remaining Duration.

Duration Equation – the scheduling formula (Duration = Work / Units) that Microsoft Project uses to calculate duration.

Earned Value – a method of measuring project performance. It indicates how much of the budget and time should have been spent, in view of the amount of work done so far.

Effort-Driven Scheduling – a Microsoft Project scheduling feature that keeps the work value constant (or fixed) and enables the duration value to increase or decrease as you assign resources to or remove resources from a task.

Elapsed Duration – an uninterrupted span of time (24-hours days; 7-day weeks) allotted to complete a task. Elapsed duration is not interrupted by project, resource or task calendars.

Entry Table – the table in the Gantt Chart view, where scheduling information is entered about the tasks in the schedule.

Estimated Variance – Variance that can be adjusted, as it includes remaining cost.

External Links – a link between two interdependent schedules, using external predecessors.

Filtering – the extraction of task or resource data that meets user-defined criteria.

Fixed Consumption Rate – the fixed rate at with a Material resource is consumed (e.g. Paint may be consumed at $75 per Gallon).

Fixed Duration a Task Type setting in which the Duration value is fixed.

Fixed Units – a Task Type setting in which the Units value is fixed.

Fixed Work – a Task Type setting in which the Work value is fixed.

Free Slack – the number of days a task can be delayed before it will delay another task(s).

Gantt Chart – a combination view in Project that includes the Entry table on the left and a graphical view on the right, which depicts the tasks in the schedule, their durations and the how they relate to one another.

Grouping – the resequencing and grouping of task or resource data into a table that summarizes the group values you specify.

Inserted Plan (also known as a subproject) – a project plan that is inserted into another project plan to create a Master Project plan.

Interim Plan (also known as an Interim Baseline) – a saved, partial copy of the original schedule. Unlike a full baseline, it only includes the current start and finish dates for all tasks and excludes resource and time-phased values.

Kanban – an application of the Agile approach that uses a visual system (called a Kanban board) for managing work as it moves through a process.

Kanban Board – a workflow visualization tool that typically uses sticky notes on a whiteboard to communicate status, progress, and issues. Kanban is the Japanese word for "visual signal" or "card."

Lag Time – the number of days a successor task is delayed after its predecessor finishes. Lag time is entered in the Predecessors field (E.g. 5FS + 2 days).

Glossary

Lead Time – the number of days a successor task can start before its predecessor finishes. Lead time is entered in the Predecessors field (E.g. 5FS – 2 days)

Manual Scheduling Mode – the scheduling mode in which Project does not automatically calculate the start, finish and duration values for a task. In this mode, users have the option of scheduling tasks manually.

Master Project (also called a Consolidated Project Plan) – a Microsoft Project file that contains multiple Inserted Project files consolidated into one project plan.

Material Resources – consumable supplies that are priced by the amount consumed.

Maximum (Max.) Units – the maximum capacity a resource(s) is available to work on tasks on any given day. This value is entered in the *Max. Units* field of the Resource Sheet view. The default value is 100%.

Milestone – a task that is used to signify the completion of a significant project event. Milestones generally don't include project work, so they have a zero duration.

Night Shift Base Calendar – one of three Base calendars in Project used to determine working times for tasks and resources. It supports a Monday night thru Saturday morning; 11:00 pm – 8:00 am (1-hour lunch break from 3:00 am to 4:00 am) schedule.

Over-allocation – the condition in which a resource is scheduled to work on tasks beyond their maximum capacity (Max. Units value).

Predecessor – a task whose start or finish date determines the start or finish date of another task or tasks.

Progress Bar – a graphical indicator on the task bar in the Gantt Chart that shows how much of a task has been completed.

Project Calendar – the Base calendar that defines the working and non-working times for the entire project. One of the three Base calendars in Project is designated as a template for the Project Calendar. It can be modified to reflect the working and non-working times for individual projects.

Project Summary Task – the summary task that displays the overall values of a project. It's the highest level of the project outline and is assigned task ID zero.

Remaining Duration – the number of remaining working days estimated to complete a task; mathematically, it is Duration minus Actual Duration.

Remaining Work – the amount of time still required to complete a task(s). Project calculates Remaining Work as Work – Actual Work.

Resource – a person or thing required to complete a project. In Microsoft Project, there are three types of resources – Work, Material and Cost.

Resource Calendar – the Base calendar that is used to define the working and non-working times for a resource.

Resource Sheet view – a view that displays resource information for the entire project in a spreadsheet-like table. It includes information like pay rates and resource groups.

Resource Leveling – the re-distribution of resource assignments or resource assignment units to resolve (or level) the condition of over-committed (or over-allocated) resources.

Resource Pool – a Microsoft Project file that only includes resource information (in the Resource Sheet view) for resources that are shared across projects.

Scrum – an application of the Agile approach, whereby teams address complex adaptive problems, while delivering incremental value on a continuous delivery cycle (usually 2 weeks).

Sharer Plan – a project plan that is linked to a resource pool.

Simple Scheduling (also known as duration-based scheduling) – a method of schedule building in which task durations are estimated and entered directly into the Duration field.

Slack (also known as Float) – the number of days a task can be delayed before it will delay another task(s) or the project schedule. There are two types of Slack – Free Slack and Total Slack.

Sorting – the resequencing of task or resource data per user-defined criteria.

Sprint – a time-boxed period (usually 2 weeks), within which to deliver value to a client.

Standard Base Calendar – one of three Base calendars in Project used to determine working times for tasks and resources. The "Standard" base calendar is the default calendar in Project. It supports a Monday thru Friday; 8:00 am – 5:00 pm (1-hour lunch break from 12:00 pm to 1:00 pm) schedule.

Status Date – the date on which the latest progress data was collected and entered in project.

Story Points – a measure of the effort required to implement a **User Story**. In Microsoft Project, this measure is most like the Work estimate.

Subtask – a task demoted beneath a Summary task.

Successor – a task whose start or finish date is determined by the start or finish date of another task or tasks.

Summary Task – a task with subtasks demoted under it. They are represented in Project in bold typeface and are used to group tasks into phases and sub-phases.

Task – an activity with a unique task ID, indicated numerically in the Entry table of the Gantt chart view. Minimally, it has a duration, a start date, and a finish date.

Task Calendar – the Base calendar that is used to define the working and non-working times for a task.

Task ID – a unique number that Project assigns to each task in a project plan.

Task Inspector – a Microsoft Project feature that allows you to view detailed scheduling information for a specific task, including Scheduling Mode, Start and Finish dates, Predecessor information, Calendars and Constraints.

Task Mode – indicates whether tasks are Automatically or Manually scheduled.

Task Relationship – a dependency (or link) between two or more tasks. There are four task relationship types – Finish-to-Start (FS), Start-to-Start (SS), Finish-to-Finish (FF) and Start-to-Finish (SF).

Task Type – a setting applied to a task that fixes the Work, Units or Duration value, and determines how Project schedules the task. There are three task types available in Project – Fixed Units, Fixed Duration and Fixed Work.

Templates – the starter project plans included in Project for typical business and personal projects.

Timeline View – a customizable view that shows a summary of the project schedule or highlights a selected section of the schedule.

Timescale – a scale shown in views like the Gantt chart view, which depicts units of time, ranging from minutes to years.

Top-Down Planning – a method of planning a project that begins with identifying the major categories of work in a project, and then breaking them down into smaller categories or tasks.

Total Slack – the number of days a task can be delayed before it will delay the project schedule.

Triple Constraints – a project management term for the trade-off between scope, schedule and cost when managing a project.

Units – the percentage an 8-hour work day a resource is assigned to work on a task.

User Story – a tool used in **Agile** software development to capture a description of a software feature from an end-**user** perspective. It describes the type of **user**, what they want and why. It helps to create a simplified description of a requirement.

Variable Consumption Rate – the rate at with a Material resource is consumed per a specified unit of time (e.g. Paint may be consumed at $75 per Gallon, and at a rate if 1 gallon per hour).

Variance – the difference between the Baseline cost and Total cost for a task, resource, or assignment. Project calculate Cost Variance as Cost – Baseline cost. Therefore, positive variance is unfavorable and negative variance is favorable.

Velocity – a key metric in the Scrum methodology that measures the amount of work a team can tackle during a single Sprint. **Velocity** is calculated at the end of each Sprint by totaling the **Story Points** for all fully completed **User Stories**.

Work – the number of working hours required to complete a task.

Work Breakdown Structure – a deliverable-oriented, hierarchical decomposition of the work required to complete a project.

Work Breakdown Structure Coding Scheme – a system of numbering tasks that shows their hierarchical position in the project outline.

Work In Progress Limits – a limit placed on the work in progress, that is determined by the team's development capacity.

Work Resources – resources that have an hourly rate and a calendar. They can be people, equipment, or rentals, such as a conference room or a crane. They can also be generic, representing a trade or professional group, such as Engineers or Architects.

Index

A

Action Indicator · 72, 73, 79
Actual Cost · 247, 249, 252, 255, 265, 292
Actual Duration · 230-233, 241, 242, 244, 386, 388, 391
Actual Finish · 230, 231, 236, 292, 386
Actual Start · 230-233, 236, 241, 242, 244, 258, 259, 261, 262, 292, 386
Actual Variance · 248, 386
Actual Work · 230-236, 258, 259, 261, 262, 310, 348, 376, 377, 386, 391
ACWP · 249
Add New Column · 76, 77, 85, 119, 124, 126, 168, 169, 197, 227, 232, 233, 241, 242, 251, 252, 258, 259, 313, 315, 344, 349, 351, 376
Agile · 271, 333-351, 353, 354, 358, 359, 361, 365, 367, 368, 376-383, 386, 389, 391, 393
Agile Manifesto · 336, 337
Assign Resources · 15, 78, 86, 104, 109, 114, 116, 117, 119, 120, 121, 124, 125, 126, 127, 129, 194, 195, 201, 251, 386
Assignments · 104, 119, 126, 195, 201, 251, 284
Auto-Filter · 215, 216, 313, 315

B

B.A.S.I.C.S. · 96-98, 106, 107, 111-113, 122, 128, 222, 224, 239, 245, 256, 329, 330, 332
BAC · 249
Backlog · 336-339, 343-353, 358, 359, 361, 362, 387
Bar Styles · 160, 164, 168
Base Calendar · 117, 130, 131, 135, 136, 139, 143, 386, 387, 390, 392
Baseline · 15, 27, 224-229, 232, 233, 237, 238, 240, 246, 248, 249, 253, 257, 260, 263, 293, 328, 329, 387, 389, 393
Baseline Cost · 249, 253
Blank Project · 12, 30, 54, 75, 107, 122, 282, 283, 350
Bottom-up Planning · 36
Budget Cost Resource · 249, 250, 387
Burndown Chart · 387

C

Calendar · 21, 65, 114, 117, 130-146, 154, 165, 180, 206, 285, 386, 387, 390-394
Change Highlighting · 6, 139, 158, 387
Change Working Time · 15, 132, 133, 134, 135, 139, 140

Combination View · 29
Compare Projects · 291, 293-295, 298
Consolidated Project · 281, 282, 288, 390
Constraint · 2, 7, 8, 9, 61, 65, 67, 100, 166, 174-183, 188, 193, 194, 200, 202, 207, 218, 222, 325, 326, 330, 386, 387, 392, 393
Consumption Rate · 114, 389, 393
Copy · 211, 227, 228, 265-267, 269, 273-280
Copy Picture · 265-267, 269, 273, 275, 279
Copy Report · 273, 277
Copy Timeline · 269, 273, 277
Cost Performance Index · 249
Cost Table · 252, 260
Cost Variance · 247, 249, 252, 253, 264, 265, 393
Critical Path · 5, 16, 157-181, 206, 237, 272, 281, 321, 388
Current date · 198, 241, 243, 258, 261, 371
Custom Field · 119, 311-317
Custom Group · 205, 211, 213, 221, 304
Customize · 302, 305

D

Deadline · 164-172, 239, 256, 359, 388
Detailed Schedule · 82-87, 90-94, 97, 104, 105, 112, 122, 234, 256, 388
Driving Predecessor · 158, 164, 388
Duration · 8, 44, 55, 56, 60, 62, 66, 70-91, 98-100, 103, 104, 108, 109, 127, 130, 137, 143, 171, 207, 226, 230-234, 241, 242, 244, 292, 311, 324, 330, 386, 388, 389, 391, 393
Duration Equation · 60, 70, 71, 73, 79, 80, 81, 87, 103, 388

E

Earned Value · 88, 89, 92, 228, 231, 247, 248, 249, 253, 254, 255, 264, 265, 272, 321, 388
Effort-Driven · 60, 71, 72, 77, 79, 81, 207, 388
Effort-Driven Scheduling · 60, 71, 72, 79, 81, 388
Elapsed Duration · 130, 137, 143, 388
Entry Table · 17, 77, 193, 261, 322, 388
Estimate at Completion · 249
Estimated Duration · 127, 128, 324
Estimated Variance · 248, 388
Exception · 6, 130-134, 139, 140, 179, 181
Exceptions · 133, 134, 139, 141, 199
Export · 30, 265, 269, 270, 273, 280, 305
External Link · 280, 286-290, 389

F

Field List · 272, 310
Field Name · 212, 217
Field Settings · 314
Filter · 205, 207, 208, 210, 214-218, 221, 232, 241-244, 258, 260-262, 310, 313, 315, 389
Finish No Earlier Than · 67, 175, 326
Finish No Later Than · 175
Finish-to-Finish · 49, 392
Finish-to-Start · 49, 50, 51, 52, 57, 77, 110, 127, 162, 170, 171, 286, 287, 392
Fixed Consumption Rate · 114, 389
Fixed Cost · 252
Fixed Duration · 73, 76-79, 89, 99, 108, 389, 393
Fixed Units · 73, 79, 80, 90, 99, 123, 389, 393
Fixed Work · 73, 74, 389, 393
Free Slack · 158, 159, 169, 389, 391

G

Gantt Chart · 5, 12-20, 27, 28, 38, 43, 44, 56, 83, 101, 107, 108, 119, 120-125, 136, 138, 142, 152, 155, 160, 168, 177, 184, 193, 200, 215, 232, 235, 237, 251, 252, 260, 265, 266, 274, 275, 279, 295, 299, 300, 308, 319,322, 331, 344, 350, 351, 388, 389, 390
Gridlines · 306, 310
Group · 116, 125, 205, 207-214, 221, 304, 389
Group by · 211-214
Group on this Field · 210

H

Hide Column · 275
Hyperlink · 144, 147-156, 292

I

Import · 305, 312
Indent Task · 15, 45, 46, 55, 76, 101, 108, 123, 327
Indicator · 65, 72, 73, 79, 110, 117, 127, 147-155, 164, 170, 172, 177, 180, 184, 198, 242, 244, 253, 259, 262, 282, 292, 299, 300, 305-307, 313, 316-319, 323, 326, 359
Insert Object · 152
Insert Task · 43
Inspect · 35, 55-57, 78, 109, 110, 125, 126, 206, 219
Interim Plan · 227-229, 389

K

Kanban · 333-346, 348, 350-356, 358, 368, 389

L

Lag · 51-53, 58, 59, 105, 389
Late Tasks · 232, 241, 243, 258, 261, 272
Lead · 51-53, 59, 157, 158, 161, 162, 166, 167, 170-174, 178, 199-202, 233, 235, 236, 390
Level Resource · 15, 189, 197, 199, 200-204
Leveling · 88, 110, 183-195, 203, 204, 387, 391
Leveling Gantt · 183, 189, 190, 204
Link · 50, 77, 110, 127, 148, 151, 155, 286, 287, 290
Lookup Table · 299, 314, 315, 316, 318

M

Manual · 19, 44, 46, 54, 60-70, 81, 186, 187, 196, 197, 203, 205, 322, 330, 390
Master Project · 280-283, 286, 288, 290, 291, 389, 390
Max Units · 116-118
Milestone · 47, 56, 76, 215, 269, 272, 323, 390
Move Project · 230
Must Finish On · 175, 180
Must Start On · 175, 180

N

Network Diagram · 21
Night Shift · 131, 387, 390
Notes · 118, 144, 146, 147, 149, 150-156, 165, 207

O

Outdent Task · 15, 45, 76, 101, 108, 123, 327
Outline · 46, 54, 55, 59, 76, 102, 138, 206, 311, 327, 328
Over-allocated · 22, 24, 110, 117, 127, 184-188, 190, 193, 194, 196-203, 271, 283, 284, 323, 324, 387, 391

P

Pan and Zoom · 268
PDF · 15, 30, 269, 270, 273
Planned Value · 249
Planning Wizard · 174, 178, 180, 182
Predecessor · 17, 42, 48, 49, 50, 52, 57, 58, 105, 162, 164, 170, 171, 188, 218, 287, 326, 331, 332, 388, 389, 390, 392
Pre-set Filters · 214, 215
Priority, Standard · 188
Project Calendar · 130-132, 136, 138, 139, 143, 206, 390
Project Information · 15, 100, 108, 123, 132, 136, 138, 139, 146, 167, 176, 198, 230, 240, 241, 243, 257, 258, 261, 325, 370
Project Overview Report · 271, 277
Project Summary Task · 16, 42, 47, 48, 58, 59, 76, 77, 108, 123, 249, 251, 282, 322, 387, 391

PV · 249

Q

Quick Access Toolbar · 13, 19, 193, 299, 300, 301, 302, 305, 319

R

Remaining Cost · 252, 253
Remaining Duration · 230-232, 241, 242, 244, 292, 386, 388, 391
Remaining Work · 230, 231, 233, 253, 258, 259, 261, 262, 292, 310, 348, 378, 380, 381, 386, 391
Replace Resource · 195, 201
Report · 14-16, 19, 30, 247, 254, 264-266, 270-279, 294, 295, 299, 300, 302, 309-311, 319, 341, 347, 348, 354, 361, 367, 376-383
Report Tools · 272, 273, 277, 309, 310
Resource Calendar · 130, 133, 140, 143, 206, 391
Resource Comparison · 295
Resource Form View · 23
Resource Graph View · 24
Resource Pool · 280, 283, 284, 285, 288, 290, 291, 391
Resource Sheet · 19, 22, 29, 104, 115, 117, 118, 119, 125, 149, 150-154, 184, 191, 199, 208-210, 249-252, 283, 284, 331, 349, 390, 391
Resource Table · 294
Resource Usage · 22, 23, 26, 183-186, 192, 195, 196, 198, 204, 236
Resource Views · 28, 115, 125, 149, 154, 186, 190, 191, 198, 199, 250, 270, 331
Respect Links · 70

S

Schedule Performance Index · 249
Schedule Variance · 249
scheduling conflicts · 69, 174, 178, 182
Scheduling Mode · 44, 60-69, 75, 81, 218, 386, 390, 392
Scroll to Task · 142, 169, 170, 179-181, 193, 200, 201
Scrum · 333,-341, 345, 350, 353, 355-358, 365, 366-369, 371, 373, 375, 391, 393
Set Baseline · 226, 227, 229, 240, 257, 328, 329
Sharer Plan · 283, 284, 391
Show Outline · 46, 102, 138, 327, 328
Simple Schedule · 83, 84, 87, 89, 90, 97, 103, 107, 112, 233, 239
Slack · 157-159, 167, 169, 170, 172, 173, 180, 181, 188, 389, 391, 393
Sort · 205, 207-209, 221, 391
Split View · 16, 29, 107, 120, 122, 138, 168, 197, 235, 267, 276, 277
Splitting a Task · 191, 192, 202
Sprint · 338, 339, 348, 349, 355-367, 369, 370-383, 392, 393

Standard Rate · 116, 125, 210, 212, 213, 253
Start date · 61, 65, 100, 108, 123, 139, 167, 198, 325, 371
Start No Earlier Than · 65, 67, 175, 179, 193, 200, 325, 326
Start-to-Finish · 49, 392
Start-to-Start · 49, 57, 163, 392
Status Bar · 19, 54, 61, 63, 215, 330
Status Date · 230, 241, 243, 258, 261, 299, 300, 305-307, 319, 392
Status Date Indicator · 299, 300, 305-307, 319
Story Points · 338, 392, 393
Styles · 160, 164, 168, 268, 308, 310
subtask · 45, 46, 56, 78, 101, 109
Successors · 42, 48, 164, 169
Summary Tasks · 42, 44, 45, 46, 59

T

Tables · 28, 252, 253, 260, 261, 263, 274
Task Calendar · 130, 134, 136, 141, 143, 206, 392
Task Comparison · 295
Task Form · 25, 119, 120, 121, 234, 235
Task ID · 52, 105, 188, 287, 392
Task Inspector · 205, 218, 219, 221, 392
Task Level · 235
Task Mode · 44, 54, 61, 63, 69, 330, 392
Task Note · 146, 147, 154-156, 207
Task Path · 157, 164, 166, 173
Task Sheet View · 26
Task Type · 60, 71, 73, 74, 76-81, 206, 389, 393
Task Usage · 19, 24, 25, 141, 251
Team Planner · 19, 26, 183, 184, 195, 196, 204
Text Styles · 160, 168, 268
Timeline · 16, 27, 107, 122, 168, 197, 265-270, 273, 276, 277, 279, 280, 299, 300, 307, 308, 319, 321, 393
Timeline Bar · 269
Timeline Tools · 267, 268, 269, 276, 277, 308
Timeline View · 16, 27, 107, 122, 168, 197, 265, 267-269, 273, 276, 277, 279, 299, 300, 307, 308, 319, 393
Timescale · 18, 19, 172, 202, 267, 322, 393
Total Cost · 127, 252
Total Slack · 158-181, 391, 393
Tracking Gantt · 27, 224, 237, 246, 260

U

Units · 8, 70, 73, 74, 78, 79, 80, 84-90, 98, 99, 103, 104, 108-110, 114-127, 183-185, 188, 190, 191, 198, 199, 202-204, 233, 323, 386, 388-390, 393
Update Project · 237
User Story · 336, 346, 362, 363, 368, 392, 393
User-controlled scheduling · 19, 322, 330

V

Variance · 17, 229, 247-249, 252, 253, 264, 265, 386, 388, 393
Variance at Completion · 249
Velocity · 338, 393
View Reports · 254, 272, 277, 310, 347, 377
Visual Report · 272

W

WBS Coding Scheme · 33, 37, 38, 41
Wizard · 174, 178, 180, 182
Work Breakdown Structure · 1, 33-41, 55, 76, 95, 98, 107-109, 122-124, 330, 394

Work Complete · 231
Work In Progress Limit · 394
Work Weeks · 130-135, 140, 143

X

XPS · 30, 269, 270, 273

Z

Zoom · 18, 202, 240, 257, 268, 275, 321

About the Authors

Jerry Reed, PMP, MCP

Jerry Reed is the Co-Founder and President of PMPlicity. He is an award-winning UCLA instructor, speaker and author. He has taught managers and technology workers from Google, SpaceX, Disney, AT&T, Blizzard, Optum Rx, the CIA, the United Nations and Netflix. With over 20 years of project management experience, Jerry has successfully delivered over 100 enterprise level projects!

Special Acknowledgement

This book would not have been possible without the tireless, professional services of my wife and co-founder, Yolanda Reed. She has been my editor, transcriber, graphic designer, typesetter, and best friend.

About the Authors

Yolanda Reed

Yolanda Reed is the Co-Founder and Principal Administrator of PMPlicity. She is an author, editor, seasoned administrator, graphic artist and certified fitness professional. She oversees project management, product development and quality assurance. Yolanda is the "secret sauce" of PMplicity. She maintains strong client relationships and is the primary liaison for PMPlicity partners and distributors, including Amazon, Apple, Vimeo, Barnes and Noble and UCLA.

Tell Us What You Think

Thank you for learning with PMplicity! We hope you've enjoyed this book and that you're now able to build reliable schedules using Microsoft Project.

If you've found this book helpful, please write a review and tell a friend!

We'd love to hear from you. "Let's Talk" at https://www.pmplicity.com/pmplicity/

Errata

We've made every effort to cross every "t" and dot every "i" to ensure the accuracy of this book.

Please let us know if you find any errors at https://mspbasics.com/errata/

Made in the USA
Middletown, DE
26 August 2019